GEOPONIKA

GEOPONIKA

Farm Work

A modern translation of the Roman
and Byzantine farming handbook
by
ANDREW DALBY

PROSPECT BOOKS

2011

First published in 2011 by Prospect Books,
Allaleigh House, Blackawton, Totnes, Devon TQ9 7DL.

© 2011, English translation and editorial matter, Andrew Dalby.

BRITISH LIBRARY CATALOGUING IN PUBLICATION DATA:
A catalogue entry of this book is available from the British Library.

Typeset and designed by Matthew Snell and Tom Jaine.
The cover illustration drawn by Andras Kaldor is of a detail from a painting by Yannis Tsarouchis (1910–1989) in the Benaki Museum, Athens.

ISBN 978-1-903018-69-9

Printed and bound by the Gutenberg Press, Malta.

Table of Contents

Acknowledgements

My thanks, first and not least, to Tom Jaine, publisher of Prospect Books. Tom's enthusiasm for bringing early food texts back to life is the cause of this new *Geoponika*, the first English translation for more than two hundred years. It is reassuring to know from Robert Rodgers that a much-needed critical edition of the Greek text is on its way. I am grateful to Harry Paris for fruitful discussion on cucurbits, Sally Grainger on fish sauce, and Sasha Grigorieva on medieval food words.

Maureen, meanwhile, watched this translation while it grew. Last and also not least, my thanks to her.

Andrew Dalby
Saint-Coutant,
31 December 2010

Introduction

The making of the Geoponika

The *Geoponika* is, in its immediate origin, a Byzantine Greek farming manual of the 10th century AD. It is dedicated to the Emperor Constantine Porphyrogenitus. 'Born in the purple chamber' of the palace at Constantinople, as all emperors should have been and few were, he succeeded to the throne at the age of eight, in the year 913, and ruled the Byzantine Empire until his death in 959.

He was a poor-to-middling ruler, by all accounts, but an assiduous scholar. Under his direction a series of anthologies was produced, distilling useful knowledge from more than a millennium of Greek and Latin writing on various subjects of practical use from diplomacy and siege warfare to farming.

These products of the imperial scriptorium would be of very little use to modern readers if it were not that the original works from which they were extracted are mostly lost. They disappeared in the aftermath of the fall of Constantinople in 1453, or in the destruction wreaked by the Fourth Crusade in 1204, or more vaguely in the gradual shrinkage of Byzantine Greek culture that was already under way in the tenth century. Indeed, if the emperor had selected the best from these works, what further need would there be to read them in full? The very existence of the *Geoponika*, the *Excerpts on Embassies* and the rest may have hastened the disappearance of some of their sources.

Nearly all earlier Greek texts on which the *Geoponika* is based are now indeed lost, although two preceding farming manuals are known indirectly. A briefer compilation made by Cassianus Bassus in the 6th century AD was translated into Pehlevi and thence into Arabic; an earlier

9

one, edited by Vindanionius Anatolius in the 4th century, was translated into Syriac and thence into Armenian and Arabic. The Greek texts are lost but the translations survive.

Its fate

The *Geoponika* itself has surfaced only at intervals. In 1137 Burgundio of Pisa, while on a diplomatic mission to Constantinople, came across the text and translated books 6 to 8, on vines and wine, into Latin. Then the work sank into obscurity for four hundred years.

In 1538, as European scholars worked feverishly to publish and translate the long-lost works of classical Latin and Greek literature, the *Geoponika* came to notice for the second time. The scholar-physician Janus Cornarius published a complete Latin translation at Venice in that year; the excitement that greeted it is shown by the fact that it was reprinted at least five times in five years. At Basle in 1539 J. A. Brassicanus produced the first printed edition of the Greek text. Between that date and 1551 two rival Italian translations, one French, one German, and a second Latin translation, appeared in turn.

Then, once again, the Byzantine farming manual dropped out of sight, until in 1704 Peter Needham was encouraged by John Moore, bishop of Norwich, to produce an edition in Greek and Latin with brief but learned notes. Published at Cambridge, it marks the first emergence of the *Geoponika* in England.

Since 1704 there have been just two editions of the Greek text. One, based on Needham's work but with a fuller commentary, by J. N. Niclas, appeared at Leipzig in 1781. The latest to date, in Greek only and with no commentary, but giving a systematic indication of variant readings in the manuscripts, is by Heinrich Beckh: it was published, again at Leipzig, in 1894.

Russian and Spanish translations now exist. Until now the only English translation has been one by Rev. Thomas Owen, who must have spent a good deal of his time between 1800 and 1810 translating the classical texts on farming into English. His *Geoponika*, self-published, appeared in two volumes in 1804 and 1805.

INTRODUCTION

The layout

The *Geoponika* is in twenty books, each with its table of contents[1] and division into chapters. Nearly every chapter break represents a real change of topic, and nearly every chapter heading characterizes that chapter's contents at least approximately. The division into chapters is a part of the organization imposed on the text by its compilers under Constantine Porphyrogenitus: aspects of this organization go back earlier, to the lost, briefer *Geoponika* that was translated into Syriac and Armenian and was incorporated into the longer version known to us.

Within each chapter the arrangement is less obvious. A common pattern (or so it will appear to the reader of this translation) is for a chapter to contain one initial paragraph, sometimes relatively long, that offers a connected explanation or solution to the issue outlined in the chapter heading. This will then be followed by other paragraphs, often consisting of a single sentence or part-sentence, that offer alternative and additional material, sometimes not wholly relevant, occasionally contradictory.

I must explain that this paragraphing is new to the present translation. It has nothing to do with the manuscripts, or the subdivisions marked by traditional sentence numbering in printed editions, or those marked with upper-case initials in Heinrich Beckh's edition. It is my fresh attempt to subdivide the text as I understand it into shorter and longer sections that appear to be self-standing, and are usually distinguished from their immediate context by style or grammar. These paragraphs represent, I think, the molecules from which the older *Geoponika* texts, and eventually the *Geoponika* that we have, were assembled. Some of these molecules are attributed to named authors; many others surely descend from various earlier texts, whether verbatim, paraphrased or summarized; others again, especially the shorter and less consequential items, will have been added from a general knowledge of the farming literature, from recent documents, and from oral tradition.

---

1. The tables of contents of each book merely duplicate the chapter titles; hence they are omitted in this translation. A full list of the contents of the text is found after this Introduction.

My aim, in dividing the chapters into paragraphs in this way, is to resolve their incoherence by visually highlighting what hangs together and what does not. Repetitions and contradictions, as part of this process, are pinned down and highlighted. Nonsense remains.

The nonsense, combined with the incoherence, went to ensure that the publishing heyday of the *Geoponika* lasted only a few years after its first printed edition: better value for money was found elsewhere. Yet even the nonsense has its value. At least one influential ancient farmer or gardener believed it. Many such beliefs were widely held. The nonsense, as well as the truth, is part of the history of farming. And occasionally what has appeared to be nonsense contains a germ of truth.

Attributions and origins

The attributions of chapters and smaller units to individual authors (see also the Index of Sources after this Introduction) are of dubious validity. The chapter attributions are the most prominent, and it is soon clear to the reader that *as chapter attributions* they are not wholly credible: the author named at the head of the chapter surely did not cite – often, for chronological reasons, cannot possibly have cited – the shorter paragraphs within the chapter that are attributed to other authors.

My conclusion, in translating, has been that the chapter attributions are not in general wholly false (though some are: this is an area in which copyists' errors can easily happen). There are convincing resemblances between the scattered chapters that are attributed to certain individual authors; and, for example, the first part of 9.19, attributed to Apuleius, is clearly translated from Latin (see note there). In many cases, I think, the chapter attributions apply to the first or principal paragraph of the relevant chapter: the rest, whether separately attributed or not, has been added by successive compilers from other sources or from experience. Having reached this conclusion I wondered whether to move the attributions out of the chapter headings and insert them at the head of the paragraphs to which I think they belong. This would be little more than a game, however, and of no help to the reader; so I have left them as they are.

Setting the attributions aside, the *Geoponika* clearly derives, in large part, from the agricultural traditions of the Roman Empire. Many resemblances can be found between it and two earlier manuals in Latin: the detailed farming textbook by Columella, written in the mid-1st century AD, and the guide arranged by the months of the farming year compiled by Palladius in the 4th century. There are particularly close links with Palladius. Yet neither Columella nor Palladius is cited.

That said, the Roman Empire was, in its intellectual culture, bilingual. The *Geoponika* is in Greek and has many evident links with the Greek-speaking eastern half of the Empire. Whenever evidence is drawn from specific geographical areas, they fall within this zone: Greece itself; the province of Bithynia and Pontus, to which it seems Florentinus refers at least three times;[1] Egypt, mentioned occasionally and the origin of much of book 20; Palestine, the context implied by observations attributed to Zoroaster;[2] Arabia (that is, the Roman province corresponding roughly with modern Jordan) where it seems that the Quintilii owned an estate.[3]

Even if not all the specific attributions can be accepted, the chronological range of the sources drawn on in the *Geoponika* is stunning. Constantine Porphyrogenitus and his team were the inheritors of more than 1500 years of literary and scientific evolution. Quotations from Homer and Hesiod, and Greek words that were already obsolete in the 3rd century BC, jostle with mid-Byzantine terminology.[4] There are some specifically Biblical words, unknown in Greek before the Jewish Bible was translated in the 3rd century BC, such as *zizanion* 'darnel';[5] there are Latin words, including *phamilia* 'household', *kritarion* 'chalk', *berikokkion* 'apricot', *damaskenon* 'plum',[6] which entered Greek in the 1st century AD and after; and a few of these denote items that were

---

1. 4.1, 5.2, 5.17. At 5.3 the attribution is to Didymos.
2. 1.10, 1.12.
3. 2.21, 2.23.
4. See for example 10.73 and 12.1.
5. 2.43 and elsewhere.
6. 2.7, 2.42, 3.1.

unfamiliar in Greek-speaking regions before the spread of the Roman Empire, such as *bikia* 'vetch, *Vicia sativa*'.[1]

Belief systems

The logic of explanations in the *Geoponika* depends, naturally, on scientific theories in vogue when it or its sources were written. Explicit rationales are supplied only rarely (see for example 10.2, 10.73, 10.75) but the sympathetic reader will soon become familiar with the theories that underlie many of the instructions in the *Geoponika*. Even if the theories are now obsolete, many of the observations are valid. For example, the modern science of allelopathy explains biochemically some of the interactions between plants that are noted in the *Geoponika* and attributed to sympathy and antipathy.

Astrological forecasting is not much relied on in the *Geoponika* but some details are given at 1.8, 1.10 and 1.12, mainly attributed to Zoroaster. The dates at which the sun was said to enter each sign are the ones familiar to us: they were defined by classical astronomers and remain standard in astrology although no longer astronomically valid.

Humoral theory is sometimes appealed to explicitly. At 5.2 'varieties that are more moist must be planted in localities that are dry and subject to drought, drier varieties in cold and wet localities; in this way what is lacking in the plants will be supplied by the nature of the soil.' At 5.26 'the most workmanlike method of manuring would be to use in sandy soil sheep or goat dung, since these are evidently the gentlest, and cow dung in white clay, which, being weak by nature, sufficiently relieves the relative sweetness and fattiness of this manure.' At 9.9 the reason given for pruning trees in autumn depends on the assumption that the moist element reduces strength; supporting evidence is added at 9.17.

The theory of sympathy and antipathy is appealed to regularly; methods based on it are described simply as *physikos*, 'natural'. This theory underlies many of the more startling assertions in the *Geoponika*, including those at 1.14; the fullest single collection of examples is at 15.1.

---

1. 2.18 and elsewhere.

Instructions based on this theory are usually attributed to Apuleius, Demokritos or Zoroaster. At 19.7 Demokritos is characterized in the text as *ho physikos*, 'the naturalist', meaning 'the expert on sympathy and antipathy'.

The lunar timetable method is set out at 1.6 and 1.7. Unlike some other theories on which the *Geoponika* relies, this one is still widely accepted: in France, for example, handbooks on gardening by this timetable remain popular.

Calendars

Knowledge of the stellar calendar was necessary in earlier classical times because the Greek world had a multiplicity of official calendars, most of which tended to get out of step with the solar year. No handbook could allow for all the variations, and in any case farmers and gardeners would find the stars a more reliable guide than any official calendar. By the time the *Geoponika* was compiled this was no longer true: the Julian calendar, relatively accurate astronomically, was in use everywhere. Hence conversion from stellar to Julian calendar was needed if readers of the *Geoponika* were to make full use of the older, traditional instructions. A guide to conversion duly appears at 1.9, and conversions are sometimes given elsewhere in the text. These do not agree precisely, because star risings and settings slowly change through the centuries and also vary according to the observer's geographical latitude – confirmation if any were needed that the sections of the *Geoponika* were written at different times and places.

The two landmarks most often appealed to in the stellar calendar are the dawn rising of Sirius on 19th, 20th or 24th July (1.8, 1.9, 2.15) which marked the beginning of the 'dog days', the 'burning of Sirius', the hottest and driest period of the summer; and the setting of the Pleiades, at dawn on 2nd, 7th or 11th November (1.1, 1.9, 2.14, 3.13) and at dusk on 16 April (1.9), punctuating spring and autumn and threatening the stability of wine.

The *Geoponika* generally applies the classical Roman form of the Julian calendar. The months are already those of our modern

(Gregorian) calendar, but in Roman usage the dates within the month were numbered differently. In this translation I have converted these dates to modern form where necessary: thus the original 'Kalends of January' is replaced by '1st January'.

Evidence of other calendars will be found from time to time. One of these is the 'Macedonian' calendar used in the Greek Hellenistic kingdoms of the successors to Alexander the Great. In that system the year began in late October with the month *Dios*, and each of the twelve months was divided into three decads (see 1.5). Another is the ancient Athenian calendar, in which the year began at a new moon in midsummer (see 1.10). The *etesiai*, 'etesian winds' or 'yearly winds', are so called because they arrived at the turn of the year in the Athenian and similar calendars.

Weights and measures

These are the standard measures used in the *Geoponika*:

> Length: 1 *stadion* = 6 *plethra* = 450 cubits = 600 feet; 1 cubit = 2 spans = 6 palms = 24 fingers; 1 foot = 4 palms = 16 fingers
>
> Dry volume: 1 *medimnos* = 2 (?) *metra* = 6 *modioi* = 48 *choinikes* = 96 pints
>
> Liquid volume: 1 *amphora* or *metretes* = 8 *choes* = 48 pints
>
> Smaller units of volume: 1 pint = 2 *kotylai* = 8 *tryblia* or saucers = 12 *kyathoi* or ladles (or fluid ounces) = 96 *kochliaria* or spoonfuls = 288 scruples
>
> Weight: 1 *talanton* = 60 *mnai* = 62½ *litrai*; 1 *mna* = 100 drams = 300 scruples; 1 *litra* = 96 drams = 288 scruples

When used as a measure of area, a *plethron* usually represents 100 feet square, i.e. 10,000 square feet. Other traditional measures, for which I offer no precise equivalents, include 1 ball or *sphairion* of tejpat leaves; 1 basket or *kophinos* of bean shucks; 1 handful or *drax* of salt; 1 bunch or *desme* of cabbage leaves; 1 handful or *cheiroplethes* of seed; 1 bean of Egyptian myrrh (a quantity of resin the size of a broad bean); 3 fingers of cumin (the quantity of seeds that could be picked up in three cupped fingers); and cuttings equated to a hand's thickness and to the little finger's thickness.

Note on the translation

The *Geoponika* is in Greek, and I have kept the proper names in it in their Greek form, with the following exceptions. I have translated the names of stars, constellations and planets. Authors' names that have a traditional English version appear in English (Aristotle, Ptolemy, Vergil, Zoroaster). Authors' names that are linguistically of Latin origin have been turned back into Latin to make them easier to read (Africanus, Apuleius, Cassianus, Florentinus, Quintilii, Varro, Vindanionius).

Among the challenges in translating a text such as the *Geoponika* are the difference in semantic range between Greek and English technical terms and the difficulty (not to say impossibility) of pinning down identities of plants, animals, diseases and pests.

The footnotes offer identifications for most of the animal and plant species mentioned in the text. These should be taken as suggestions. Even when obviously valid they obscure the fact that such terms in any one language seldom coincide precisely in semantic range with those in any other, or with scientific classifications.

Where a Greek term is more specific than any comparable English one, or cannot be securely identified, I retain the Greek word in the text, discussing its meaning in a footnote on its first or major occurrence.

For the two common names of larval insects, *skolekes* (which burrow into flesh and wood) and *kampai* (which eat leaves and spoil fruit) I have usually used 'grubs' and 'caterpillars'. For *theria*, unwanted creepy-crawlies in general, I use 'vermin'. For *herpeta*, creepy-crawlies that bite or sting, I use 'pest'.

Two notes on wine. I have translated *oinos melas* as 'black wine', the literal meaning of the words, because a distinction is sometimes required between this and *oinos erythros* 'red wine'; a roughly equivalent distinction in English would be between dark and light red wines. The taste-quality *austeros*, literally 'austere', can often be translated 'dry', but this translation does not work well in the *Geoponika*. The word means 'dry, full, round' – a typical flavour of good red wine; it is never used for white wine. At 5.15 its opposite is *glykys* 'sweet', but at 7.15 its opposite is *chaunos* 'loose, spongy, empty'. In the same chapter we learn that must or grape juice (*gleukos*, always and by definition sweet) may be *austeros*. So as not to mislead, I have usually adopted the literal translation 'austere'.

[...] indicates that there appear to be words missing in the manuscript text.

Occasionally several Greek words appear in the translation without explanation. This is because the text is (I think) untranslatable at these points. In one or two cases these words must not be translated, because they are spells to be pronounced verbatim by the reader; elsewhere the manuscript text is clearly faulty.

List of Books and their Chapters

26

10. *Keeping and storing citrons.* Sotion.
11. *Planting pistachios.* Diophanes.
12. *More on planting pistachios.* Damegeron.
13. *Planting and care of peaches.* Florentinus.
14. *Making* persika *carry writing.* Demokritos.
15. *Making peaches red.* Same author.
16. *Making peaches stoneless.* Africanus.
17. *Grafting peaches.* Didymos.
18. *The season for planting apples and their general care.* Anatolios.
19. *How to make apples red.* Berytios.
20. *Grafting apples.* Diophanes.
21. *Keeping apples.* Apuleius.
22. *The planting of pears, their care, and how to prevent grittiness in the fruit.* The Quintilii.
23. *More on growing pears.* Diophanes.
24. *Cleft-grafting pears.* Tarantinos.
25. *Keeping pears.* Demokritos.
26. *Growing quinces.* Didymos.
27. *Making quinces take a particular shape.* Demokritos.
28. *Keeping quinces.* Same author.
29. *Planting, treatment, and general care of pomegranates.* Florentinus.
30. *So that pomegranates will not split.* Africanus.
31. *Growing seedless pomegranates.* Same author.
32. *Pomegranate fronds ward off vermin.* Same author.
33. *Making pomegrates redder.* Didymos.
34. *How to make a sour pomegranate sweet.* Paxamos.
35. *Making pomegranates bear plentiful fruit.* Demokritos.
36. *How to tell, after picking a pomegranate, how many segments it contains.* Africanus.
37. *Grafting pomegranates.* Florentinus.
38. *Keeping and storing pomegranates.* Berytios.
39. *Growing plums.* Pamphilos.
40. *Keeping plums.* Same author.
41. *Planting cherries.* Florentinus.
42. *Keeping cherries.* Florentinus.
43. *Growing jujubes.* Vindanionius.
44. *Keeping jujubes.* Same author.
45. *The season for planting figs and their care.* Didymos.
46. *To ensure when planting figs that they will be free of maggots.* Same author.
47. *Producing figs with writing.* Demokritos.
48. *To ensure that a fig tree does not shed its fruit.* Same author.
49. *To tame a wild fig.* Africanus.
50. *Scab on fig trees.* Leontinos.
51. *To produce laxative figs; to produce early figs. From* Demokritos.
52. *Cleft-grafting fig trees.* Leontinos.

List of Sources Cited in *Geoponika*

This list sorts the references to and citations of the various ancient sources relied upon by the compilers. In the majority of cases, the source is indicated in the chapter heading, but there are many instances of sources being referred to in the body of the text. In this list, no distinction is made between the two forms of citation.

Africanus is Sextus Julius Africanus, prolific Roman author of the early 3rd century AD, part of whose miscellany *Kestoi* survives. He was fascinated – as the reader will soon see – by the paranormal, the unexplained and the downright untrue.

    1.14, *On hail;* 1.15, *More on hail;* 1.16, *On thunderbolts;* 2.18, Ensure that seed is not damaged in any way after sowing; 2.7, On water and the collecting of rainwater; 2.28, To increase the volume of grain stored in granaries; 4.2, More on tree-trained vines; 5.24, Good fruiting and good wine; 5.30, To stop the vine producing phtheires or caterpillars and prevent damage by frost; 5.45, When to harvest the grapes; signs that they are ripe; 5.48, Treatment against pests that damage the vines; 5.49, Against kantharides and larger pests that damage the crop; 7.9, Separating wine from water; 7.14, An infallible verse to ensure that wine never turns; 7.29, To spoil wine; 7.30, So as not to smell of wine after drinking; 7.31, So as not to be drunk after drinking a lot of wine; 9.8, Making olive trees heavy-fruiting; 9.14, The olive-grape; 10.9, How to make citrons take the form of any kind of bird, or of a human face or that of any animal; 10.16, Making peaches stoneless; 10.30, So that pomegranates will not split; 10.31, Growing seedless pomegranates; 10.32, Pomegranate fronds ward off vermin; 10.36, How to tell, after picking a pomegranate, how many segments it contains; 10.49, To tame a wild fig; 10.53, To produce figs that are white on one side and black or red on the other; 10.55, On olynthoi or unripe figs; 10.56, How figs can be kept as fresh as if still on the tree; 10.59, Making bitter almonds sweet; 10.66, To make trees bear walnuts without rinds; 10.82, To make all trees* *fruit more heavily;* 12.11, *To harm the gardener;* 12.38, *Sorrel;* 13.3, *Weasels;* 13.13, *Bats;* 13.18, *Frogs;* 14.3, *To make pigeons stay and attract others to join them;* 14.10, *Producing eggs with writing;* 14.15, *To stop a cat harming a bird;* 17.6, *Predicting the offspring;* 17.11, *Preventing cattle being troubled by flies;* 18.4, *To make sheep follow you;* 18.5, *To prevent a ram attacking;* 18.12, *Milk, and how to make farm animals yield plenty of milk.*

Amphiaraos was a legendary figure, revered as a healer and seer at his shrine at Oropos. He was King of Argos, the son of Oecles and Hypermnestra, and husband of Eriphyle.

2.35, *Broad beans.*

Anatolios see **Vindanionius Anatolius Berytius**.

Apsyrtos, otherwise unknown, is among the writers on horses quoted in book 16.

16.1, *Horses;* 16.3, *Cures for various diseases;* 16.4, *Fever;* 16.5, *Ophthalmia;* 16.6, *Cataract;* 16.7, *Nerves;* 16.8, *Bowels;* 16.13, *Dysuria;* 16.14, *Blood in the urine;* 16.15, *Ulceration;* 16.16, *Inflammation;* 16.19, *Leeches;* 16.21, *Asses suitable for mating.*

Apuleius shares a name with the author of the fantasy novel *Metamorphoses* (also known as *The Golden Ass*) and with the compiler of a Latin herbal, but no link is visible between those surviving writings and the citations in the *Geoponika*.

1.5, *Predicting whether the spring will come early or late;* 1.14, *On hail;* 2.8, *On large farms there should be forested mountains; how to plant them;* 2.18, *Ensure that seed is not damaged in any way after sowing;* 2.39, *Lupins;* 5.33, *On rust;* 6.11, *Duties of those responsible for the kanthelia; treading the grapes; how the treading team should work in the troughs;* 7.26, *To stop moistness in wine;* 8.38, *To keep sour vinegar;* 8.39, *Making pepper vinegar;* 8.40, *Testing whether vinegar contains water;* 9.19, *Making unripe olive oil;* 10.21, *Keeping apples;* 12.8, *So that there will not be caterpillars in vegetables or trees;* 13.5, *Field mice;* 13.8, *Snakes;* 13.9, *Scorpions.*

Aratos is a Greek poet of the 3rd century BC. His astronomical poem *Phenomena* actually contains the information credited to him in the *Geoponika*.

11.2, *Signs of calm weather;* 1.3, *Signs of bad weather; how to foretell rain;* 1.4, *Signs of a long winter.*

Aristotle, philosopher of the 4th century BC, is credited in the *Geoponika* for four details that are not found in his surviving works.

13.16, *Beetles;* 14.26, *Vultures;* 15.1, *Natural sympathy and antipathy;* 15.9a, *Box-tree honey.*

Asklepios is cited only in the mysteriously useless chapter 20.6; the known individuals who bore this name have no link with the subject of that chapter.

20.6, *Fishing.*

Berytios see *Vindanionius Anatolius Berytius.*

Cassianus Bassus, dated to the 6th century AD, was the compiler of a farming manual that is the direct ancestor of the *Geoponika*.[1]

5.6, *When to plant vines;* 5.36, *Star-struck vines.*

Damegeron is a Greek farming writer of whom nothing else is known.

2.30, *Keeping barley: how to make it last as long as possible in the granary;* 2.31, *Keeping flour;* 5.21, *Care of vines;* 5.22, *How many shoots to leave on a four-year vine; what vine-props to tie in to;* 5.37, *Diseased vines;* 7.13, *A wonderful preparation to stabilize wines, called 'panacea';* 7.24, *To make aggressively young wine old;* 9.18, *How to make oil without olives;* 9.26, *Imitating Spanish olive oil;* 10.12, *More on planting pistachios;* 10.63, When to plant chestnuts; 10.64, When to plant walnuts; their care; 10.65, Cleft-grafting walnuts; 11.30, Growing ivy; 12.12, Mallow and its medicinal use in various illnesses; 12.35, Spearmint.*

Demokritos shares a name with a Greek philosopher of the early 4th century BC. The writings on natural history and on antipathy that are attached to this name seem to belong in truth to a Hellenistic Egyptian author, Bolos of Mendes.[1]

---

1. In addition to these citations, he is also named, in the Greek text, in the tables of contents to books 7, 8, 9.
1. See Columella, *On Agriculture* 7.5.17; Palladius, *Agriculture* 14.32.6.

1.5, *Predicting whether the spring will come early or late;* 1.12, *The twelve year cycle of Jupiter;* 2.6, *Finding water;* 2.14, *The season for planting wheat and barley;* 2.41, *How to produce beans that will cook easily;* 2.42, *The lion plant;* 4.7, *The seedless grape;* 4.10, *To prevent wasps attacking vines, grapes or other fruit;* 5.2, *Vine varieties;* 5.4, *The lie of the land;* 5.5, *Seaside and riverside districts;* 5.35, *Vines that bear no fruit;* 5.43, *How to find out before the vintage whether it will be plentiful and good, or poor;* 5.44, *Hedging;* 5.45, *When to harvest the grapes; signs that they are ripe;* 5.50, *A Democritean remedy, based on natural antipathy, to prevent vines, fruit trees, standing crops or anything else being infected by any pests, particularly larger creatures;* 6.19, *Helping must that is turning sour;* 7.4, *How to cure and stabilize the wine from grapes that have absorbed much water before picking, also from grapes similarly watered after harvesting;* 7.8, *Testing wine and must for water;* 7.27, *Curing wine spoiled by vermin venom;* 7.32, *How to stop the craving for wine;* 8.31, *Making konditon;* 8.41, *Stretching vinegar;* 9.12, *So that olive trees do not shed their fruit;* 9.25, *If a mouse or other creature falls into the oil and spoils its aroma;* 10.5, *How to make date palms fruit plentifully;* 10.14, *Making persika carry writing;* 10.15, *Making peaches red;* 10.25, *Keeping pears;* 10.27, *Making quinces take a particular shape;* 10.28, *Keeping quinces;* 10.29, *Planting;* 10.35, *Making pomegranates bear plentiful fruit;* 10.47, *Producing figs with writing;* 10.48, *To ensure that a fig tree does not shed its fruit;* 10.51, *To produce laxative figs; to produce early figs;* 10.60, *Producing almonds with writing;* 10.61, *Making a barren almond tree bear fruit;* 10.67, *To dry up a walnut or any other tree;* 10.73, *Explanations of the names of fruits and nuts;* 10.74, *The difference between opora and akrodrya;* 10.79, *Star-struck trees;* 10.80, *To keep birds off a tree;* 10.89, *A natural Demokritean method to prevent animals damaging plants and seeds;* 11.5, *Planting cypress;* 11.13, *The willow;* 11.16, *Growing rosemary;* 11.18, *Roses; how to make them more aromatic; how to ensure that they do not fade;* 12.6, *How to make the garden flourish and flower;* 13.1, *Locusts;* 13.8, *Snakes;* 13.9, *Scorpions;* 13.11, *Mosquitoes;* 13.14, *Bugs;* 14.5, *To stop snakes entering the pigeon-house;* 14.8, *How to hatch chickens without a hen;* 15.2, *Bees* 15.7, *Honey and its improvement;* 15.9, *To kill the drones;* 17.4, *Preventing weakness in oxen;* 17.9, *Preventing exhaustion in working oxen;* 17.14, *Unknown illness in cattle;* 18.6, *To diagnose the colour of the lamb that a ewe is carrying;* 19.4, *Hares;* 19.7, *Treatment of pigs;* 19.8, *Wild boar;* 20.4, *Collecting all kinds of fish in one place;* 20.6, *Fishing.*

Didymos is a Greek farming writer of whom nothing else is known.

1.5, *Predicting whether the spring will come early or late;* 2.3, *In what places and exposures you should site the farm buildings, and facing what star; and on baths;* 2.14, *The season for planting wheat and barley;* 2.17, *Seed from one spot should be sown in another;* 2.26, *Making the threshing-floor;* 2.33, *How to make very nice bread without yeast;* 2.35, *Broad beans;* 2.48, *Neither farm workers nor plants should be transferred from better to worse ground;* 4.3, *How layered vines can be planted on easily and quickly;* 4.13, *Grafting by piercing;* 4.14, *To make the same vine bear different fruits (grapes), both white and black or tawny;* 5.3, *The nursery;* 5.14, *The difference between layered vines and those from cuttings;* 5.27, *Propping;* 6.5, *Testing pitch;* 6.6, *Preparing pitch;* 6.10, *Equipment for the vintage;* 6.18, *Using gypsum;* 7.18, *How to manage grapes so that the wine they yield will be sweet;* 7.19, *How to produce sweet wine from the must;* 8.22, *Making Aminaean wine;* 9.5, *The nursery;* 9.6, *Planting holes for olives;* 9.7, *Selecting new olive trees;* 9.15, *Manure suitable for olive trees;* 9.31, *Conserve of olives with grape pressings;* 9.32, *Bruised olives;* 9.33, *Kolymbades;* 10.3, *Which trees are to be grown from seed, which from cuttings; which from slips, and which from branches;* 10.6, *Use of palm stems in weaving;* 10.11, *Planting pistachios;* 10.17, *Grafting peaches;* 10.20, *Grafting apples;* 10.26, *Growing quinces;* 10.33, *Making pomegrates redder;* 10.37, *Grafting pomegranates;* 10.43, *Growing jujubes;* 10.45, *The season for planting figs and their care;* 10.46, *To ensure when planting figs that they will be free of maggots;* 10.68, *The Pontic nut or hazelnut;* 10.71, *Planting medlars;* 10.76, *Crown-grafting and cleft-grafting; what stocks will take that slips in crown and cleft-grafting;* 10.77, *When and how to bud-graft;* 10.84, *Treatment of trees;* 10.87, *To prevent trees shedding their fruit;* 10.90, *Avoiding damage to trees and vines by grubs and other pests;* 11.5, *Planting cypress;* 11.18, *Roses; how to make them more aromatic; how to ensure that they do not fade;* 11.25, *Growing narcissus;* 12.3, *Soil suited to vegetables;* 12.4, *What manure is suitable for vegetables;* 12.14, *How to grow lettuce that produces celery, rocket, basil and the like from the same root;* 12.18, *Asparagus;* 12.22, *On radishes;* 12.24, *Mint;* 12.25, *Rue, cultivated and wild;* 12.27, *Cress;* 12.28, *Chicory or endive;* 13.2, *Brouchos;* 13.4, *House mice;* 13.14, *Bugs;* 14.2, *To make pigeons stay and mate;* 14.9, *Caring for chickens;* 14.18, *Peacocks;* 14.23, *Ducks;* 14.24, *Turtle-doves, quails, thrushes and other small birds;* 15.3, *Bees;* 15.4, *To stop bees flying away;* 15.5, *When to harvest honey;* 16.22, *Camels;* 17.3, *Bulls;*

17.8, *Care of calves;* 17.20, *Feverishness;* 18.3, *Mating and lambing;* 18.8, *When and how to shear sheep;* 18.15, *Scab;* 18.16, *Ticks;* 19.7, *Treatment of pigs;* 19.9, *Salting of all kinds of meat;* 20.3, *Catching river fish.*

Dionysios. This is not Cassius Dionysius of Utica (2nd century BC), who made the Greek translation in 20 books of Mago's 28-book Punic farming manual (the translation from which Diophanes worked). The only passage for which 'Dionysios' is cited is 1.11, and it is not about farming but about the Greek names of winds.

1.11, *On the names of the winds, how many there are, and where they blow from.*

Diophanes (1st century BC) wrote a summary in 6 books, dedicated to king Deiotarus of Galatia, of the 20-book translation by Cassius Dionysius (see **Dionysios**) of Mago's 28-book Punic farming manual.

1.6, *On the lunar month;* 2.7, *On water and the collecting of rainwater;* 2.11, *More on testing the soil;* 5.7, *How to predict what kind of wine a future vineyard will produce;* 5.31, *Preventing damage to vines from hoar-frost and rust;* 5.44, *Hedging;* 6.12, *How the vats are filled with must after treading is completed;* 6.15, *Settling must rapidly for use;* 7.3, *The difference between young and old wine, and between wine from white and black grapes;* 7.17, *Stabilizing wine for export by sea;* 9.20, *Making aromatic oil;* 10.11, *Planting pistachios;* 10.20, *Grafting apples;* 10.23, *More on growing pears;* 10.29, *Planting;* 10.76, *Crown-grafting and cleft-grafting; what stocks will take what slips in crown and cleft-grafting;* 11.3, *Propagating bay with grafts;* 11.26, *Growing saffron crocus;* 12.9, *How to destroy leek moth larva;* 13.9, *Scorpions;* 15.7, *Honey and its improvement;* 18.14, *Hunting wolves.*

Florentinus is a Roman author on farming of the early 3rd century AD, one of the favourite sources of the *Geoponika* or its predecessors.[1]

1.1, *On the subdivisions of the year, the solstice and equinoxes;* 1.11, *On the names of the winds;* 2.22, *Preparation of manure;* 2.25, *When to harvest;* 2.32, *Assaying wheat; how to verify the weight of bread;* 2.33a, *[Other notes on yeast and bread.]* 2.34, *Ptisane;* 2.36, *Chickpeas;* 2.37, *Lentils;* 2.38, *Millet;* 2.39, *Lupins;* 2.44, *The overseer or farm manager;* 2.45, *The supervisor should keep a journal of farm work; how he should organize*

---

1. See Dalby 1996 pp. 80, 100, 150.

Fronto is a Roman author on farming of whom nothing else is known.\

> 5.15, *Grape varieties should not be grown intermixed, particularly not white and black grapes*; 7.12, *Precautions to ensure that wine stabilizes and does not turn*; 7.22, *To clarify wine*; 12.10, *Interplanting to help vegetables*; 19.2, *More on dogs*.

Hesiod, dated to about 700 BC, author of *Works and Days*, is quoted once.

> 7.6, *Racking wine; when to rack wines; the quality of wine that has been replaced in the same vat.*

Hierokles is a Greek writer on horses, cited frequently in the *Hippiatrika* and occasionally in the *Geoponika*.

> 16.9, *Horse Colic*; 16.10, *Horse Pneumonia*; 16.11, *Horse Cough.*

Hippokrates shares a name with the semi-legendary medical writer; otherwise unknown, he is cited once.

> 16.20, *Curing the bites of scorpions and other poisonous creatures.*

Homer, legendary author of the 7th century bc Iliad and Odyssey, is quoted three times.4

> 7.31, *So as not to be drunk after drinking a lot of wine*; 10.87, *To prevent trees shedding their fruit*; 11.13, *The willow.*

Juba, king of Numidia and Mauretania in the early 1st century AD, wrote copiously on African history and geography and other topics.

> 15.2, *Bees.*

Leontinos or **Leontios** is a Greek farming writer of whom nothing else is known.

> 2.13, *What kinds of seeds to plant when the soil is wet and what when it is thoroughly dry*; 2.24, *Earthing over and weeding after sowing*; 5.47, *How to save unripened or otherwise spoiling grapes, and to treat the wine that will be made from them*; 7.34, *Aside from wine, certain other beverages are also intoxicating*; 8.32, *Making the best grape syrup*; 9.11, *Olives are planted in many different ways*; 10.4, *Growing dates*; 10.50, *Scab on fig trees*; 10.52, *Cleft-grafting fig trees*; 10.78, *When to prune trees*; 11.21, *The*

iris; 12.33, *Pennyroyal;* 14.11, *Making hens produce large eggs; keeping eggs;* 14.12, *To stop cocks crowing;* 14.25, *Jackdaws;* 15.8, *To prevent enchantment of beehives, fields, houses, animal sheds and workshops;* 18.13, *Treatment of diseases of sheep.*

Mago (before 150 BC), the Carthaginian farming writer, is not cited in the *Geoponika* but some of his work survives here indirectly in texts attributed to Diophanes.

Manetho is cited only in the mysteriously useless chapter 20.6; the known individuals who bore this name have no link with the subject of that chapter.

    20.6, *Fishing.*

Nestor of Laranda in south-western Anatolia was a minor Greek poet of the early 3rd century AD. He is cited on medicines and antidotes.

    12.16, *Various vegetables and their medicinal effects;* 12.17, *Cabbage and its medicinal effects;* 15.1, *Natural sympathy and antipathy.*

Oppianos of Korykos in south-eastern Anatolia, a Greek poet who wrote on fishing in the 2nd century AD, is probably the author credited at 20.2 and perhaps also at 20.10.

    20.2, *Bringing fish together.*

Orpheus a figure of myth connected with medicine, agriculture, music and astrology. He is cited once, on beans.

    2.35, *Broad beans.*

Pamphilos is probably the philologist of the first century AD, author of a vast dictionary or encyclopaedia of obscure words.

    2.20, *How to achieve an adequate quantity in sowing;* 5.23, *Pruning;* 7.20, *To make wine aromatic and pleasant to the taste;* 10.39, *Growing plums;* 10.40, *Keeping plums;* 10.86, *How one can keep seeds for a period and then grow them;* 13.15, *Fleas in the house;* 14.14, *To prevent abortion in hens;* 15.1, *Natural sympathy and antipathy.*

Paxamos was a Greek author on cookery and other technical subjects who worked in Rome. He must have been (very roughly) contemporary with Cato, but independent of him; occasional resemblances can be seen between the preoccupations of these two authors, including a shared enthusiasm for cabbage. Paxamos is cited for certain details of vine and olive growing, and for one recipe, but his real utility to the *Geoponika* was apparently in his extensive knowledge of wild plants, including prescriptions for their use in human and animal medicine and in agriculture.[1]

10.54, *How dried figs, called ischades, are kept without going mouldy;* 2.4, *Finding water;* 2.43, *Which crops are spoiled by which weeds;* 4.9, *The perfumed grape;* 5.29, *Second thinning;* 7.10, *At what time of year wines usually turn;* 7.23, *To make wine go further in mixing, so that a smaller quantity will serve more people;* 9.17, *How and when to select and harvest olives;* 10.12, *More on planting pistachios;* 10.34, *How to make a sour pomegranate sweet;* 10.62, *Cleft-grafting almonds;* 10.84, *Treatment of trees, curing every malady;* 12.17, *Cabbage and its medicinal effects;* 12.32, *Hartwort;* 12.40, *Purslane;* 13.4, *House mice;* 13.7, *Mole rats;* 13.10, *Ants;* 14.17, *Particular treatments for poultry;* 15.6, *To avoid being stung when gathering honey;* 15.10, *To avoid being stung by wasps;* 17.13, *Care; to prevent them swallowing bones;* 18.21, *Quick way to make melke;* 20.6, *Fishing.*

Pelagonios was a 4th century AD Latin author on veterinary medicine.
16.2, *Signs in horses;* 16.17, *Plaster for joints;* 16.18, *Mange.*

Philostratos was possibly a Greek historian, but it is not clear from what kind of text the one citation in the *Geoponika* derives.
1.14, *On hail.*

Plato, the 4th century BC philosopher, is cited twice.
15.1, *Natural sympathy and antipathy;* 16.2, *Signs in horses.*

Plutarch, prolific Greek author of the 2nd century AD, is cited twice.
13.9, *Scorpions;* 15.1, *Natural sympathy and antipathy.*

Ptolemy (Claudius Ptolemaeus), 2nd century AD Greek writer on astronomy and geography, is cited once.
1.13, *On the sun and moon.*

1. See Dalby 1996 pp. 164-165.

Pythagoras, the philosopher and mathematician of the 6th century BC, was notorious for his refusal to eat beans.

> 2.35, *Broad beans;* 8.42, *Making squill vinegar.*

The **Quintilii** (Sextus Quintilius Valerius Maximus and Sextus Quintilius Condianus) were brothers who famously did everything together. Their political careers, in the Roman Empire of the 2nd century AD, ran closely parallel until both were murdered on the orders of the emperor Commodus; their farming and their agricultural writing was also the work of both equally. One reference (11.3) is to a single Quintilius.

> 1.9, *Rising and setting of major stars;* 2.21, *On manure;* 2.40, *On pulses, hemp, linseed;* 3.1, *Calendar of work to be done during each month; January;* 3.2, *February;* 3.3, *March;* 3.4, *April;* 3.5, *May;* 3.6, *June;* 3.7, *Making khondros;* 3.8, *Making tragos;* 3.9, *Making ptisane;* 3.10, *July;* 3.11, *August;* 3.12, *September;* 3.13, *October;* 3.14, *November;* 3.15, *December;* 5.8, *Selection of stems for cuttings; from what part of the vine they should be taken, and whether from young or ageing vines;* 5.14, *The difference between layered vines and those from cuttings;* 7.1, *How grape harvests differ;* 7.2, *What kind of wines should be in the open air, and what kind under a roof;* 9.10, *How to make olive trees flourish and fruit heavily, and how to treat them when sick;* 10.2, *At what season and in which part of the month to plant trees;* 10.22, *The planting of pears, their care, and how to prevent grittiness in the fruit;* 10.88, *Treatment of trees that lose their blossom or shed their leaves;* 11.3, *Propagating bay with grafts, seeds and suckers;* 12.19, *On gourds and melons: their therapeutic uses, how to make them seedless, and how to grow them early;* 14.6, *The pigeon-house;* 14.22, *Geese;* 17.5, *Mating;* 18.11, *Preventing the loimike nosos in sheep and goats.*

Sotion is a Greek farming writer of whom nothing else is known.

> 1.13, *On the sun and the moon;* 2.19, *What to do and what to avoid for a good harvest;* 2.29, *To prevent ants attacking the heaped grain;* 2.42, *The lion plant, also called broomrape;* 5.10, *At what date in the lunar month to plant vines;* 5.16, *The vineyard should not have a single variety but several, planted separately;* 5.19, *How to work the soil;* 5.20, *Trenching;* 5.28, *Thinning;* 5.38, *Weeping vines;* 5.39, *Vines that shed their fruit;* 5.40, *Vines that run to wood;* 6.17, *Testing whether must contains water;* 7.6, *Racking wine; when to rack wines; the quality of wine that has been replaced in the*

same vat; 7.15, *Signs and predictions that wine will turn or will be stable;* 7.25, *So that wine does not have anthos;* 7.35, *Making wine without grapes;* 8.35, *Vinegar to promote digestion and good health;* 8.36, *Preparing sweet vinegar;* 8.37, *Preparing sour vinegar;* 9.9, *Care of mature olive trees;* 9.27, *Imitating Istrian olive oil;* 10.10, *Keeping and storing citrons;* 10.87, *To prevent trees shedding their fruit;* 11.28, *On misodoulon or basil;* 12.15, *Beet and how to make it grow bigger;* 12.29, *Leeks;* 13.6, *A cat;* 14.4, *To stop the cat disturbing the pigeons;* 17.7, *Horsefly or gadfly;* 17.12, *Fattening cattle.*

Tarantinos is a Greek farming writer of whom nothing is known except that his name connects him with the southern Italian city of Taras, modern Taranto.

2.12, *What seeds to sow in rich soil, what in middling and what in thinner soil;* 2.27, *On the granary or horreum and the storage of wheat;* 4.4, *The myrtle-grafted grape;* 4.5, *The early grape;* 4.6, *The late grape;* 5.11, *What else to grow in vineyards;* 7.16, *Treating wine that has begun to turn to vinegar;* 9.21, *How to make olive oil clean;* 9.22, *Treating rancid oil;* 9.23, *Treating bad-smelling olive oil;* 9.24, *Settling cloudy olive oil;* 10.24, *Cleft-grafting pears;* 11.23, *Growing violets;* 12.41, *Growing mushrooms;* 13.4, *House mice;* 13.8, *Snakes;* 13.9, *Scorpions;* 20.6, *Fishing.*

Theomnestos of Nicopolis is cited twice on veterinary medicine. A Greek writer on veterinary matters (specifically horses) from the 4th century AD, his work has not survived except as part of later compilations.

16.12, *Unknown illness [in horses];* 19.3, *Care of dogs.*

Theophrastos, Aristotle's successor and a major writer on botany of the late 4th century BC, is cited three times.

3.3, *Calendar of work. March* 3.4, *Calendar of work. April;* 15.1, *Natural sympathy and antipathy.*

Varro was a Roman politician and polymath of the 1st century BC. He wrote a handbook on farming – the citations in the *Geoponika* have no close resemblance to this surviving work – and a great deal else. Varro and the Quintilii together are credited with the farming calendar of book 3.

1.1, *On the subdivisions of the year;* 2.2, *Boys are best suited to agriculture; Select workers for their physical suitability to the work, and choose separately those adapted to each task; 2.23, When to clear each kind of soil; 2.49, Smiths, carpenters and potters need to be at the farm or nearby; 3.1, Calendar of work to be done during each month; January; 3.2, February; 3.3, March; 3.4, April; 3.5, May; 3.6, June; 3.7, Making khondros; 3.8, Making tragos; 3.9, Making ptisane; 3.10, July; 3.11, August; 3.12, September; 3.13, October; 3.14, November; 3.15, December; 5.17, The differences between grape varieties; 5.41, Vines that rot their fruit; 5.42, Vines injured by the fork; 6.9, Aromatizing the vats; 7.21, Making white wine black and black wine white; 8.33, Making a different vinegar; how to make wine into vinegar; 8.34, Making vinegar without wine; 9.13, Pruning olives; 10.81, Care of young trees; 12.16, Various vegetables and their medicinal effects; 12.39, Artichokes; 14.19, Pheasants, guinea-fowl, partridges and francolins; 15.2, Bees; 17.10, From what age cattle must be prevented from mating; 19.1, Dogs.*

Vergil, Rome's 'national poet' if that concept is not anachronistic, is cited twice in the *Geoponika*.

    2.18, Ensure that seed is not damaged in any way after sowing.

Vindanionius Anatolius Berytius (apparently one person, variously cited under three names: Berytius means 'from Beirut') was the author of a farming manual directly ancestral to the *Geoponika*. He wrote in the 4th century AD and apparently had a Roman political career. The citations are divided between the three attributions in the text itself.

Anatalios

    2.10, Testing the soil; 5.10, At what date in the lunar month to plant vines, and whether with the moon above or below the earth; 5.18, How to plant layers; 5.25, When to dig mature vines; the benefits of digging; 5.26, How to manure at the time of trenching; 6.3, Preparing vats; 6.4, When and how to pitch; 6.13, Making the so-called thamna from grapes taken straight from the trough after treading; 7.28, Settling wine that is full of lees or cloudy; 10.8, More on growing citrons; 10.18, The season for planting apples and their general care; 10.72, Planting cornels; 10.85, How one can transplant large trees and those that are carrying fruit; 11.20, Lilies; 12.7, So that vegetables will not be eaten by flea beetles or damaged by phtheires or birds; 12.36, Grape hyacinth bulbs; 13.4, House mice; 13.12, Flies; 13.17, Leeches; 14.21, Hunting partridges and other game birds; 18.17, Various diseases.

Berytios

2.9, *What soil is best;* 4.11, *How to keep grapes on the vine until the beginning of spring;* 5.11, *What else to grow in vineyards;* 5.33, *On rust;* 7.33, *To restore sobriety in drunkards;* 8.24, *Making Coan wine;* 10.19, *How to make apples red;* 10.38, *Keeping and storing pomegranates;* 10.69, *On mulberries and how to make them white;* 10.70, *On keeping and storing mulberries;* 12.37, *Squill;* 13.12, *Flies;* 14.13, *To blind hens;* 14.20, *Partridges;* 18.18, *Herds of goats;* 18.19, *Cheesemaking;* 18.20, *Testing milk.*

Vindanionius

II.16, *The selection of seed, the quality of seed to be sown, and how long it lasts;* V.34, *Treatment for vines that dry their fruit;* VII.36, *An infallible preparation for wine that maintains health until old age;* X.43, *Growing jujubes;* X.44, *Keeping jujubes;* XII.5, *How all kinds of vegetables can be grown on waterless sites.*

Xenophon, Athenian historian of the 5th and 4th centuries BC. Among other works, he composed books on the household and agriculture (*Oeconomicus), On Horsemanship,* and *On Hunting.*

19.5, *Deer.*

Zoroaster shares a name with the prophet of the *Avesta,* a semi-legendary figure of the 6th century BC. The Zoroaster of the *Geoponika* wrote about astrology and magic.

1.7, *The importance of knowing whether the moon is above or below the earth;* 1.8, *The rising of Sirius and what can be forecast from it;* 1.10, *Schedule of forecasts from the first thunder after the rising of Sirius in any year;* 1.12, *The twelve year cycle of Jupiter, and what its presence in each of the twelve houses of the zodiac foretells;* 2.15, *Forecasting which crops will thrive;* 5.46, *What house the moon must be in at vintage; Grapes must be harvested when the moon is waning and is under the earth;* 7.5, *Opening the vats, and what precautions to take at this time;* 7.6, *Racking wine; when to rack wines; the quality of wine that has been replaced in the same vat;* 7.11, *How to ensure that wines are not turned by thunder and lightning;* 10.83, *To make a barren tree produce fruit;* 11.18, *Roses; how to make them more aromatic; how to ensure that they do not fade;* 13.9, *Scorpions;* 13.16, *Beetles;* 15.1, *Natural sympathy and antipathy.*

GEOPONIKA

Preface

This great city has been beautified by many other noble kings; it stores up their achievements and noble deeds like treasures of high price, but it would confess that it has had none better than you, and can show no greater achievements than those of your reign. Counting the efforts of other kings as minor, you have emulated the first Christian king, Constantine, this city's founder and protector, and you have left him far behind in good works, in trophies, in victories and all other prowess.

The tale of what you have done to benefit your subjects and to drive off your enemies is long, requiring much time and a copious narrative. Beyond this you are working for the improvement of mankind and the advantage of those who are to come. First you have skilfully and wisely restored philosophy and rhetoric, which had fallen from memory and were plunged in a yawning pit of oblivion, and have stretched your powerful hand over them. Next you have renewed every other science and art. Then, conscious of the tripartite division of the state – army, priesthood and agriculture – you have bestowed not the least of your efforts on the last of these, which, as is well known, is the staff of human life.

Hence with high inspiration and profound intelligence you have gathered and expounded, as a work of utility to all, the discoveries that are owed to the assiduity and observation of various ancient authorities in farming and gardening; the seasons and soils and methods proper to each species; the finding of water; the planning of buildings, their site, their orientation, their structure; and much else. Whoever encounters this work of yours may study whatever constitutes his own livelihood. He may explore, neatly and logically arranged, the necessary and essential arts on which human life rests and in which he himself invests; he may regard not only the essential but also those luxury arts whose aim is to please the senses of sight and smell.

In your love of workmanship – or, if I may speak more truly, your love for humanity – you gather useful information by every means and with every care, always having in mind the welfare of your subjects. May you prosper, O most just lord Constantine, delightful flower of the Purple; may you go forward with God; may you conquer every one of your enemies and always confer the best on us over whom you reign.

Book 1

I have compiled this work by collecting the writings of several early authors on farming, the care of trees and crops, and other useful subjects. It is a selection from Florentinus, Vindanionius, Anatolios, Berytios, Diophanes, Leontios, Tarantinos, Demokritos, the *Paradoxes* of Africanus, Pamphilos, Apuleius, Varro, Zoroaster, Fronto, Paxamos, Damegeron, Didymos, Sotion and the Quintilii. I decided it was necessary and appropriate to prefix to the whole work the elementary facts that those taking up farming need to know in advance: this first book therefore includes signs of good and bad weather, the rising and setting of major stars, and the effects of the natural environment.[1]

1. *On the subdivisions of the year, the solstice and equinoxes.* Florentinus.

The manager of a farm must be familiar with the seasons, the solstices and the equinoxes: he can then direct the farm workers to suitable tasks at each period and in this way be of greatest benefit to the farm.

Most authors, and among them *Varro* the Roman, say that the beginning of spring is when *zephyros* generally begins to blow, which is on 7th February,[2] when the sun is in Aquarius and is at

1. This section is indeed something new in farming manuals. Parts of it are attributed to agricultural authors, Florentinus, the Quintilii, Dionysios, Didymos and Diophanes, but the majority to others. The astronomical authors Ptolemy and Aratos are cited only in this book.
2. In this chapter the original text employs the classical Roman calendar (7th February, for example, is literally 'seven days before the Ides of February').

three or five degrees, that is, has been in the sign for three or five days.[1] Spring ends on 7th May. Summer begins on 8th May, when the sun is in Taurus, and ends on 7th August. Autumn begins on 8th August, when the sun is in Leo, and ends on 9th November. Winter begins on 10th November, when the sun is in Scorpio, and ends on 6th February.

The winter solstice [is on 25th December. The summer solstice] is on 24th June, but some think that it is on 2nd July.

The spring equinox is on 25th March; some say 24th March. The autumn equinox is on 24th September or on 26th September.

The rising of the Pleiades begins on 10th June. Their setting begins on 2nd November.[2]

The feast of the *Bruma* is celebrated on 24th November.[3]

2. *Signs of calm weather.* Aratos.[4]

If the moon appears smooth and clear when it is in its third or fourth day, this means calm weather. If it appears clear when it is full, this signals calm weather. If it appears clear at half moon,[5] this predicts calm weather. If it appears reddish this signals wind. If some part of it appears darkened, this means rain.

When the sun is clear as it rises, this means calm weather. If there is some slight cloudiness before it rises, it will be calm, and if there is scattered cloud around it when it sets, this signals no rain. If it is clear of any cloud when it sets, this signals that the next day will also be calm. If at sunrise and sunset the sun's rays appear narrowed, with clouds compacted around it, this means calm weather; if there

---

1. According to the Latin translation, 'twenty–three days'. I make it nineteen! I don't understand this bit, and I suspect the author didn't either.
2. Compare 1.9.
3. Compare 1.5. The feast is given a Latin name, *Brumalia*, by Ioannes Lydos, *On the Months* 4.157–158.
4. 1.2–1.4 draw on a much longer series of weather signs in Aratos, *Phenomena* 779–1154.
5. The meaning would normally be 'If it appears clear half way through the lunar month', but that duplicates the previous sentence (full moon is half way through the lunar month). With Cornarius and Owen I take *dichomenos* as 'at half moon', a sense that would be influenced by Aratos's use of the word *dichoosa* 'halved' in the same context (Aratos, *Phenomena* 799).

is airy cloud, but not touching the mountain, so that the peak is visible clearly, this means calm weather. If cloud is seen over the sea, it means winter has ended. If the sun sets free of cloud, and much reddish cloud comes after, it will not rain either that night or during the following day. Scattered reddish clouds around sunset mean no rain.

The little owl[1] singing repeatedly at night, and a crow[2] cawing early in the morning, and ravens[3] in large groups celebrating, as it were, and cawing, are all signs of no rain.

3. *Signs of bad weather; how to foretell rain.* Same author.

If the moon's cusps appear blunt and dark when it is in its third or fourth day, this foretells rain. If its disk appears red or fiery, this signals bad weather. At full moon if some part of it is seen darkened, it means rain. If there are two or three rings around the whole moon, this means that there will be a severe storm, particularly if they are rather dark.

If the sun when rising is red and rather dark, this means rain. If, when the sun rises, a dark cloud appears beside its rays, this means rain. If, when the sun sets, there is a mass of black cloud to the right of it, you must expect rain soon.

From whatever direction there is thunder and lightning, that is the direction from which the storm will come. If lightning comes sometimes from the south, sometimes from north and east, you should expect rain from the south, wind from the north-east.

If many shore and water birds bathe in pools, this means bad weather. If the rainbow appears double, this means heavy rain. If sparks appear on a jar or bronze bowl, this means heavy rain. If a crow bathes itself or dips its head at the shoreline and crows repeatedly at night, this foretells heavy rain. If barnyard fowl frequently dust themselves and cackle, if many ravens and jays[4] appear and caw, if swallows fly noisily over pools, reservoirs and rivers, these signs

---

1. Greek *glaux*: *Athene noctua* (Scopoli, 1769).
2. Greek *korone*: *Corvus* spp., e.g. *Corvus corone* Linnaeus, 1758.
3. Greek *korax*: *Corvus corax* Linnaeus, 1758.
4. Greek *koloios*: *Garrulus glandarius* Linnaeus, 1758.

indicate rain. If flies bite a lot, if geese go to their food noisily, if spiders are airborne when there is no wind, if the flame of a lamp is darkened, if sheep skip, these signs indicate a coming storm. If oxen look towards the south, and lick around their hooves, and are lowing as they go to their stalls, this means heavy rain. Likewise a wolf[1] approaching habitations boldly, and dogs digging the ground, mean a storm. The tree frog[2] croaking in the early morning, and birds flying towards the sea, indicate a storm. Cranes[3] flying fast mean that a storm is imminent. Mice squeaking foretell a storm. When several of these signs occur together, the prediction is more certain.

It is especially necessary to observe the first and last quarters of the lunar month, which reverse the movement of the air.

4. *Signs of a long winter.* Same author.

Holly oaks[4] and oaks[5] fruiting heavily mean that the winter will be a long one. Nanny-goats and ewes, mating and wanting to mate repeatedly, foretell a rather long winter. If cattle dig at the soil, and stretch out their heads towards the north, they predict a hard winter.

5. *Predicting whether the spring will come early or late.* Didymos.

It is quite useful to know in advance whether the year will begin early or late: it is best to use a relatively large quantity of seed if spring comes late, because some seed will perish meanwhile. If rain comes after harvest and before the setting of the Pleiades,[6] spring will be early. If rain comes as the Pleiades set, it will be middling. If rain begins after the setting of the Pleiades, spring will be late.

Demokritos and *Apuleius* say that the coming winter can be predicted from the weather on the day of the feast that the Romans

---

1. Greek *lykos*: *Canis lupus* Linnaeus, 1758.
2. Greek *ololygon*: *Hyla arborea* Linnaeus, 1758.
3. Greek *geranos*: *Grus grus* Linnaeus, 1758.
4. Greek *prinos*: *Quercus coccifera* L., kermes oak, and *Q. ilex* L., holm oak.
5. Greek *drys*: *Quercus robur* L.
6. Between 2nd and 11th November (1.1, 1.9, 2.14, 3.13).

call *Bruma*, that is, the fourth day of the last decad of *Dios*,[1] 24th November.

Others claim that it is shown by observation that the weather in December will be like that of the fourth day of the last decad of *Dios*, 24th November, the day of the *Bruma*; January will be like the fifth day of the last decad of November; February will be like the sixth day of the last decad of November. Sometimes this is the case, sometimes not.

Some claim to have observed that from 7th to 14th March the air turns colder. It was during those days that the forty martyrs were consigned to the ice and suffered martyrdom.[2]

6. *On the lunar month.* Diophanes.

Some instruct that nothing should be planted when the moon is waning, everything when it is waxing; others advise planting between the fourth and eighteenth days of the lunar month. Some recommend planting only on the three days 'before the moon', the first three days of the lunar month; others advise against planting anything from the tenth to the twentieth, lest the moon and the plants be 'buried' together.[3] Truer and better than any of the preceding instructions is this: plant when the moon is under the earth, cut wood when it is over the earth.

7. *The importance of knowing whether the moon is above or below the earth.* Zoroaster.

Since various farming tasks must be carried out when the moon is above the earth, and others when it is below, it is necessary to know for each day from one new moon to the thirtieth following at what hours of night and day the moon is above and below the earth. At new moon the moon begins to be below the earth at half an hour past sunset, and remains there till half an hour past sunrise. On the

---

1. The first month of the Hellenistic ('Macedonian') calendar as used in Egypt and Syria.
2. The Forty Martyrs of Sebaste in Cilician Armenia were sentenced to be exposed on the ice of a frozen lake in the year 320. Their feast is celebrated on 9th March.
3. As the moon decreases towards the end of the month.

2nd, from one hour and a half of night to one hour and a half of day. On the 3rd, from two hours and 4½ twelfths of night to two hours and 4½ twelfths of day. On the 4th, from three hours and two twelfths of night to three hours and two twelfths of day. On the 5th, from three hours and 11½ twelfths of night to the same time of day. On the 6th, from four hours and 9 twelfths of night to the same time of day. On the 7th, from five hours and 6½ twelfths of night to the same time of day. On the 8th, from six hours and 4 twelfths of night to the same time of day. On the 9th, from seven hours and 1½ twelfths of night to the same time of day. On the 10th, from seven hours and 11 twelfths of night to the same time of day. On the 11th, from eight hours and 8½ twelfths of night to the same time of day. On the 12th, from nine hours and a half of night to the same time of day. On the 13th, from ten hours and 3½ twelfths of night to the same time of day. On the 14th, from eleven hours and 3 twelfths of night to the same time of day. On the 15th it is there from sunrise to sunset, and this is excellent since the work can be done throughout the day. On the 16th, from half an hour past sunrise to the same period past sunset. On the 17th, from one hour and 7 twelfths of day to the same time of night. On the 18th, from two hours and 4½ twelfths of day to the same time of night. On the 19th, from three hours and 2 twelfths of day to the same time of night. On the 20th, from three hours and 11½ twelfths of day to the same time of night. On the 21st, from four hours and 9 twelfths of day to the same time of night. On the 22nd, from five hours and 6½ twelfths of day to the same time of night. On the 23rd, from six hours and 4 twelfths of day to the same time of night. On the 24th, from seven hours and 1½ twelfths of day to the same time of night. On the 25th, from seven hours and 11 twelfths of day to the same time of night. On the 26th, from eight hours and 8½ twelfths of day to the same time of night. On the 27th, from nine hours and 6 twelfths of day to the same time of night. On the 28th, from ten hours and 3½ twelfths of day to the same time of night. On the 29th, from eleven hours and 3 twelfths of day to the same time of night. On the 30th, from sunset to sunrise.

8. *The rising of Sirius and what can be forecast from it.* Same author.

The rising of Sirius is at dawn on 20th July.[1] It is necessary to note which house the moon is in when this takes place. If the moon is in Leo when the rising of Sirius takes place, there will be a plentiful harvest of wheat, olive oil and wine; all other supplies cheap; clamour, killings, appearance of a king, mildness of air, invasion by one people of another; there will also be earthquakes and tidal waves. If it is in Virgo, much rain, happiness, deaths in childbirth, slaves and beasts cheap. If in Libra, movement of a king, profit in beasts, clamour of mobs, dearth of olive oil, failure of wheat, plenty of wine and shelled fruits.[2] If in Scorpio, clamour of priests, death of bees, a state of pestilence. If in Sagittarius, a good season and much rain, abundance of wheat, wellbeing among people, deaths among the newborn, fecundity among fowl. If it is in Capricorn when the rising takes place, movement of armies, much rain, plentiful harvest of wheat, wine and olive oil, all supplies cheap. If it is in Aquarius when the rising takes place, release of a king, failure of wheat, attack of locusts, lack of rain, pestilence. If it is in Pisces when the rising takes place, there will be much rain, fecundity of fowl, good harvest of wine and wheat, sickness among people. If it is in Aries when the rising of Sirius takes place, there will be fecundity of farm animals, much rain, very poor harvest of wheat, good harvest of olive oil. If in Taurus, much rain, hail, wheat rust, many vendettas. If in Gemini, extremely plentiful harvest of wheat, wine and all crops, the extinction of a king, deaths among people, movement of armies. If in Cancer, drought and famine.

9. *Rising and setting of major stars.* The Quintilii.

It is essential for farmers to know the rising and setting of major stars. I have compiled this information, therefore, so that even the completely illiterate may listen and easily learn the dates of these risings and settings.[3] At the new moon of January Alpha Delphini

1. Compare 1.9.
2. Greek *akrodrya*. The word is defined at 10.74.
3. This compilation is not entirely consistent internally. It differs in detail from statements at 1.1 and 1.8.

rises. On 26th February[1] Arcturus rises in the evening. At the new moon of April the Pleiades set at nightfall. On 16th April the Pleiades set in the evening. On 23rd April the Pleiades rise at sunrise. On 28th April Orion sets in the evening. On 30th April the Hyades rise at sunrise. On 7th May the Pleiades show at dawn. On 19th May the Hyades show at dawn. On 7th June Arcturus sets in the morning. On 23rd June Orion begins to rise. On 10th July Orion rises in the morning. On 13th July Procyon rises in the morning; on 24th Sirius rises in the morning. On 26th July the *etesiai*[2] begin to blow. On 30th July the bright star at the breast of the lion[3] rises. On 25th August Alpha Sagittae goes down. On 15th September Arcturus rises. On 4th October Alphecca rises in the morning. On 24th October the Pleiades go down at sunrise. On 11th November the Pleiades set in the morning and Orion begins to go down. On 22nd November Sirius goes down in the morning.

10. *Schedule of forecasts from the first thunder after the rising of Sirius in any year.* Zoroaster.

The next thunder after the rising of Sirius must be counted as the first of the year.[4] It is necessary to note which house of the zodiac the moon is in when this first thunder occurs. If the moon is in Aries when this first thunder occurs, it foretells some excitement in the country; there will be contention, men fleeing; afterwards a settled state. If the moon is in Taurus when it thunders, it foretells failure of wheat and barley, an attack of locusts, joy in a royal house, affliction and famine in the east. If in Gemini when it thunders, it shows clamour and sickness, failure of wheat, ruination of Arabs. In Cancer, failure of barley, lack of rain, death of oxen; much rain in March and April. In Leo, failure of wheat and barley in mountain parts, itch and tetter. In Virgo, ruin of a king, another to rule the country in his place; danger at sea, rust in grain crops. In Libra, wars and scourges galore, failure of crops. In Sagittarius, earth tremors,

---

1. In this chapter the post-Roman calendar is used.
2. A summer north-west wind.
3. Regulus.
4. According to the Athenian or a similar calendar.

a good harvest of wheat in mountain parts, failure in the plains. If in Capricorn, it foretells rain for fifty days, treachery of kings, spite and unseemly speech and the appearance of a new king in the east who shall rule the whole world. There will be fruitfulness, death of honoured men, good lambing. In Aquarius, fierce wars on the coast, ruination of pulse crops and failure of others. In Pisces, partial failure of wheat, death of a strong man.

11. *On the names of the winds, how many there are, and where they blow from.* Dionysios.[1]

From the four cardinal points four major winds blow, *apeliotes, zephyros, boreas, notos.*[2] *Apeliotes*, blowing from the east, has *euros* and *kaikias* blowing on either side of it; *zephyros*, from the west, has *iapyx* and *lips* on either side of it; *boreas*, from the north, has *thraskias* and *aparktias* on either side of it; *notos*, brought from the south, has *libonotos* and *euronotos* on either side of it, so that there are twelve winds in all.[3]

Zephyros, more than all the other winds, is the farmer's friend: so says *Florentinus*, and we agree.

Wind is presaged by the sea rising into waves and breaking loudly on the shore; by mountain peaks showing clear; by thistledown and dry leaves swirled by the winds. In summer, look for wind from the direction from which thunder and lightning come. You should expect wind from the direction towards which setting stars tend.

---

1. On the winds see Aristotle, *Meteorologica, De Mundo.*
2. *Apeliotes* means 'from the sun' in the old Ionic Greek dialect; this was widely used in common Greek as the proper name of the east wind. Latin translations of the *Geoponika* give *Subsolanus, Favonius, Boreas* and *Auster*. In various other Latin sources the loanword *Apheliotes* (from a non-Ionic Greek form) is used for the east wind.
3. Latin translations of the *Geoponika* give *Africus* for *lips* and *Aquilo* for *aparktias*, but they simply adapt the remaining six names from the Greek. In other words, Latin as used by the translators had only six native names for major winds. Greek as used by the author of this chapter had ten, and he added the compound words *libonotos* and *euronotos* to make the number up to twelve. Aristotle (*Meteorologica* 364b11) in his listing of the winds saw no need for the added two: he denied that a SSW wind existed, and doubted whether a SSE wind existed.

12. *The twelve year cycle of Jupiter, and what its presence in each of the twelve houses of the zodiac foretells.* Zoroaster.

The zodiac is divided into twelve houses: three for spring, Aries, Taurus, Gemini; three houses for summer, Cancer, Leo, Virgo; three for autumn, Libra, Scorpio, Sagittarius; Capricorn, Aquarius and Pisces for winter. When Jupiter's star is in each of these houses it foretells the following.

When Jupiter's star is in Aries, the house of Mars, the whole year will have *boreas* with an admixture of *euros* winds; winter will be icy and snowy, rains persistent, rivers full. After spring equinox the weather will change to fine and dense rain. Summer will be temperate and healthy, autumn very hot; then there will be diseases, especially of the head, with catarrhs and coughs. As to country, the plains will bear a better harvest. Pray that no wars will arise. *Demokritos* says that wine will be fine and will keep well, and the year will be suitable for the planting of vines only; wheat at the threshing-floors must be secured against the rains; there will be few birds; it will be good to work in gardens.

When it is in Taurus, the house of Venus, winter will begin temperate and rainy, continue snowy and finish cold. Particularly if there is wintry weather from midwinter until spring equinox, spring will be temperate and very moist until the rising of Sirius; summer very hot; autumn icy and unhealthy, especially to the young. There will be ophthalmias. Plains will yield better than mountain parts; wine will suffer because grapes will have to be gathered late. There will be a good harvest of tree fruits and few birds. The year will be unfavourable to mariners. This year a well-known man will die. *Demokritos* says there will be much hail and snow this year; the *etesiai* will be irregular. Pray for no earthquakes and no movement of the army.

When Jupiter is in Gemini, the house of Mercury, the whole year will have *notos* and *libykos* winds.[1] Winter will begin windy, continue temperate and finish icy and windy; spring temperate, with light rains, and there will be plenty of wheat; summer temperate because the

---

1. *Libykos*, apparently identical with *lips*, is a west wind and is so called from an Egyptian or Palestinian point of view (it blows from *Libya* or Africa).

etesiai will blow keenly for a long time. The grain on the threshing-floors will not keep its promise, particularly in Syria. There will be sickness around autumn, especially in the young and middle-aged and women; if autumn is very hot there will be ophthalmias, and death among women. Tree fruits will yield well. Sources of water will fail. It will be wise to store crops against the failure of next year's harvest. *Demokritos* says there will be damage from hail. Pray for no epidemics.

When Jupiter is in the Moon's house, Cancer, winter will be mostly easterly, cold, with hail and dark clouds, with full rivers. About the winter solstice the rain will hold off. After spring equinox there will be frequent hail. Hilly country will yield the better harvest. The year will be healthy, except autumn. *Demokritos* says that in autumn there will be eczemas around the mouth; hence, in spring, apply herbs, purge the bowels (especially in the young) and use unmixed wine. Olive trees will bear well.

When Jupiter is in Leo, the Sun's house, winter will begin cold and wet with winds strong enough to bring down trees, continue temperate, and finish very cold; spring will have little rain, summer just like spring; in summer the sources of water will fail, as will pasture for beasts. Autumn will be very hot and unhealthy, with catarrh and cough; so take less bread and more wine. Wheat will produce moderately; vines and olives will bear well. It will be a good year for grafting, not so good for planting. Farm animals will lose their young but there will be many young in the wild. A notable man will die. Pray for no earthquakes or wars.

When Jupiter is in Virgo, the house of Mercury, winter will begin cold, continue temperate, and end stormy with frequent frost and rain and full rivers, with widespread floods. Spring will be very rainy and difficult for trees; as spring ends there will be scattered hailstorms. Summer will be rainy with dark cloud. The grain harvest must be completed quickly so that the crop is not spoilt by rain. Autumn will be windy and healthy; vines will bear well. It will be a suitable year for planting vines. Wheat will spoil easily. The whole year will be healthy without any sickness. Pray for the harvest.

When Jupiter is in Libra, the house of Venus, winter will begin wet, [continue] temperate and windy, and end very wet and frosty;

spring temperate and headachy; summer will begin like spring. This year will be dangerous for pregnant women. *Demokritos* says that throughout this year there will be no full rivers and not much hail. Autumn will be very wet.

When Jupiter is in Scorpio, the house of Mars, winter will begin cold with hail, continue warm, end mild. Spring will be wintry until the summer solstice, with rain and thunder; sources of water will fail. Wheat middling; vines and olives will bear well; death among cattle. *Demokritos* says that there will be full rivers, and sicknesses around autumn (therefore pray for no epidemics). He advises the taking of less food and of more drink.

When Jupiter is in his own house, Sagittarius, he will have a temperate and wet winter, neither warm nor cold. Rivers will be full. As winter ends there will be life and wind. Spring will be southerly and fairly wet; summer temperate and stormy. The threshing-floors must be protected from rain. Thanks to the *etesiai*, autumn will be without danger. Early and late crops will be good, middle-season crops bad; wheat will do well on the plains and in hilly country. Wine harvested relatively late will keep well. All trees will bear well. The year will be suitable for planting and all other work. Farm animals will have plenty of young; dogs will lose their young. The sea will be stormy, with strong winds late in the year. A prominent man will die.

When Jupiter is in Capricorn, the house of Saturn, winter will begin temperate, continue very wet and very cold, and end windy. The wet weather will be damaging to seed and other crops; there will be severe spells of rain, frost and snow. Before the rising of Sirius the summer will be bad; after that date very hot and disease-ridden. The *etesiai* will blow steadily; there will be earthquakes. The plains will bear a better harvest. There will be little wine because of the frost, but tree fruits in plenty. The year will be ideal for small animals but unlucky for larger beasts, especially cattle. In autumn there will be illnesses, headaches, ophthalmias, itch. Pray for no frost or wind damage to the crops.

When Jupiter is in Aquarius, the house of Saturn, there will be plenty of wind beneficial to cereal crops and particularly to tree fruits. Winter will begin very cold and end windy. Spring will be wet, rather stormy and frosty. Summer will be fresh owing to the strength of the *etesiai*. There will be summer rains sufficient to waterlog some of the standing grain. In autumn winds will bring rain and damage to crops. Acute diseases, resulting from the damp, will attack young and middle-aged. Frost will harm the grapes in many places. Seed crops will be excellent, both early and late. There will be death among birds and wild animals. There will be many shipwrecks. A very famous man will die. Pray for no epidemic, earthquakes or thunderbolts. When Jupiter is in Pisces, his *own* house, winter will begin wet, continue windy, and end in hail and snow. Strong *zephyroi* will blow in spring. Summer will be very hot, autumn feverish, especially to women and girls. Hot winds will blow, scorching the tree fruits. Seed crops will do well. The threshing-floors must be protected against the rains. The year will be dangerous for pregnant women. *Demokritos* says vines and olives will bear well. Pray for no earthquakes.

13. *On the sun and moon.* Ptolemy.

The sun by the dryness of its own fire draws out the moist element. Conversely the moon is in itself moistening, effecting mixture and dilution.

Sotion gives the name of 'moonless days' to those from the 29th of the lunar month to the 2nd; in these, owing to the rays of the sun, the moon is concealed and is not seen by humans.

14. *On hail.* Africanus.

If a menstruating woman displays her private parts to the hail she will ward it off; all wild animals, too, recoil from this sight.

Take a girl's first towel, bury it in the middle of your land, and the vines or crops will not be injured by hail.[1]

If a thong made of sealskin is hung on one of the prominent vines there will be no damage from hail, according to *Philostratos* in *Historical Research*.

Some say that if you display a mirror to overhead clouds the hail will pass by.

1. Plutarch, *Symposium Questions* 700e and Pliny, *Natural History* 28.77–78 allude to these beliefs.

Also if you carry the skin of a hyena or crocodile or seal around your land, and hang it at the farm gate, hail will not fall. And if you hang a large number of keys of different buildings on cords, all around your land, the hail will pass by. If you set up wooden bulls before your house you will effectively protect it. Take a tortoise, as found in marshland, in your right hand, turn it upside down and carry it around the whole vineyard. When you have completed this, go to the centre of the vineyard and place it there upside down, alive, heaping up a little earth all round it so that it cannot turn itself over and walk away: it will be unable to do so, finding no hold without earth under its feet, and will stay where you put it. If you do this hail will not fall on that field or anywhere of yours. Some insist that the carrying round and placing of the tortoise must be done at the sixth hour of day or night. *Apuleius the Roman* says that if you draw a grape cluster on a tablet and set it up as a shrine in the vineyard, sounding a lyre, the fruit will not be damaged. You must begin to sound the lyre on 23rd November and sound it for the last time on 4th February. So much for what the ancient sources say. I think that some of these methods are quite improper and to be avoided; I advise readers not to trust them completely. I copied them so as not to be thought to have omitted anything said by the ancient sources.

Pieces of the hide of a hippopotamus, placed at each boundary marker, prevent damage by hail.

15. *More on hail.* Africanus.

Xyla daphnesas parthenou knemas alleoresai: tes de hekastou kath' hekaston klema chre einai te kai chosai.

16. *On thunderbolts.* Africanus.

Bury the skin of a hippopotamus in your land, and no thunderbolts will fall in it.

1. Greek *peganon*: *Ruta graveolens* L.
2. Greek *malache agria*: *Malva* spp. and *Althaea* spp.
3. Wine flavoured with wormwood, *Artemisia absinthium* L. Instructions for
4. Greek *skilla*: *Urginea maritima* (L.) Baker.
6. I use 'adder' to translate Greek *echidne* and 'viper' to translate *echis*, the two names of *Vipera berus* (Linnaeus, 1758).
7. Greek *phalangia*: European black widow, malmignatte or karakurt: *Latrodectus tredecimguttatus* (Rossi, 1790).
8. Greek *ophis* and *mygale* ... (Linnaeus, 1758); neither is venomous in the usual sense, but their bites can cause dangerous infections. Owen identifies *mygale* with Italian *toporagno*
1. For *taurous*, 'bulls', Hamblenne suggests *staurous*, 'crosses'.
2. I do not understand this text; nor did Cornarius. Owen's text did not include this chapter.

Book 2

1. *The master's presence is very helpful to the farm.*

The continuous presence of the master improves the farm greatly. He persuades all to work diligently; he ensures that forgotten tasks are remembered; he praises those who work enthusiastically and scolds the slackers, resulting in a shared aim of care and assiduity.

2. *Boys are best suited to agriculture. Select workers for their physical suitability to the work, and choose separately those adapted to each task.* Varro.

Each period of life has its own suitability to farm work, but in terms of age boys are specially adapted to it: they are bred up to labour, obedient, and keenly responsive to whatever arises. They can easily bend down to pull out dog's-tooth grass[1] or to remove vine leaves.[2] They learn about nature from experiment, from their own work and from their elders' teaching.

The ploughman needs to be rather long-bodied: he has to bear down on the plough-handle strongly and weight the whole ploughshare, so that the furrow will not be superficial; also blows fetched downwards from above will strike home on the oxen. Those who work the vineyard need not be so tall, but four-square; one of that build will not be stooping down from on high to tend the vines; being at ground level he will work without tiring. We will choose cowmen to be strong and tall, with rather harsh voices. If they

---

1. Greek *agrostis*; *Cynodon dactylon* (L.) Pers. No recipe for squill wine is given.
2. To encourage full ripening: compare 5.29.

are small, the cattle in front will hide them. They need to be able to see well ahead; a rough voice will enable them to dominate the cattle. Goatherds must be light and fast-moving to keep up with the quickness of the goats.

3. *In what places and exposures you should site the farm buildings, and facing what star; and on baths.* Didymos.

Sites near the sea, in the mountains and on north-facing slopes are in general healthier. Sites near marshes and lakes, in hollow places, facing the south wind, or sloping towards the west, are unhealthy. The farm buildings should be on a relatively high site: this is most convenient for health, for observing your lands and for protecting them. The whole orientation of the farm buildings should be eastwards and its entrance on that side. East winds are healthiest, and the sun's heat, entering more rapidly, will thin and disperse the heavy and dank air. The buildings should not be made low or confined, but open, broad and lofty. Some advise orienting the buildings towards the south, so that they will get most sun; but I say an east orientation is better because the *notos*, blowing from the south, is damp, irregular and very unhealthy.

Bathhouses, however, should not have a northerly outlook, facing the *borras*; they should face the winter sunset or the south. They need to be well-watered and open to clean air. If there are no dungheaps and foul-smelling sites close at hand, clean air can enter. Their furnaces should be at ground level, inward-facing and with a downward slope, so that wood when thrown in stays and does not fall out: a fire deep within will give a lot of heat to the structure.

4. *Finding water.* Paxamos.

You must dig where the chaste tree grows (called by some agnus castus),[1] or fleabane,[2] or *othleis*,[3] or reeds,[4] or *kolymbatos* on its

---

1. Late Greek *damaskenon*: *Prunus* spp., e.g. *P. domestica* L.

4. Greek *kerasea*: *Prunus* spp., e.g. *P. cerasus* L.

5. This sentence, with its unexpected simile, belongs to one of the oldest identifiable strata in the *Geoponika*: it comes from a text of the 4th century BC by

1. The two Greek names are *lygos* and *agnos*: *Vitex agnus-castus* L.

2. Greek *konyza*: *Inula* spp.

3. Unidentified.

4. Greek *kalamos*: *Arundo donax* L.

own,[1] or the so-called *triphyllon*,[2] or pondweed,[3] or where rushes[4] appear without being planted.

A more reliable test of the presence of water is as follows. In a place you choose dig a pit three cubits deep, and have ready made a lead bowl of hemispherical shape or a jug. As the sun goes down, whatever it is should be smeared all over with olive oil. Then take some wool, washed, dry, clean, about filling the hand, and fasten a small stone in the middle of the wool, and fix the wool inside [the base of] the bowl with wax so that it cannot fall. Then turn the bowl over [and put it in] the pit, making sure, as the bowl tilts, that the wool hangs down halfway inside the bowl. Then screen the bowl all round at the height of one cubit, and leave it there for the night. At first light, before the sun rises, remove the screening and turn over the bowl. If the place has any water, you will find droplets inside the bowl, and the wool will be wet. If there is a lot of moisture, so that it is dripping, the water is close underground. If it is simply damp, then there is still water but deep down. If no such sign appears, make the same test in another place, and another again, having in mind your own human judgement as to promising sources of water.[5]

5. *More on finding water.*

High and very rocky mountains are likely to be well-watered, particularly the slopes that face the *borras* and the north; likewise black and fatty soil, also rocky soil. If the stones are black and fiery, in particular, it will be very well-watered. In the plains, where the soil is clayey with pebbles and pumice and looks parched and bare, in other words dried-up and naked of vegetation, it is likely to be without water; similarly potter's earth, and land that refuses and repels rain and storms.

1. Possibly great burnet, *Sanguisorba officinalis* L.
2. Possibly caltrop, *Tribulus terrestris* L.
3. Greek *potamogeiton*: *Potamogeton natans* L.
4. Greek *schoinos*: *Juncus* spp.
5. Similar to the last section of 2.6.

There is water underground where you find dog's-tooth grass, plantain,[1] turnsole,[2] sedge,[3] bramble,[4] horsetail,[5] horse-mint,[6] slender and tender reeds,[7] maidenhair fern or adiantum,[8] melilot,[9] curled dock,[10] cinquefoil,[11] broad-leaved *polygonos*,[12] rush, *stryphnos*,[13] *stratiotis*,[14] coltsfoot,[15] teasel.[16]

Where plants are plentiful, thick, green and flourishing, water will be plentiful too.

Crabs are useful in streams; they open up springs and they kill leeches.

Districts with black soil and rich soil have rather persistent and vigorous streams; very muddy districts more so, and, if the water tastes sweet, more so still.

If water appears in some porous spot, accept what comes but do not look for more, for fear that existing waters will dry up.

1. Greek *arnoglosson*: *Plantago* spp., notably *P. major* L.

2. Greek *heliotropion*: *Chrozophora tinctoria* (L.) A.Juss.

3. Greek *boutomon*: *Carex hyalinolepis* Steud. (syn. *Carex riparia*).

4. Greek *batos*: *Rubus fruticosus* L.

5. Greek *hippouris*: *Equisetum* spp., notably *E. sylvaticum* L.

6. Greek *kalaminthe*: probably *Mentha longifolia* (L.) Hudson.

7. Greek *kalamos leptos, kalamos hapalos*: if these are different kinds (which is not certain) they are presumably common reed, *Phragmites australis* (Cav.) Trin. ex Steud., and small reed, *Calamagrostis* spp.

8. Greek *kallitrichos* and *adiantos*: *Adiantum capillus-veneris* L.

9. Greek *melilotos*: *Trigonella graeca* (Boiss. & Spruner) Boiss.

10. Greek *oxylapathos*: *Rumex crispus* L.

11. Greek *pentadaktylos*: probably *Potentilla* spp., e.g. *P. reptans* L. The same term is used at 18.10.

12. Greek *polygonos he platyphyllos* 'broad-leaved polygonos', probably a relative of the plant elsewhere called 'male *polygonon*' (knot-grass, *Polygonum aviculare* L.); therefore possibly water-pepper, *Persicaria hydropiper* (L.) Spach.

13. Possibly bittersweet, *Solanum dulcamara* L.

14. Unidentified; perhaps in some way resembling *stratiotes*, which was water-lettuce, *Pistia stratiotes* L., familiar to Greeks as a plant of the Nile; or perhaps a second name for plantain, already mentioned in this list. Plantain contains a coagulant and has been used as the 'soldier's herb' in treating wounds.

15. Greek *chamaileuke*: *Tussilago farfara* L.

16. Greek *chamaileon*: *Dipsacus fullonum* L. This is not one of the usual identifications of the Greek name, but it agrees with Pseudo-Apuleius, *Herbarius* 25.

Some sources well up from below, some flow transversely; those that well up are more persistent. Therefore dig deeply to capture the root of the spring, so that the flow will be persistent and uninterrupted. The sources that flow transversely are less long-lasting; they derive from storms and spring rains.

To predict whether a place has water, some do as follows. They dig a hole one cubit wide and three cubits deep, place in the hole at midday a dry sponge and leave it there for three hours, covering it with a thatch of green reeds or other fresh herbage. If it picks up moisture, there will be water; if it is dry, there will not.

You should go up to some elevated spot and observe the first ray of the rising sun, before the air whitens; if something misty seems to be drawn up into the ray, before it dissipates, that will be a sign of water.

Look in the first light of the sun for mosquitos, flying directly upwards on a converging path like meteors: this too will indicate water.

You need to watch from an elevated spot, in summer at noon, when the air is clear and the land at its driest. That is when moisture rises in places where there is water; it will look like a little cloud. In winter such places give off a vapour like that from rivers, lakes and wells (but from those it is plentiful and cloudy, while above underground water it is thin and airy).

If water is brackish we grind up coral and throw it in; or grind barley, wrap it in a rag and submerge it in the water.

Leeches are destroyed by eels and river crabs thrown into the water.

Rush, reed, clover[1] and bramble are signs that indicate a source of sweet water.

6. Demokritos *on finding water.*

We shall now discuss the art of finding water, water-divining, as some call it. Those who have engaged in the business tell us that plains are in general waterless, wider plains more so than narrower

---

1. Greek *lotos*: *Trifolium fragiferum* L. and *Trifolium resupinatum* L. But this identification is only one among the many meanings of the Greek word.

ones. Most mountains are well-watered, the foothills more so than the heights, bushy and forested parts more so than bare. Water that is found in the plains is in general saline; that found in mountains and foothills is sweet, except in cases where the taste is spoiled by local particularities of the water, whether it is raw, saline or alkaline; whether it contains alum, sulphur or some such mineral.

The physical explanation given for these facts is as follows. The sun always draws up the minutest and lightest element of waters. It dominates the plains throughout the day, sucking out and vaporizing their moisture. Some therefore become wholly waterless; where a certain amount of water remains it is at all events found to be salty, the light and sweet element of it having been extracted (just as is the case with the sea). Mountain waters do not suffer the same effect because the sun's rays burn them all day, and, because of the slope, fall on them obliquely. Hence, it is argued, northward-facing slopes are better watered than southward; east- and west-facing slopes have more water than the south-facing but less than the north-facing; forested tracts are more moist than bare tracts because they are shaded. Foothills are more moist because water is borne downwards, from the heights towards the lowlands and down into the roots of the mountains.

That is why most springs, and the biggest of them, are in such districts, with massive, high and forested mountains above them, with deep valleys and ravines. In such places rainwater collects and filters through the earth each year to replenish the springs. Some of the water that is present in these mountain foothills is not seen, but is carried for a space through underground passages and eventually expelled. In general it emerges in the country neighbouring the sea; but veins carry some of this water a great distance through the earth, so that it gushes up in the sea, as with the undersea well at Arados[1] and the one at Herakleia on the Black Sea;[2] and they say

1. See Strabo, *Geography* 16.2.13 on the undersea well at the Phoenician island of Arados, used with the help of special equipment when besiegers cut off the inhabitants from their usual water sources.

2. No such phenomenon is described by other sources at Herakleia Pontike, although near that city was a deep cave said to be an entrance to the underworld (Mela 1.19; Pliny, *Natural History* 27.4).

that springs are fed from a high elevation under intervening lands near the mountain called Saokes,[1] not far from whose summit are rough tracts and ravines well able to absorb all the rains: it is for these reasons, so they argue, that the springs are so abundant. There are in most parts of the earth veins that carry water; just as in living beings the whole of the body is densely traversed by veins and arteries, so in the earth there are porous places, filled with air, and also veins, filled with water (in some parts very dense and interwoven, in other parts more rarefied) which, owing to their number and density, are easily hit on by those who dig wells. Springs, then, it is explained, are the openings of veins; hence they are persistent, are fed from a great distance and by transfer among the veins. But pools are supplied by percolating rainwater and water standing in the ground in shady and covered places, as if contained in vessels, not the outflow of veins; hence pools are not persistent but quite rapidly die away if they happen not to be very copious.

Springs wax and wane depending on the state of the weather: when there are droughts they decrease; when the season is rainy they increase. Their own waters are fed, as already explained, by the rains; hence they increase especially around the winter solstice, when the sun is less than usually bright and the rains increase, while around the summer solstice and the [rising of] Sirius they show the opposite effect. Springs and pools can thus be distinguished in the following way. A spring when discovered, one fed by a good vein, flows easily from the beginning, will show a slight increase and retain this volume for a time, or else will continue with the same volume originally seen except when it wanes or waxes with changes in the weather; but a pool, they say, behaves differently, initially flowing violently and plentifully but, after a short time, diminishing. Such a flow should not be relied on.

Thus they advise those searching for water first to explore the district, to identify its orientation and its type, making use of the indications already given – also whether there are fords for use in hunting, and other signs from landforms and plant life.

They say that signs of water in a particular spot will be that the rushes known as club-rush[1] grow there, and sedge, and brambles, and the *kypeiros* that some people call *zerna*;[2] also plentiful and thriving dog's-tooth grass; also the reeds known as Indian or giant reed *or halites* or pipe-reed,[3] thickly-growing and tender; likewise a flourishing colony of the creeper called bindweed;[4] and wild fig,[5] and monk's pepper,[6] and wild elm,[7] and horsetail, and cinquefoil,[8] and crowfoot or 'gold-flower'.[9] In general any of these growing without dog's-tooth grass, having been planted, self-seeded, green and vigorous and dense, are evidently fed by underground water. Relying on these signs and setting out upwards from the location (if the site is inclined) you must dig to locate the spring that will lie somewhere above.

The origin of the name horsetail is evident from the etymology. It is like a horse's tail, with leaves like the hairs, and the stem, rising from the root, continually narrows towards the top. This stem is hollow, like a reed, with distinct joints, and the hair-like leaflets grow from these joints. From its nature it is called *salpingion* 'little tube'.

Sedge grows in marshes. It has leaves like narcissus. Cattle like to eat it. Each root sends up a thicket rather than a single stem.

Cinquefoil sends up numerous stems about a span in length, like little sticks, from each root; it is these that bear the fruit. It has leaves like mint, five (rarely more) on each stalk, serrated all round; the flower is pale yellow.

Crowfoot or 'gold-flower' has leaves like celery but bigger, and a golden flower. The whole plant is no bigger than two palms.

1. Greek *holoschoinos* and other spellings, here and at 2.40: *Scirpoides holoschoenus* (L.) Soják.

2. Possibly *Cyperus rotundus* L. (sometimes called coco-grass, with bitter but edible tubers) or a relative.

3. *Arundo donax* L.

4. Greek *malakokissos*: *Calystegia sepium* (L.) R.Br.

5. Greek *syke he agria*, but this is probably an error in the text. More likely is the almost-homonymous squirting cucumber, Greek *sikys he agrias*: *Ecballium elaterium* (L.) A.Richard.

6. Greek *pisax*, another name for *Vitex agnus-castus* L.

7. Greek *ptelea agria*: *Ulmus* spp., e.g. *Ulmus glabra* Huds.

8. Greek *pentaphyllon*: *Potentilla reptans* L.

9. Greek *batrachion* and *chrysanthemon*: *Ranunculus muricatus* L. and *Ranunculus chius* DC., related to buttercup and lesser celandine.

11. Bindweed is a creeper like ivy; it cannot stand up straight and its leaves and stems are tender enough to be woven at any point. It grows particularly in reed-beds and places with rich soil.

The *kypeiros* sometimes called *zerna* has thin leaves like just-germinated leek, a stem like that of rush but thinner, a seed at the top like millet, a root like a black olive stone, aromatic to the taste.

If we reject the evidence offered by all the above plants and shrubs, we shall be at a loss in places that have no water either from streams, springs or wells; but where these plants appear, they indicate that underground water exists. When inspected, the weedier they appear, the closer the water will be to the surface, and therefore less powerful and less persistent; the sturdier and greener they appear, the deeper and more persistent the water is shown to be.

It is also necessary to observe the type of soil. They say that it will be altogether waterless if it is clayey and pumice-like and parched by nature, but if it is sticky or fiery or muddy, or with black and fatty soil, or with pebbly layers, no conclusion can be drawn. The pebbly part should not be mixed through the soil, but present in it horizontally, and in general variously coloured soil should have thick and well-marked layers; when neighbouring rocks are somewhat blackish, this colouring should not have the appearance of stains but marble-like; if there is to be water present; when rocks that are whitish are lying on soil such as has been described, there will be water under their footings where they are embedded in the underlying stratum: these are the signs that indicate its presence in such cases. Irregular groups of rocks will also indicate water when they are in terrain oriented as described earlier.

In land that is pebbly, black, thick, and similarly sticky, there will be many surface pools. Here, therefore, conduits should be dug following the pools, and in this way the most possible water will be collected. In porous and rocky places whatever springs are found must suffice.

Investigators should also look for water in the following way. Have ready a lead basin of hemispherical shape, containing about one *chous*, and in them two or three hanks of wool, well carded, tied around their middles with linen, and the linen fixed with wax to the inside bottom of the basin. The basin should be rubbed with olive oil. Then a well should be dug, down to about three cubits, in the place where it is thought there might be water as a result of the signs described; the basin should be turned upside down and placed in the well, and green leaves of reeds or other plants placed over it, and the earth replaced to about one cubit. This is to be done when the sun is setting. At sunrise the earth is to be cleared away, the leaves gently removed, and the basin turned over and inspected. If there is the likelihood of springs, you will find the wool saturated with water and the surface of the basin covered with droplets of condensed water. You can sample the water, too, by tasting what is squeezed out from the wool; this will, however, be sweeter than the water of the spring, because the minutest and lightest element will have been taken up.[1]

Enough has now been said about finding water.

7. *On water and the collecting of rainwater.* Diophanes.

Above all, pay attention to water: not just for the pleasure of having it, but because water tempers the air during a drought.

It is especially fortunate to have water from a spring. Lacking this, collect sufficient rainwater for our own and the whole household's[2] use; not in sheepfolds (as some do), because sheep and other animals may foul them with dung, but in structures which must be carefully and frequently cleaned. Use wooden pipes to channel the water cleanly into cisterns.

Africanus: Water is made healthy by steeping bay leaves[3] in it. We make foul water healthy as follows. Put it into jars and leave it in the open air until it has settled, then pour it off carefully into other containers, leaving behind the sediment it has thrown.

1. Similar to the second section of 2.4.

2. For 'household' the Latin loanword *familia* is used. A Greek author as early as Diophanes would not have chosen this word.

3. Greek *daphne, Laurus nobilis* L.

8. On large farms there should be forested mountains; how to plant them. Apuleius.

It is good to have forested natural mountain on your property: if you have none, it is not difficult to plant mountains with wood. There are seeds of wild trees, which if scattered will produce a forest, though this is harder to achieve in dry places. Willow,[1] tamarisk,[2] white poplar,[3] fir,[4] manna ash,[5] elm and all similar kinds like damp places; pine[6] flourishes in sandy soil; experience shows that only pomegranates[7] and olives[8] do really well in more arid places. Oaks and sweet chestnuts (called 'Zeus acorns')[9] should be put in places that get continual rain.

9. What soil is best. Berytios.

Black soil is best and is highly commended by all because it can bear both rain and drought. Next come yellow soil[10] and alluvial soil (called 'slimy') and sweet and hot: these have been seen as suitable for vines, trees and seed crops. Rich soil is also commended, so long as it is crumbly, not difficult to dig, and not meant only for tree-planting. Red soil is best for other uses but is unsuitable for tree-planting.

10. Testing the soil. Anatolios.

Testing for the best soil can be done by observation: that is, if during a drought it does not crack excessively; if after violent rains it does not become swampy, but absorbs all the rainwater into its substance,

1. Greek *itea*: *Salix* spp., e.g. *Salix alba* L.
2. Greek *myrike*: *Tamarix* spp., e.g. *Tamarix gallica* L.
3. Greek *leuke*: *Populus alba* L.
4. Greek *elate*: *Abies alba* Miller and *Abies cephalonica* Loudun.
5. Greek *melia*: *Fraxinus ornus* L.
6. Greek *pitys*: especially Aleppo pine, *Pinus halepensis* P. Mill. and Scotch pine, *Pinus sylvestris* L.
7. Greek *roia*: *Punica granatum* L.
8. Greek *elaia*: *Olea europaea* L.
9. Greek *kastanea* and *Dios balanos*: *Castanea sativa* Mill.
10. *Pyrros*, 'fire-coloured', between yellow and red.

and if during a frost its spine does not appear covered with a shell, such soil has been judged good in general.

Early authors found another excellent method of testing, again under the heading of observation. If the wild trees growing on it are big and woody it may be evaluated as of top quality; if they are less vigorous, it is moderate; if it has thorn thickets, small bushes and low-growing herbage, it is weak and not good for much.

Others, not satisfied with testing by observation, devised a method using other senses. Having dug to a certain depth at the relevant place they extract some soil, and first of all evaluate it by smell. Not yet satisfied, they put it in a vessel, pour on drinking water[1] and carry out an examination by taste; the taste of the water, after this mixing, shows how the soil will be. For seed crops the soil should be taken at one foot depth; for vines, three feet; for fruit trees, four feet. Some assume that the soil is sweet on the evidence of club-rush, reed, clover or bramble growing in it – the same plants that act as evidence for water-finders – but better evidence is the actual taste.

Salty earth must be avoided, so the ancients thought. Since we keep salt out of compost, and experts tell us to apply only *amorge*[2] from unsalted olives to the roots of trees, and we water compost-heaps with sweet and not salty water, it is no surprise that they condemn salty soil, which is indeed unsuitable for anything except date palms: these, however, will flourish and fruit heavily. This is why in our own country, where the soil is entirely salty, the date palm is the only tree that gives a good crop. In salty soil, then, plant only date palms, or give it up, or improve it so far as possible, mixing sweet soil with it in the same way that compost is added.

Bad-smelling soil is wholly useless and must be altogether avoided.

1. 'Drinking water' because unsalted, the opposite of 'seawater'.
2. *Amorge* is the bitter, watery by-product of olive-pressing, Latin *amurca*. As explained at 9.19, salt was sometimes sprinkled on olives before pressing, but the *amurca* called for here (and also at 5.23, 9.10 and 18.15) must contain no salt.

11. *More on testing the soil.* Diophanes.

Others determine the best soil in this way. They dig a hole and take out a certain quantity of earth, then they turn the earth into the hole again. If the dug earth fills the hole, or more than fills it, they judge that the soil is very good. If dug earth does not fill the hole it shows that the soil is not good.

12. *What seeds to sow in rich soil, what in middling and what in thinner soil.* Tarantinos.

It is better to sow wheat in rich soil and in the plains, barley in middling soil, pulses in thinner soil; but pulses can be sown in the plains, after the wheat harvest, for next year's crop. Pulses rest and relieve the soil, because (with the exception of chickpeas) they are shallow-rooting.

13. *What kinds of seeds to plant when the soil is wet and what when it is thoroughly dry.* Leontios.

Barley should be sown when the ground is not wet but rather uniformly dry. Wheat[1] should be sown in muddy and wet soil, because it grows better in such conditions; it is necessary, however, not to delay the sowing of wheat.

Broad beans and peas should be sown when the soil is muddy. In wholly dry ground they are broken before they shoot, and so die; those that are not broken will grow poorly. Other pulses can succeed even if sown in wholly dry soil, but they grow better and finer if sown in well-moistened soil.

14. *The season for planting wheat and barley.* Didymos.

The earlier the better with sowing.

It is best to begin on rich soil when it has had a little rain.

Some think it correct to sow from autumn throughout the winter; in colder places until 15th March or until the spring equinox, that is, 25th March. Others, more carefully specifying the dates for

1. Greek *sitos*: *Triticum* spp.

sowing, make a distinction: they advise that the sowing of barley can begin at the autumn equinox, that is, 30th September, and that of wheat at the setting of the Pleiades, that is, 11th November (as *Vergil* instructs),[1] and that both should stop at the winter solstice, that is, 24th December.

Demokritos, however, advises that it is preferable to sow around the setting of Alphecca, and gives a physical explanation: not only are there frequent rains at that period, but also the earth has a naturally receptive tendency to enhance procreativity in seeds sown at that time. In the region of Phoenicia the setting of Alphecca begins on 25th November.

One who sows seed must avoid northerly days and those with very cold breezes. Clearly on such days the earth does not accept the seeds, groaning and as if bristling; on fine days, southerly and otherwise warm, the earth is ready to receive the seeds, to start them rooting, and to produce sturdy crops.

Some advise that sowing should take place when the moon is waxing, that is, from the fourth of the lunar month until full moon, the fifteenth.

Some take the precaution, considering the uncertainty of the future, of not sowing the whole crop early but deferring to a second, third and fourth occasion.

15. *Forecasting which crops will thrive*, Zoroaster.

Some use the following method to find out in advance what crops will thrive. At a certain spot, a few days before the rising of Sirius, they sow a small quantity of each seed experimentally. When Sirius rises, it harms some of the crops, in its usual way, but not others. Having made this test they sow the crops that were not damaged by the rising of Sirius, and abandon those that were dried up. The rising of Sirius takes place on 19th July; the experimental seeds should therefore be watered 20 or 30 days beforehand so that they will have begun to grow.

---

1. Repeated more concisely at 5.18.

1. Vergil, *Georgics* 1.221 (Vergil calls the Pleiades *Atlantides*).

16. *The selection of seed, the quality of seed to be sown, and how long it lasts.* Vindanionius.

Select, as it grows, wheat that is noble, sturdy, tall and smooth, golden in colour, and highly productive (as shown in breadmaking). Avoid wheat that is beaten down or that is shrivelled. Select barley that is full, sturdy, fresh, white and very heavy, and not beaten down. All other pulses should be selected for similar qualities.[1]

Some select the stronger ears, those that have full and well-developed grains, keep back this finer part of the harvest, and store it for sowing.

The best seed is that of the current year; two year seed is weaker, and three year seed very poor. Older seed produces nothing.

17. *Seed from one spot should be sown in another.* Didymos.

Some say that it is conducive to high yield to sow seed from one kind of ground in another, for example, seed from mountain land in the plains, from damp ground in parched ground, and vice versa, because there is a desire for opposites both in seeds and in soil.[2] But let it be a move from worse fields to better, not from better fields to worse.

18. *Ensure that seed is not damaged in any way after sowing.* Africanus.

If you soak the seed in the juice of houseleek[3] before sowing it will not be attacked by birds or mice or ants and will produce better plants.

If you mix a little of the wheat with hellebore and sow it at the edge of the field, surrounding the rest, the crop will not be harmed by birds.

1. Either there is a missing sentence on how to select beans for sowing, or the meaning is that 'all pulses, i.e. all other seed crops' selected for sowing should have qualities similar to those of barley.
2. Repeated more briefly at 2.19.
3. Greek *aeïzoon*: *Sempervivum* spp.

If you put river crabs, that is, *pagouroi*, into water for eight days, and then sprinkle this water around the edge of the crop, the seeds and plants will not be harmed by birds. If you mash cypress[2] leaves and mix them with the seed, this will protect them from animal pests.

Some grind up stag's horn or elephant tusk and sprinkle it over the seeds, either dry or mixed with water.

Apuleius says that seeds sprinkled with wine will suffer less disease.

You will also help them a lot by drizzling them with water and *amorge*.

It is better to use natural antipathy. If the seed, while in the container in which you measure it, is wrapped round for some days with a hyena skin, it will take on the natural force and smell of the animal, and will not easily be attacked. If after sowing your seed and covering it with earth you mix a little wheat with hellebore and sow that over the top, when birds taste it they will die; take the dead birds, stick them on reeds and hang them by their feet, and no other birds will be able to approach. If you crush squirting cucumber roots, soak them all day and night, and drizzle the water liberally over seeds you are about to sow, cover them with a cloak the next day, and then sow them; the sown seed will not be attacked and will be all the better. Vetch[3] seed will not be eaten if you mix a little fenugreek seed with it at the time of sowing.

Vergil advises drizzling natron[4] and water over the seeds being sown.

Also seed sown at full moon will not be attacked by pests.

Apuleius says that before the land is dug a toad (a land frog, that is) should be carried round it at night, fastened in an earthenware container, and buried in the middle of the field; then, when it is time

Similarly 5.50 and 10.89.

2. Greek *kyparissos*: *Cupressus sempervirens* L.

3. Latin *vicia*, medieval Greek *bikia*: *Vicia sativa* L. The species was unfamiliar in earlier Greece; hence it was known to the Byzantines under a form of its Latin name.

4. Greek *nitron*; mainly sodium carbonate, Na_2CO_3. Vergil in fact advises *amurca*, not water. Vergil, *Georgics* 1.193.

84

to sow, it should be dug up and thrown off the land. This will ensure that the harvest is not bitter.

It is again *Apuleius* who says that it is advisable to mix a little prepared lentil[1] with the seed being sown: by nature it opposes the maleficence of the wind.

With old urine and excrement of dogs, mixed and smeared on crops, fruit trees or vines, you will keep them all uninjured.

19. *What to do and what to avoid for a good harvest.* Sotion.

Write the word *Phryel* on the plough, when working fallow land and when sowing, and it will bear well.

They say that it is conducive to high yield to sow seed from one kind of ground in another, for example, seed from mountain land in the plains and vice versa.[2]

For good yield some mix in birds' dung, especially that of pigeons, when sowing; in parched land, however, this should not be done because it could burn the seeds.

The sower must take care that seeds do not fall on the ox's head. Some call such seeds 'horn-struck', saying that their produce will be barren and useless, so that not even the power of fire will soften it.[3]

Seed will go further if the sieve is of wolf's skin, with thirty holes, big enough for a finger.

20. *How to achieve an adequate quantity in sowing.*
    Pamphilos.

Spread out the fingers of your hand and press it on the earth; then lift it up again and count the number of seeds in the imprint. There should be at the most 7 wheat seeds, at the least 5; between 7 and 9 barley seeds; between 4 and 6 broad bean seeds. If the quantity falls in this range it is adequate. On snow-covered ground sow a little more thickly, because some of the seed will be destroyed by the frost.

---

1. Lentil as prepared for soup, Greek *phake*, not whole lentil seed.
2. Repeated from 2.17.
3. An ancient belief, used in a metaphor by Plato, *Laws* 853d and denied by Theophrastos, *Plant Physiology* 4.12.13. See also 15.1.

21. *On manure.* The Quintilii.

Manure makes good soil better; it improves poor soil even more.

Good land does not need much manure; light and weak soils need plenty.

Do not manure in heaps, but evenly. Soil that is not manured shivers. Soil that is heavily manured burns.

When manuring plants you should not put it straight to the roots, but first add some fairly light soil, then the manure, then again soil to cover the manure. In this way you avoid either burning the plants by putting the manure to them directly, or stifling them with its heat unshielded by the soil.

The manure of all kinds of birds is good, except that of geese and water birds, which is too wet – but this also is usable when mixed with others. Best of all is pigeon, because it has plenty of heat; for this reason some do not prepare it but use it as it is, spreading it on rather thinly when sowing. It is helpful to infertile land, nourishing it and giving it more potency to produce and nourish, while at the same time attacking dog's-tooth grass. Next best after pigeon is human manure, which is rather like it, and has the property of destroying all weeds. (In Arabia they prepare it thus: they dry it completely, soak it with water, then dry it again. They assert that human manure is the most suitable for vines, but owing to its foulness it is preferable to moderate it by mixing with other manures.) Third is donkey manure, very potent by nature, and particularly suitable for all plants. Fourth is that of goats, being very sharp. Next is that of sheep, which is more gentle. After these is ox manure. Pig manure is better than these, but is unsuitable for newly sown crops because of its great heat: it burns them up at once. Least valuable, weaker than all of them, is horse and mule manure, at least if used alone; if mixed with sharper manures it becomes useful.

More than anything else it is necessary to ensure that labourers do not use fresh manure, that of the same year. It does not help at all; in fact it hinders, and produces a great many vermin.[2] Three and four-year manure is particularly good; with the passage of time its foul-smelling element is dissipated and its roughness is smoothed.

1. Repeated from 4.5.

2. Owen understands this to mean 'among the bearing branches', i.e. 'among the Greek *theria* 'creatures'.

Do not manure when the moon is waxing; it would encourage the growth of weeds, as we have explained sufficiently elsewhere.

22. *Preparation of manure.* Florentinus.

Some people dig a deep pit and cart all manure to it, the better with the worse, and rot it: into this goes ash from bread ovens, food waste, dung from all animals and (better) human dung, and (best of all) human urine, which on its own is good for all fruiting plants and particularly vines. They also add the refuse from tanning. Many people cut the straw, after the grain harvest, and use it as bedding for animals, so that as it is trampled and rotted with their urine it turns into manure. Then they put it in the pit with everything else listed. If there is any muddy refuse, or any ash from burning chaff, brushwood, dry sticks, or timber, they throw this in as well. They also add algae thrown up by the sea, having carefully washed it in fresh water. After all these things are mixed together in the manure pits, they add fresh water so that everything will rot more quickly. After this they shift it around with shovels until it is completely mixed and blended and the manure has liquefied.

It is particularly helpful if we channel into the manure pit rainwater that runs off the road. This water, full of slime and mud, will not only increase the volume of the manure but also aids putrefaction and thus improves it.

23. *When to clear each kind of soil.* Varro.

Different soils are not cleared in the same way. If it is dense, with many roots and bushes, it is dug deeply with local implements[1] at a period when there is serious drought; the soil will be more crumbly and the roots will be burned by the force of the sun, so that they cannot hold. Likewise rich soil, solid, heavy, fat, is considerably easier if turned during a drought.

Light soil becomes ashen when burned by the sun; it expires in the burning, and all the fatness in it is destroyed; for this reason it must be cleared around the autumn equinox, not with forks or spades but

---

1. Not with a plough.

with a plough, and then immediately manured. Generous manuring will help it most. In Arabia they refuse to plough light soil because it has too little strength: it will be opened up by the ploughing and lose what moisture it has. Before ploughing, they sow barley[1] in the *gordaton* as they call it, and it often produces well, especially if there has been plenty of rain.[2]

As with light soil, so soils that are yellow, red, sandy, black, white, dry, thin, and white clay, and also hilly places, are to be cleared in winter.[3]

Salty soil should be turned with small ploughs at the beginning of winter after rain and then sprinkled with chaff. Bean shucks are best, better than from grain; next best are barley and wheat husks. As this rots in, the salty ground, cleared and sweetened, will no longer emit its salty moisture into the air. Then leave it for the whole year, in autumn manure it with ox and horse dung, which are sweeter than the rest, and sow barley and shallow-rooted pulses.

Terrain that is mountainous, or with hard winters, or more shaded, or north-facing, should be worked in summer and in dry periods, as with rich soil, which, as we have said, is better dug with forks.

If digging with forks is impractical because of the large area of ground to be sown, then summer ploughing is possible, beginning in the evening and continuing through the night till sunrise. Thus the moisture and fatness will remain shaded by the raised earth; the oxen, which would have sickened when burned by the sun, will work unconcernedly; and the soil will be made a little more tender by being worked at night. In ploughing it is necessary to yoke four oxen, not two, using so-called double yoking. Work the ground two or three times, and use a rather heavy ploughshare, so that the fatness of the soil will be worked deeply and the clods well turned.

1. Greek *krithe*: *Hordeum vulgare* L.
2. This section might come from the Quintilii, whose work is linked with 'Varro' in book 3. A preceding chapter, 2.21, attributed to the Quintilii, mentions farming in Arabia.
3. Partly repeated at 3.1.

24. *Earthing over and weeding after sowing.* Leontinos.

[Cereal] seeds when sown are best earthed over by hand, so that they are all covered; if that is not possible, they can be hoed using oxen. When the point is reached at which the growing plants hide the soil, they can be hoed, so that weeds are killed and roots laid bare by the rain are buried. Twice hoed is twice as good. When they are in the ear they can be weeded: thus the ground will be broken up for their benefit, and the grain when harvested will be clean and generally serviceable.

25. *When to harvest.* Florentinus.

When some areas of the crop begin to turn yellow, harvest the whole, especially in the case of barley. Pulses should be harvested much earlier than this: they will be easier to cook and nicer to eat, so you should not wait until they are all fully ripe. If you wait, you will lose the first of the crop, which will have dried and will drop when harvested. A drier crop keeps longer but is less in quantity. A yellowish crop will be better to eat and the pods, too, will be better as fodder. All produce should be gathered early in the day, from first light, when still covered in dew. Wheat and barley, when winnowed, should be left on the threshing-floor for not just one but two days, or at least [a day and] a night, and then removed before sunrise so as to be stored in the granary when still cold: this allows it to be kept much longer.

26. *Making the threshing-floor.* Didymos.

The threshing-floor should be laid out at an elevated spot so that it readily catches the wind. It is essential, though, to avoid placing it upwind of the farm buildings or pleasure gardens. The winds will take the chaff, that is, the lightest part of the husks, and carry it – it cannot be prevented – into people's eyes, inflaming their pupils: many have lost an eye from this cause and some have lost both. The chaff also damages fruits, particularly grapes. Like dung, chaff is appropriate to apply to roots but very harmful to shoots and leaves. It is especially bad for green vegetables: it rests on and pierces the leaves, and when pierced they burn.

The threshing-floor must be frequently drenched with *amorge* and flattened with a roller: this will prevent injury from ants. When all has been threshed the threshing-floor must be watered with *amorge* again so that it stays clean with no mess.

Corn placed on the threshing-floor should have the cut end pointing south: it will be fuller and more readily threshed.

27. *On the granary or horreum[1] and the storage of wheat.*

Wheat is best stored in lofts lit from the east. The location should be moderately open to *borras* and *zephyros* but protected from *notos* and other such winds. There must be plenty of vents so that warm air can escape and fresh breezes can enter. There must be no dampness, foul odour or unpleasant fumes. It should preferably be well away from stables, cowsheds and such places and from all sources of heat. The walls should be covered with mud mixed with hair (instead of chaff) and then both inside and out with the so-called white clay. Then soak the roots and leaves of squirting cucumber in water for two days; mix this water into what is called cement and coat the inner walls with it.

Some mix the urine of farm animals into this cement to make it injurious to animal pests. They also use this urine in mixing the concrete that coats the floor.

Some sprinkle the ash from burned oak fronds on the wheat; others, dry cow dung; some place dry sprigs of wormwood[2] or southernwood[3] in it, and also dry leaves of houseleek.

It is better to mix the cement with *amorge*, which kills all vermin. It also makes the wheat firmer and thicker; which is why some boil *amorge* down to half its volume and sprinkle the walls with it, let it dry, and then store the harvest.

Better than anything is to prepare some dried clayey soil, or some dried and sifted pomegranate leaf; then, when the wheat is stored, mix in with each *medimnos* of wheat a *choinix* of clayey soil or pomegranate leaf.

1. A Latin loanword, familiar in Byzantine Greek but not earlier.
2. Greek *apsinthion*: *Artemisia absinthium* L.
3. Greek *abrotonon*: *Artemisia abrotanum* L.

Most useful is to spread semi-dried leaves of fleabane on the ground under the wheat, and after ten *medimnoi* of wheat to spread more fleabane over it, and then continue till all the wheat is stored. Wheat stored in this way not only remains whole for a long time but also keeps its full weight in breadmaking.

Wheat naturally blackens and becomes bitter as it ages. That is why the aforementioned precautions are necessary.

28. *To increase the volume of grain stored in granaries.* Africanus.

You can make wheat increase in volume as follows. Pound natron and flower of natron fine; mix them with fine soil and add them to the stored grain. This procedure also keeps the grain unbruised.

29. *To prevent ants attacking the heaped grain.* Sotion.

Ants will not attack the heaped grain if you scratch around the heap with white earth or put wild oregano[1] around it.

30. *Keeping barley: how to make it last as long as possible in the granary.* Damegeron.

You will keep barley unspoiled if you place in it dry leaves of the fruiting bay, and any wood ash but particularly that of bay.

Similarly dried houseleek and horse-mint in gypsum, mixed in the barley.

Some fill a bucket with vinegar, put a lid on it, and put it in the middle of the heaped barley.

It is necessary to know that barley becomes bitter when aged.

31. *Keeping flour.* Same author.

Flour keeps unspoiled for a time if you split resinous pine wood and put it in the flour.

Some grind equal amounts of cumin and salt, make dry cakes of this mixture, and put them in the flour.

1. Greek *agrion origanon*: *Origanum* spp.

32. Assaying wheat; how to verify the weight of bread.
Florentinus.

Take unspoiled wheat, clean and sift it carefully, weigh it. If the weight is 40 *litrai*, demand the same weight of bread, because what is lost by the removal of bran will be saved in the grinding and subsequent processes when water is added.

The baking of bread reduces its weight by three-twentieths, so that from a weight of 10 *litrai* 1½ *litrai* are lost. It should be assumed that the same weight will be lost in the baking of white bread and of second-quality bread.

33. How to make very nice bread without yeast. Didymos.

Some make bread without yeast by adding natron: it makes bread more crumbly (meat, too).

Others make bread without yeast in the following way. One day in advance they put grapes in water, then take out the floating grapes, squeeze them and use the juice from them instead of yeast: it makes the loaves nicer and better-looking.

[Other notes on yeast and bread.]

If you want to have yeast for a whole year, when the must foams in the vats take some of the foam, mix it with millet flour, knead it well and make cakes with it, dry them in the sun, store in a damp place; take whever you need from them and use it instead of yeast.

All breads made without yeast are particularly stimulating sexually.

Florentinus says that crock-baked bread, shaped thin and dried off in the sun, is easily digested. Bread baked in ovens is heavier in digestion.

34. Ptisane.[1]

Husk barley by pounding in a mortar, dry it in the sun, pound it and sun-dry it again. Put it aside and sprinkle on it the sharps produced in the pounding, as this conserves it.

1. Pale green; not recorded elsewhere as a variety. Theophrastos, *On Odours* 52, who describes it as robust and with a good aroma (the robustness could be alleviated by the...) Similar to 3.9.

When the *ptisane* is taken rather liquid it is particularly nourishing, so *Florentinus* was told.

35. *Broad beans.* Same author.[1]

Never sow bean seed[2] at the roots of a tree: it could dry up the tree.

Beans must be sown early, because they like muddy soil. To grow beans that cook well, soak the seeds in water mixed with natron for one day before sowing.

Scientists say that beans dull the hearts of those who eat them. Because beans are flatulent they are thought also to obscure clear dreams.[3]

They also say that if barnyard fowl eat beans continually they become sterile.

Pythagoras says that beans should not be eaten because of the grievous letters written on their flowers.

They say that a bean which has been nibbled will be restored when the moon is waxing.

Beans should not be boiled in salty water; hence not in seawater.

The first to abstain from beans was *Amphiaraos*, owing to the practice of foretelling the future from dreams.

Verses such as these are quoted from *Orpheus*: *Fools! withhold your hands from beans!*[4] and: *To eat beans is as much as to eat your parents' heads.*[5]

Beans watered with seawater will not be attacked; likewise those watered with an infusion of *magodaris*.[6]

1. But the previous chapter has no general attribution. Cornarius and later editors attribute it to Didymos.

2. Greek *kyamos*: *Vicia faba* L.

3. This was important because of oneiromancy, the practice of foretelling the future from dreams.

4. Whose line was this really? Empedocles's, according to Aulus Gellius (*Attic Nights* 4.11).

5. Attributed to Pythagoras at *Epitome of Athenaeus* 65f.

6. *Cachrys ferulacea* (L.) Calestani, an umbellifer that resembles the extinct aromatic silphium.

36. *Chickpeas.* Florentinus.

If you soak the chickpeas in lukewarm water one day before sowing them, the chickpeas you produce will be bigger.

Some, more assiduously, wanting to have much larger chickpeas, soak them in advance in their pods, with natron, and then sow.

If you want to make them produce early, sow them at barley time.

So that nothing can eat them when they are coming ripe, steep the seeds of squirting cucumber[2] and wormwood in water and sprinkle them with this each day before dawn for five days. During the next five days the dew will wash the bitterness off them.

37. *Lentils.*[3] Same author.

Lentils germinate faster and better if coated in dry cow dung before sowing. Lentils grow bigger in their pods if the seed is soaked in lukewarm water with natron before sowing. They keep without rotting if sprinkled with vinegar containing fig sap.

Egyptian lentil soup produces cheerfulness in those who eat it.

38. *Millet.*[4] Same author.

Millet likes slimy and moist ground; sandy, too, as long as it is frequently watered. It requires little seed to sow a whole field. It wants to be hoed and weeded regularly. It is sown after the spring equinox, that is, 23rd April. If it is sown too thickly its growth will be harmed: a *plethron* will not take more than a handful. When hoeing, the weeds must be pulled up; worked in this way, the *plethron* will reliably yield 40 *modioi*.

1. Greek *erebinthos: Cicer arietinum* L.
2. Greek *sikyos agrios: Ecballium elaterium* (L.) A. Rich., squirting cucumber.
3. Greek *phakos: Lens culinaria* L.
4. Greek *kenchros: Panicum miliaceum* L., broomcorn millet.

39. *Lupins. Same author.*

Lupins[1] should be sown before other crops, after the spring equinox, without waiting for the rains. Before it flowers drive in cattle, which will browse all other plants but not touch the lupins because they are bitter.

Apuleius[2] says that each day they follow the sun in its course, indicating the hours to farmers even if the sky is clouded over.

Lupins are sweetened by steeping them in seawater or river water for three days; when they begin to be sweet they are dried and stored, and are given to animals for food with chaff.

At bakeries adequate loaves are made when lupin flour is mixed with barley or wheat flour.

Lupins are to be sown in weak soil and they need no manure. They are their own manure, in fact; they manure any exhausted soil and make it yield well in the future.

They flower three times.

They must be harvested after rain, because if dry they fall out of their pods and are wasted.

Ground and applied to the navel they expel worms.

They need not be sown deeply, and they do well if neglected, like the caper bush.[3] They are driven away if they sense anyone working the soil.

40. *On pulses, hemp,*[4] *linseed.*[5] *The Quintilii.*

Pulses like extremely dry soil, with the exception of broad beans, which like moist soil and ground that is well-watered.

Hemp likes valley land and soil that is continually humid. It is sown from the rising of Arcturus, that is, 27th February, until the spring equinox, that is, 25th March.

1. Greek *thermos*: *Lupinus albus* L.
2. What follows agrees in part with Pliny, *Natural History* 18.133–136.
3. Greek *kapparis*: *Capparis spinosa* L.
4. Greek *kannabis*: *Cannabis sativa* L.
5. Greek *linon*: *Linum usitatissimum* L.

Linseed likewise likes muddy ground, and is sown from the autumn equinox until the rising of Altair,[1] that is, 4th January.

41. *How to produce beans that will cook easily.* Demokritos.

In sowing, mix with dung and natron; this is how to produce beans that are readily cooked.

If, as it happens, you did not do this, but you want beans that will cook quickly, put a bit of mustard[2] in the cooking pot; this will immediately break down whatever you are cooking, be it meat or pulses. If you add a larger quantity of mustard, what you are cooking will break down and dissolve completely.

42. *The lion plant, also called broomrape.* Sotion.

Osproleon, sometimes called broomrape,[3] will not invade the fields if at the four corners and in the middle you stick branches of oleander.[4] This keeps all pulses safe from attack.

If you want this plant not to make an appearance, take five potsherds, draw on them with a bit of chalk[5] or some other white substance a picture of Herakles throttling the lion, and place them in the four corners and at the middle.

Another preventative exists, relying on nature and antipathy, reported by *Demokritos*: a virgin girl ripe for marriage, barefoot and naked,[6] completely uncovered, her hair loosened, carrying a cockerel in her hands, should go around the field. The lion weed will

1. The text repeats 'rising of *Arktouros*', which is clearly wrong; 'rising of *Aetos*', i.e. Altair = Alpha Aquilae, is an emendation suggested by the text of Columella, *On Agriculture* 2.10.17.

2. Greek *sinepi*; *Sinapis alba* L.

3. Greek *orobakche, osproleon, leōn botanē*: *Orobanche lutea* Baumg., *Orobanche ramosa* L. and perhaps, depending where and when this was written, *Orobanche crenata* Forskål; the last has spread south-eastwards in Europe in historic times. All three are parasitic on the roots of *Vicia* and other species.

4. Greek *rhododaphne*: *Nerium oleander* L.

5. The word used is *kritarion*, a loanword from Latin known only in Byzantine Greek.

6. In place of 'ripe for marriage, barefoot and naked' manuscript F has 'with the blood of marriage ... naked', some text having been erased.

immediately retreat and the pulses will improve, possibly because this lion plant is afraid of the cockerel.

Some, on the basis of experience, want the seed you are about to sow to be sprinkled with the blood of a cockerel: then it will not be attacked by the lion plant.

Some write the word *Iabo* and bury the potsherd in the middle of the field.

It is necessary to avoid letting the bean seeds that you are sowing touch the ox's horn. Any that do will be barren and worthless.

43. *Which crops are spoiled by which weeds.* Paxamos.

Broomrape destroys broad bean and chickpea by embracing them. Darnel, the so-called *zizanion*,[1] kills wheat, and if mixed in bread it causes blindness in those who eat it. Goatgrass[2] is harmful to barley; the weed called *pelekinos*[3] damages lentil.

44. *The overseer or farm manager.* Florentinus.[4]

The person entrusted with overseeing the farm must be an example to all who work there, so that when they observe him, his life and his habits, they are ashamed – rather than afraid – [to fall short]. He must be respectable, approachable, avoid wine as far as possible (because excessive drinking of wine causes inattention); he must not be grasping or greedy about loans; he must be satisfied with a little, always ready with what the labourers need, alert, waking up before the rest; avoiding lies and false oaths, God-fearing, following local religious cults and not desecrating sacred trees or the like, but guiding them all towards religious observances;[5] strict when it is time for work, affable and generous at times of relaxation, helping

---

1. *Lolium temulentum* L. The first Greek name, *aira*, is classical; the second, *zizanion*, seems to be Near Eastern in origin and was introduced to Greek (after the time of Paxamos) by way of the Greek New Testament. See also 10.87.
2. Greek *aigilops*: probably *Aegilops geniculata* Roth.
3. Perhaps crown vetch, *Coronilla varia* L. (which has its uses, as did *pelekinos*) or a close relative such as *Securigera securidaca* (L.) Degen & Dörfl.
4. This chapter is to be compared with Cato, *On Farming* 5.
5. To Cato, religion was potentially divisive; he was concerned that the farm manager should observe only those rituals that the owner approved.

to ensure that the weekly holiday is observed – not giving orders for anything that is forbidden on that day[1] but enjoining rest – and more especially the monthly and annual festivals. He must not work on others' account, nor take profit from his master's land, nor lend generally on his master's account,[2] but carry out his master's instructions; and if he has a better idea, he must consult his master before acting on it, unless the advantage is so pressing that he cannot wait for his master's order.

45. *The supervisor should keep a journal of farm work; how he should organize working parties.* Same author.

The supervisor should keep a diary, carefully compiled from the shared views of experienced workers on the farm, including every day of every month, so that he will know and remember how the work goes and not forget any chronological landmark. If any such day is forgotten, the sequence is thrown out, and it is not only this year's harvest that suffers, but the ground itself will be in a poorer state [for next year].

If there are many workers they should not all be working [at the same tasks], because they will gladly take it easy; nor in twos and threes, because they will need more foremen. So they should not work all together or in very small groups, and the supervisor should determine the size of working parties. It is best, if there are many of them, to organize them into tens; if there are fewer, into sixes and not fives. With even numbers of diggers, a regular sequence is maintained, and the lazier ones, lifting and planting the spade to the same rhythm, are forced to be like the keener ones.

46. *Apportioning farm work.* Same author.

Some give the rule that whether the ground being dug is to be vineyard, rosebed, kitchen garden or whatever other type of planting,

---

1. For lists of work forbidden on rest days see Cato, *On Farming* 2; Vergil, *Georgics* 1.268–272; Columella, *Agriculture* 2.21.1–5.
2. Meaning that he must not deal for his own profit in the farm's labour, or produce, or income.

dug to a depth of three feet, it takes seven men to dig each *plethron*, or in very difficult ground eight.

The *plethron* of old vines, in easily worked ground, with no weeds, even on a hillside, is often worked by three people, or if more difficult and weedy by five. New vines, for the first five years, are often worked by three. *Aminnios*[1] is much easier to work than other grape varieties; *Syrentinos*[2] is the opposite, and needs more workers. Four men can trench a *plethron*, so the experts assure us, if the width of the trench is two and a half feet, the depth one foot; this is prescribed as the best measure. It has been observed that four men can prune a *plethron* [of vines]. It takes one man [per *plethron*] to thin the shoots the first time this is done; much less than that the second time.

It is not possible, nor indeed desirable, for even the handiest vineyard worker to work more than eight *plethra* of vines, so classical authors assert.

47. *Health of farmers.* Florentinus.

It is a good idea to station a doctor at the farm. Otherwise you must learn to treat whatever illnesses afflict your people from having observed similar illnesses in others. When people who live in the same district and have nearly the same way of life fall victim to the same illnesses, they will be cured by the same treatments.

It is better to prevent workers' illnesses and to treat them in advance so far as possible.

Since the hot sun injures the bodies and veins of those who work in the sun and are unable to bear the burning, it is necessary to control their food, so that they do not eat just once or twice a day but several times at frequent intervals; this will restore them to health and improve their digestion.

1. A group of varieties recorded from Cato onwards, generally as high in quality and low in yield. They originated in Italy or Sicily and were later grown in Asia Minor. In the 3rd century AD there was a type of wine, presumably a varietal, with this name. See Dalby 2003 p. 165.
2. Named after the southern Italian city of Surrentum, which produced fine wines in the 1st century AD. No other sources mention this grape variety.

Some boil up rue[1] and wild mallow,[2] make a watery mixture of this with sour wine, and give it among other food. Some mix milk and water, add a little sour wine, and give it before food. They do this from the beginning of spring until autumn. Some give vermouth:[3] this works not only before food but also after it, or if taken in food. If we have no vermouth we give wormwood, put into very hot water and boiled. Squill-flavoured[4] wine has the same effect; squill vinegar is also made. If it is to be squill wine, give it before food; give squill vinegar after the meal.[5]

Marsh wine – wine produced in marshland – is very salutary, maintaining health in those who drink it. *Ptisane* is also very nourishing and restorative. Clay-oven bread, kneaded dry, and [afterwards] dried in the sun, is very useful for health; bread baked in what are called bread-ovens makes digestion slower.

If the water is not good, not drinkable, causing sickness, it should be boiled until a tenth part has boiled away, then cooled; it will then not be harmful. In the same way seawater, when boiled, becomes sweet.

When farm people are frequently troubled by venomous creatures (adders,[6] widow spiders,[7] poisonous snakes and rats,[8] also scorpions)[9] including kinds found indoors, they must be persuaded that the theriac grape provides adequate treatment for the bites of all such

1. Greek *peganon*: *Ruta graveolens* L.
2. Greek *malache agria*: *Malva* spp. and *Althaea* spp.
3. Wine flavoured with wormwood, *Artemisia absinthium* L. Instructions for making it are at 8.21.
4. Greek *skilla*: *Urginea maritima* (L.) Baker.
5. This section seems to be of cures for intestinal worms: rue, wormwood (and therefore vermouth) and squill all have anthelmintic properties.
6. I use 'adder' to translate Greek *echidne* and 'viper' to translate *echis*, the two names of *Vipera berus* (Linnaeus, 1758).
7. Greek *phalangia*: European black widow, malmignatte or karakurt: *Latrodectus tredecimguttatus* (Rossi, 1790).
8. Greek *ophis* and *mygale*. I take it that these two are, respectively, colubrid snakes and *Rattus rattus* (Linnaeus, 1758); neither is venomous in the usual sense, but their bites can cause dangerous infections. Owen identifies *mygale* with Italian *toporagno* 'shrew'.
9. *Scorpiones* such as *Leiurus quinquestriatus* (Ehrenberg, 1829) and *Androctonus australis* (Linnaeus, 1758).

creatures. It is not only the wine made from this grape that stops the pain in those who are bitten, but also the vinegar, the grape itself and the raisin; in addition, when the leaves and stems are burned, the ash, applied to the bite, stops the pain and saves life. The ash from burning a vine stem of any kind has the power to treat the bites of dogs, often even rabid dogs; when the power of the theriac vine is added, it intensifies the benefit of the heat.

How the theriac vine is grown, and how vermouth and squill wine are made, will be explained separately in the appropriate place.[1]

48. *Neither farm workers nor plants should be transferred from better to worse ground.* Didymos.

Some advise that plants (and farm workers) should not be transferred from healthy sites to unhealthy ones but rather from worse to better or from like to like or to those that are very little worse. Those who are moved are alienated and disturbed by the change to a worse position, and the very wise believe that this is to be applied not only to people but also to plants.[2]

49. *Smiths, carpenters and potters need to be at the farm or nearby.* Varro.

It is undesirable for labourers from the farm to have to go to cities for equipment and repairs. Frequent delays in the use of equipment hinder the labourers, and frequent visits to the city make them lazier. Therefore smiths and carpenters need to be at the farm itself or close by.

It is quite essential, too, to have potters for all types of work. Assuredly potters' clay can be found in every terrain. Either on the surface, or deep down, or in hidden nooks and crannies on the farm you will find earth suitable for making pots.

1. See 4.8, 8.21 and (for squill vinegar) 8.42. No recipe for squill wine is given.
2. Compare what is said of sheep at 18.2.

Book 3

1. *Calendar of work to be done during each month.* Varro *and* the Quintilii. *January.*

In January prune tree-trained vines, avoiding the hours of dawn and dusk.

In the same month fell timber for building and woodwork, at a time when the moon is in conjunction and is under the earth, because moonlight makes the wood softer. Wood felled at this period will not rot.

In the same month manure fruit-bearing trees. The manure must not touch the roots. In the same month cleft-graft the fruit trees that blossom first, such as peaches, plums,[1] apricots,[2] almonds,[3] cherries.[4]

In the same month you may also prune ground-trained vines, using very sharp knives, keeping to windless days and hours.

Vines and other fruit trees can be planted from 13th January onwards for as long as that particular ground will take planting.

In the same month sowing is ruled out, because the soil is wet and heavy, full of vapour and like badly-carded wool.[5]

Manure alfalfa;[6] harvest green tree-medick.[7]

1. Late Greek *damaskenon*: *Prunus* spp., e.g. *P. domestica* L.
2. Late Greek *berikokkion*: *Prunus armeniaca* L.
3. Greek *amygdalea*: *Prunus dulcis* (Mill.) D.A.Webb.
4. Greek *kerasea*: *Prunus* spp., e.g. *P. cerasus* L.
5. This sentence, with its unexpected simile, belongs to one of the oldest identifiable strata in the *Geoponika*: it comes from a text of the 4th century BC by Kleidemos. His work is lost, but this information was cited, and attributed to him, by Theophrastos, *Plant* Physiology 3.23.2.
6. Greek *medike*: *Medicago sativa* L.
7. Greek *kytisos*: *Medicago arborea* L.

Dry, thin, white, hilly, light and sandy soils, and soil full of roots and shrubby plants, if not broken up in October, should now – before manuring – be ploughed with short ploughs, and then at once manured. Salty soil should be turned over with small ploughs and scattered with bean shucks, or, if none, wheat and barley husks.[1]

2. *February.*

In February we plant out from the nursery two or three-year-old layered vines, but never one-year-old, because they are too weak. Transplanting of vines produces generous fruit and improves the wine.

This month we plant reeds, before they begin to shoot.

This month vines, all fruit trees, roses and lilies should be planted while the moon is waxing.

In the same month sow three-month wheat, sesame[2] and hemp.

The ground where you plant alfalfa is now ploughed a second time.

3. *March.*

In March we will take scions for cleft-grafting, and do the grafting itself, with vines and other fruit trees.

This month, before the equinox, plant reeds.

This month we will deal with the olive trees that need treatment.

This month we will put pig manure to the roots of almond trees, because it makes bitter ones sweet, and big and juicy too, so *Aristotle* says. *Theophrastos* says that urine should be poured on to the roots.

This month we will plant all kinds of fruit trees, including chestnuts, taken as slips, particularly in cold and damp places.

This month it is necessary to hoe vines and other fruit trees; if they are hoed now they produce abundant and fine fruit.

This month it is necessary to pick off young shoots from three-year-old vines, while the shoots are still tender. Some do it with the

1. The same instructions are given at greater length at 2.23.
2. Greek *sesame*: *Sesamum indicum* L.

hands: early authors considered that up to the third year an iron blade should not be applied to vines. Layering of three-year[1] vines is also best done in this month.

This is the month in which all cleft-grafting can be carried out, before the buds sprout but when the trees are considered to have abundant sap. When taking scions of apples and pears for cleft-grafting, take care to cut them off carefully and precisely with a very sharp pruning-knife. These trees have particularly tender bark, and some prefer to take them off with the hands rather than with a pruning-knife.

Those preparing a new field for sowing should now plough it for the first time. If turned over now it will not grow many weeds and will be more crumbly. It is not enough to plough it once: do it again, and even a third time.

It is now time to sow white wheat, the kind called *setanion*,[2] also the *melanather*[3] and the long type called *Alexandrinos*,[4] into soil that is thin, with good exposure to the sun, mountainous, with pools, sandy and unwatered: do this before 25th March. Sow barley of the type called *leptitis* in ground formerly used for wheat. In suitable ground grow sesame, einkorn,[5] emmer,[6] millet and hemp. When the sown crop is in ear, weed it, so that the grain will be clean and healthy.

Harvest green tree-medick.

4. *April.*

In April it is still possible to plant olives, but, especially at this time, they must be well trimmed; if properly pruned thy will produce better fruit.

Theophrastos says that in this month olive, pomegranate and myrtle,[7] taken as slips, can be planted in damp and irrigated ground.

---

1. 4.3, on layering, recommends layering from ten-year-old vines.
2. 'This-year' wheat, a term familiar from the 4th century BC onwards.
3. Known from papyri from Egypt. See *P. Col. Zen.* 69.9.5–6; Crawford 1979 p. 141.
4. Widely known under the Roman Empire: see e.g. Pliny, *Natural History* 18.66–68.
5. Greek *tiphe*: *Triticum monococcum* L.
6. Greek *zeia*: *Triticum turgidum* L. subsp. *dicoccum* (Schrank) Thell.
7. Greek *myrsine*: *Myrtus communis* L.

Early in this month we will cleft-graft and bud-graft olives and other fruit trees. Bud-grafting of figs, chestnuts and cherries also begins now.

The second hoeing of new vines ought to be completed this month, and the new vines should be pruned; the damage is lighter on them if it is done now. Some consider, particularly early authors, that up to their third year an iron blade should not be used on vines.

In this month elm seed should be gathered, and immediately planted.

Layered figs can now be transplanted, even if they are already putting out leaves.

5. *May.*

May is considered the ideal time to cleft-graft the vine, before the buds sprout. Some, however, cleft-graft it after the grape-harvest.

In this month we will prune the olive trees.

In this month we will rack wines. The jar must be filled to just below the neck, so that the wine is not stifled but has some breathing space.[1]

In this month, as already said,[2] vines can be cleft-grafted, when the crown is beginning to sprout; the sap is then sticky. The scions – meaning those that were taken some time earlier, before any sprouting – will have been packed away carefully, in the ground or in a pot, ensuring that they do not begin to sprout.

In this month the vines must be hoed, and preferably when there is no rain. Hoeing encourages the thirsty vine, allows it to breathe; the soil, raised by the hoeing, cools the thirsty vine. The nursery must also be hoed now (the nursery is the ground from which we take young [vines] after two or three years to transplant them).

In this month the newly cleft-grafted trees should be sprinkled, every evening, with water from a sponge.

Some people plant in this month, but of course only in wintry, very cold and very damp places or where it is possible to irrigate. They

1. Repeated at 7.6.
2. Just above.

do this not only throughout May, but on as far as 13th June: any plant whose buds have not swollen in readiness for sprouting is able to be planted out. Once the buds have sprouted, a plant cannot come into bud again, except for figs; but some plant vines after sprouting.

Also in this month lupins should be dug in, those that were sown to manure or clean the ground. Before the 15th of the month, before the vine blossoms, cut down [the lupins], when they are wet, and leave them there to rot for a short time. Then plough, so that the cut lupins are dug in and the roots destroyed.

In the same month we will turn over land that is overrun with dog's-tooth grass, and allow all the uprooted plants to dry where they lie. Sixteen days after new moon, we will pile them all together and take them off our land. Antipathy will help to prevent their growing in the same place again.

The wine-jars into which wine is racked from the vats must be rubbed and cleaned with broom:[1] if this is done there will not be too much sediment, and what there is will not get dried out:[2] that is most damaging to wines.

6. *June.*

In June cleft-grafted vines must be hoed – before the 13th of the month, if possible – for the second and third time, the first time having been before 15th May. Thinning the shoots must be completed during this month. Now, too, additional shoots on young vines must be removed, even if on the upper part of the plant; the young vine must be limited to one shoot.

In this month any branches of mature tree-trained vines that are hanging free and that have no fruit should be removed.

In this month we hang caprifigs and wild figs in the fig trees.

In this month, and until 15th July, we cleft-graft and bud-graft every kind of fruit tree; figs even beyond that date.

In the same month trees that have been trenched round and left bare should be earthed up.

---

1. Spanish broom, Greek *sparton*: *Spartium junceum* L.
2. Seems illogical: how can it dry out? Presumably, solidify and adhere to the surface.

Before 13th June reed-beds and willow plantations can be hoed.

This is also the time to plant celery,[1] *amaranton*[2] and marshmallow[3] in kitchen gardens.

In the same month cut the so-called vetch, the green [fodder] plant, and put it in the dark to dry it completely, so that it will be sweet. After cutting, water the fodder-field immediately, and plough for new use.

Thresh from 24th June. There are no rains or dews during those days.

7. *Making* khondros.

Pound emmer spikelets, crack them, put in boiling water, squeeze them out. Then pound white gypsum and sift it fine; a quarter part of the whitest and finest sand, with each part of gypsum, to be gradually mixed with the emmer as it is being husked. This is made in the dog days,[4] so that it will not go sour. When it is all husked, pass it though a rather coarse sieve.

The best is the first-sieved *khondros*; the second is next best; the third is poorer.

8. *Making* tragos.

Soak and pound *Alexandrinos* wheat and dry it in hot sun. Then repeat the process until the glumes and fibrous parts of the wheat are all removed.

Tragos from good-quality emmer can be dried and stored in the same way.

9. *Making* ptisane.[5]

Soaked barley is pounded and dried in the sun, and then stored as follows. The sharps should be sprinkled back on to it, because this

1. Greek *selina*: *Apium graveolens* L.
2. Perhaps feverfew, *Tanacetum parthenium* (L.) Schultz-Bip.; at 8.37 this species is called *pyrethron*.
3. Greek *althaia*: *Althaea officinalis* L. Like feverfew it is used medicinally, not in food.
4. See introduction.
5. Similar to 2.34.

preserves the rest. The water should be one-tenth the volume of the barley. Pound rough salt and mix with it.

A similar *ptisane* can be made with wheat.

10. *July*.

In July the vines should be hoed, up to the second hour of daylight and in the late evening, but not deeply; and remove weeds, especially dog's-tooth grass. The disturbed soil should then be smoothed and levelled, so that the sun does not burn what is below. Mature vines should be earthed up a little, because dirt ripens and expands the grapes.

In this month all weeds and thistles should be pulled up.

In this month wood can be cut if need arises, but of course when the moon is on the wane and is under the earth.

The ground where broad beans and grass peas[1] have been harvested should be ploughed. All land should be ploughed immediately after harvesting the crop, before it dries out.

Foliage for animal feed can be cut and stored.

Around 15th July one will uproot bracken,[2] sedge, rush and reed.[3]

Rub flowering lupins with lye[4] and spread this on to the cut ends of the roots in the earth; it dries them up.

[Note on lupins.]

If the ground is full of roots, sow lupins in it. When they flower, cut them and plough it so as to dig in the cut plants, add light manure, and leave it. After 12 days plough a second time and sow what suits the soil, mixing a small proportion of prepared lentil with the seed.

1. Greek *lathyros*: *Lathyrus sativus* L., used as human food (especially when other crops fail) and animal fodder.
2. Greek *pteris*: *Dryopteris filix-mas* (L.) Schott.
3. Perhaps 'cut' rather than 'uproot'. These plants have their uses, and they are cut a second time in August.
4. Greek *konion*: caustic soda, NaOH, or quicklime, CaO; but the word is homonymous with hemlock, Greek *koneion*: *Conium maculatum* L.

11. *August.*

In August, in warmer regions, ripe grapes should be harvested. Those not yet ripe should be hoed moderately – also olive groves. Break up the sods to arouse the dust: when this falls on the fruit it will ripen it more quickly. This is why olives and vines growing beside the road have more luxuriant fruit, because of the dust stirred up by passers-by. The only vines that should not be hoed are those in light soil when the soil is already dry; they will parch rapidly, being shallow-rooted because of the light soil.

In the same month cleft-grafted trees should be sprinkled with water from a sponge when the sun is setting.

In the same month the vats should be dried in the sun, and then, 20 days before they are to receive the wine, pitched.

In the same month the late-fruiting vine should be thinned. This thinning makes the fruit bigger and better and makes it ripen more quickly. With young and heavy-cropping vines some portion of the grapes should be removed, otherwise the stems will be weaker and the fruit poorer.

Grapes taken for keeping should be taken when they are ripe. This is the time, too, in warmer regions, to take figs that are for drying; also to prepare the planting holes in which, in the autumn, we will plant olives and other fruit trees.

In the same month, those vegetable plots that we irrigate should be irrigated. We will cut for the second time bracken, rush, reed and sedge. We will plough new ground that is dense and heavy and rich; in ground that is mountainous, suffers bad winters, is always shaded, or faces the north wind, we will dig to full depth with ploughs or forks.

We will thresh until 25th August, because during these days, too, there is no rain or dew.

12. *September.*

In September heavy-cropping and poor-cropping vines should be marked, to graft the former and to cut out the latter. Make the mark with red earth mixed with olive oil and pitch.

In this month the chaff and plane leaves in which grapes are to be stored should be dried in the sun.

Also walnuts should now be knocked down, dried, and stored.

Sowing is risky until 27th September, because if there are dry spells the seeds will die. Then, from 28th September, sow lupin, because it does not demand rain.

After the 13th September, when the rains come, light soil, and soil that is full of roots and shrubby plants, should be ploughed before manuring, and then immediately manured.

13. *October.*

In October it is good to gather the grapes. The first gathering makes more wine, the second makes better wine, the third makes wine that is better-flavoured.

Some people plant in this month, after the equinox and the first rains and until the setting of the Pleiades (they begin to set from about 7th November).

In the same month it is good to trench around the vines, and put to them lye[1] or dust or dry ash or old human urine or wine lees or chaff.

In this month almonds, cherries and figs are to be cleft-grafted.

Olive, almond, cherry and all fruit-bearing trees can be planted in parks, also elm, white poplar, manna ash, pine and fir – but never fig at this season. It is also worthwhile to sow seeds of all trees.

In the same month we begin the making of young olive oil, collecting unripe olives. In the same month, in wintry places, we protect citron trees.[2] We wrap gourd leaves around the base of their trunks, and put ash from the burning of gourds to their roots.

In this month it is better to start pruning the vines, and also, after the harvest, to hoe the ground so that what was trodden by the harvesters becomes porous again and transmits the autumn rains to the roots. Weeds will also be fewer, because all their roots will be damaged and will be attacked by the frost.

Apples to be kept over the winter should be picked and put away in sawdust of aromatic wood; other fruits similarly. The roots of marsh asparagus,[3] too, should now be cleared of weeds.

1. Greek *stakte* (see du Cange 1688 s.v.).
2. Greek *kitron*: *Citrus medica* L.
3. Greek *asparagos ho heleios*, the cultivated species: *Asparagus officinalis* L.

In this month many begin the sowing [of cereals]. If you irrigate after 14 days, all crops will flourish; even if you do not irrigate they will not be damaged. It is not advisable to sow before 1st October. Note the rising and setting of Alphecca:[1] sowing during this period will be particularly successful.

14. *November*

In November, after the first rains, plant vines in rather warm and waterless places.

Some people prune at this period in rather warm places. In general autumn pruning improves the roots and stem; spring pruning produces more fruit.

15. *December.*

In December, too, it is possible to plant vines.

In November and December the must, after it has finishing fermenting, should be cleaned; scum and foam from around the neck of the vats should be wiped off with a fenugreek[2] plant or with clean hands.

In December and November it is good to plant and cleft-graft suckers of all early-fruiting trees; also to fell timber for building, while the moon is waning and is under the earth.

Also young and mature vines should be hoed round, and the mature ones manured: it is not necessary to put manure to young vines. It is also a good time to prune olive trees, once they have dropped their fruit; the new branches give more fruit. It is a good time to hoe around these and other fruit trees, and add a sufficient quantity of goat manure, or 20 *kotylai* of *amorge* to weak trees. It is also appropriate to plant a chestnut plantation.

This is also the right time to sow broad beans.

---

1. Alphecca = Alpha Coronae Borealis: the dawn rising on 4th October, the setting on 25th November (1.9, 2.14). Compare Vergil, *Georgics* 1.222.
2. Greek *tilis*: *Trigonella foenum-graecum* L.

Book 4

1. *Tree-trained vines.* Florentinus.

Tree-trained vines are more advantageous than all others. They yield wine that is better, better-keeping and sweeter, and since they are planted at wider intervals they allow the intervening ground to be sown once every two years.

Tree-planted vines cannot be put to every kind of tree, but to those that are single-rooted, such as the white poplar, or have compact roots and not too heavy a crown, so that the grapes are not too shaded; suitable are elm, black poplar,[1] manna ash and maple.[2] They need a height of about [thirteen] feet. In the *Tarsena* and *Boana* districts in Bithynia[3] the trees on which the vines are carried rise to [sixteen] feet, and no harm is done;[4] they produce a better wine in fact, especially the *Aminnios*. On good soil such trees can be allowed to grow to the height just stated; on light soil, however, they should be pruned at 8 feet, so that not all the strength of the soil goes into the trees. The vine stems should be trained towards east and west so far as possible. These trees, like the vines, should be trenched round and manured moderately.

Vines grown in this way need to be tall and strong, and it is better to use layers. Some take rooted layers from the nursery and

1. Greek *aigeiros*: *Populus nigra* L.
2. Greek *sphendamos*: *Acer monspessulanum* L.
3. *Tarsena* from around Tarsia, east of Nicomedia; *Boana* unknown. This is the only mention of either kind.
4. The manuscript text gives heights of 'thirty and ten' followed by 'sixty'; these seem much too high. The text is emended on the basis of Pliny, *Natural History* 23.35; Columella, *On Agriculture* 5.7.1.

replant them; others take a flourishing and already almost mature vine, trim it, uproot it, and replant it in a planting hole beside the tree with which it is to be paired.

The vine is set as follows. Plant it at a distance of three cubits from the tree. Then, when it has taken well, so that it is adequate for uniting with the tree (as will be evident from its thickness) lay it down and dig it in in the direction of the tree. At a distance of one foot from the tree leave the remainder of the stem free, with as many of the eyes as possible. Rub out with your fingernail all of them except the top one (or two) so that this will thrive better, and as it grows guide it gently towards the support of the tree. You must make sure that this part of the tree is carefully pruned, removing anything tending towards the root [of the vine], so that nothing covers the root. Remember that these vines – the tree-vines – must be cut long in pruning, so as to leave shoots of not less than two cubits. The shoots must be trained to the branches of the tree in such a way that the fruit-bearing parts rise high and are shaken by the wind.

The rows should be 15 cubits apart. This will produce more and better wine. Small-rooting fruit trees such as pomegranates, apples and quinces can be planted between the rows. Olives can also be inter-planted, though some deny this. Some insist that fig trees are a suitable companion to vines, but experience shows this to be false: figs do better if planted around the outside of the vineyard. We have found in Bithynia that tree-vines like cherry trees, particularly the *Oporike*;[1] for the *Aminnios* too this pairing produces plenty of fruit and plenty of wine. As said above, this kind of vineyard can also be sown once every two years. Those who have tried it not only assert that the vines are not harmed by this adjacent crop, but also report that a better wine is obtained.

Since by this method the vine encircles the tree as it climbs, it will happen in time that in its union with the tree it is compressed and, as it were, stifled. Many people in Bithynia insert a wedge between the vine and the tree, so as to separate them, and thus give the vine some space to relax.

---

1. An otherwise unknown variety name. Cornarius took it to be a variety grown for fruit; Liddell and Scott 1925–1940 took it to be one ripening at harvest time.

2. *More on tree-trained vines.* Africanus.

Insert three goats' horns upright around the tree-trained vine, point downwards, and dig them in so that a little earth covers the end of each horn but so that falling rain will moisten them. The vine will then fruit very heavily.

3. *How layered vines can be planted on easily and quickly.* Didymos.[1]

When we have trenched well-grown vines a couple of times – begun to dig around them, that is – there will be a big reward for all our labour. From a newly mature vine, ten years old or more, selecting the longest and finest new branch from the lower part, that is, within a one-foot height from the ground, lay it down and place it in an already-dug furrow a foot deep and long enough to take four eyes, because that is the length that needs to be buried. It should be done so that what remains, emerging from the ground after the four eyes have been buried, consists of not more than two or three eyes. If it is much longer, enough for a second buried section, then you will get two layers from the same new branch; bury it in the same way to the same lengths already given. Any that remains beyond these two layers is best removed: it will generally be of no use. It is important to watch it carefully to ensure that the part between the old vine and the first buried section does not put out any side-shoots: if these intervening two or three eyes shoot, they will prevent the rooting of the buried section. Those dealing with this should therefore remove the eyes with a fingernail so that they will not shoot, and, if there are any offshoots, clear them off as well. We instructed that there should be two or three eyes on the *embrochas* as it is called, the new layer that emerges from the ground: the corollary is that only one of the side-shoots from these eyes, the best of them, should be kept. The side-shoot that is retained should be tied to a thin stick or reed, so that while tender it will be supported by the reed and not be bent or broken off. The roots strengthen if the branch is cut in the second year,[2] cut from the vine,

---

1. Repeated more concisely at 5.18.
2. About a year after the branch was laid down.

that is, so that it does not damage the mother plant by excessively long proximity and does not absorb the mother's strength.

Farmers in Bithynia at the end of the [first] year make a single cut to the new branch. This does not separate it completely from the mother plant, since it is not yet fully rooted; nor does it trouble the mother unduly. What the cut does is to ensure the autonomy of the two. The final cut is made when it is time to replant the layer, that is, at the beginning of the third year.[1]

Quite good, then, are rooted layers grown on in the nursery. But better still are hardwood cuttings, well grown and when appropriate transplanted. These can be reared in the most suitable way without troubling the mother plant; they can be more quickly planted out in the field and become an independent vine.

4. *The myrtle-grafted grape.* Tarantinos.

The myrtle-grape has myrtle-berries on its lower branches. It is made by cleft-grafting vine stems on to a myrtle.

5. *The early grape.* Same author.

If you cleft-graft black grape on to cherry you will have grapes in the spring, because the vine will bear grapes at the season at which the cherry bears its own fruit.[2]

The vine will come into bud quickly if you mix smooth natron with water to the thickness of honey and coat the eyes plentifully with it immediately after pruning. It will bud within eight days.

You will produce early grapes if, when planting vines, you throw on a good number of sweet grape seeds (not vinegary, that is) around them; better still if you put these grape seeds into the ground with the vine at the moment of planting.

6. *The late grape.* Same author.

The grapes that appear first should be removed: others will grow after them.

---

1. Just under two years after the branch was laid down.
2. Repeated at 4.12.

Give particular care to the plant and it will put out a second crop; when these ripen they will be late grapes. Take these bunches, insert them in an earthenware vessel pierced at the bottom and cover the top carefully, tying the vessels to the vine so that they will not move in the wind.

7. *The seedless grape.* Demokritos.

Some produce seedless grapes as follows. When about to plant a cutting, they split open gently whatever length is about to be buried and remove the pith with an ear-pick, then bind damp papyrus[1] around it and plant it. It is better if you wrap the whole section that is to be buried in a squill, and then plant it, because squill aids growth and healing.

Others operate on a vine that is already fruiting. They make a cut in a fruiting shoot, and with an ear-pick remove the pith from it, as deeply as possible, not taking the shoot off but, as above, leaving it undamaged; then they dilute Cyrenaic silphium resin[2] in water to the thickness of grape syrup and insert this mixture. They restore the shoots to their position, tying them to vine-props, and ensure that the resin does not run out. They treat the shoot with the resin for eight days, until it buds.

You can do the same with walnuts and cherries if you want the fruits to be seedless.[3]

1. Dried sections of the stem of *Cyperus papyrus* L., used as paper in the ancient world.
2. The ancient spice of Cyrenaica. Silphium was extinct, according to the more convincing ancient sources, by the 1st century AD (Dalby 2003 pp. 303–304): it was perhaps available to 'Demokritos' but certainly not to Constantine Porphyrogenitus. Asafoetida (*Ferula assa-foetida* L.) was adopted as a substitute.
3. The absurdness of the last sentence (who wants seedless walnuts?) would be reduced if the text said 'pomegranates and cherries'. So it did, apparently, at an earlier stage. Hence Palladius, *Opus Agriculturae* 3.29.3 says: 'The Greeks affirm that this can also be done with pomegranates and cherries;' the Syriac version of Vindanionius (9.6) says: 'The same is to be observed with pomegranates, if you want them seedless, and with cherries.'

8. *The theriac and purging vines.* Florentinus.

The theriac vine is of course useful for many purposes, and particularly for bites of pests.[1] You shall now learn how it is grown.[2] We split the lower part of the vine stem that we are going to plant, take out the pith and insert the antidote into the stem, then bind around the split stem with papyrus and plant it. Those who do it more carefully also pour some of the antidote on to the roots.

We grow the purging vine in a similar way, splitting the stem and inserting hellebore.[3]

It is necessary to know that a cutting taken from the theriac vine does not have the same power; it is diluted by planting on and by grafting, the antidote weakening in the course of time. For the same reason it is necessary to rub the roots with the antidote from time to time.

Drinking the wine [made from this vine] is useful against bites of pests, likewise the vinegar, and the grapes themselves and the raisins when eaten; if these are not available, the leaves pounded and applied; and if none of these can be had, the ash from the burning of the stem of the theriac vine, applied, saves life.

Aside from the theriac vine, the stem of any variety of vine is useful against the bites of dogs, even of rabid dogs.

Florentinus says this in books 1 and 2 of his *Georgica*.

9. *The perfumed grape.* Paxamos.

If you want to fill the whole of your land with a good aroma, split the vine cuttings that you are planting and insert perfume in them using the method just described.

Better than this, soak the cuttings in perfume, and, while still wet, graft or plant them.

---

1. Greek *herpeton* (see introduction).
2. This takes up a promise made at 2.47 (also attributed to Florentinus).
3. Most likely what is elsewhere called 'black hellebore', i.e. *Helleborus* spp.; 'white hellebore' is *Veratrum album* L. For a different method see 8.18.

10. *To prevent wasps attacking vines, grapes or other fruit.* Demokritos.

Take mouthfuls of oil and spray it over the vines and the grapes and over other fruit.

11. *How to keep grapes on the vine until the beginning of spring.* Berytios.

Alongside vines in a very shady spot dig a ditch to a depth of two cubits and fill it with sand, sinking vine-props in it. Wind the shoots around them once or twice, turning them carefully on the grape-bunches, and having tied them to the props cover them so that they are not rained on and do not touch the ground.

12. *Cleft-grafting vines.* Florentinus.

The vine selected as stock for grafting must have a thick trunk, so that it can take either a single scion or two.

Some make the graft below ground level; they go down to a depth of half a foot and make the graft almost in the base of the vine. Some graft at ground level, and this is better. The graft that is made above ground level unites with difficulty because it is caught by the wind; if the graft has to be made at a height, because there is [no] smooth place lower down, then prepare in advance a stake and fasten the scion to it against the wind. Some graft to the shoulder of the vine.

If you graft vine on cherry you will have very early grapes, because it will bear grapes at the season when the cherry bears its own fruit, that is, in spring.[1]

The season for grafting is the spring, when the frosts are over, and when, if the vine is cut, the sap is seen to be not abundant or watery but thick and sticky. Stems selected as scions for grafting must be round, sturdy, with buds close together, and preferably among the shorter ones.[2] The scion needs only two or three buds, or if it is

1. Repeated from 4.5.
2. Owen understands this to mean 'among the bearing branches', i.e. 'among the arms'.

grafted below ground level three or four. It is not a good idea to take more than two slips for grafting from one shoot. What is beyond the first seven buds is unproductive and useless. The scions that unite most reliably are those that consist of new shoot with a section of last year's shoot.

We will not graft scions as soon as we have taken them from the vine; after cutting we will put them away, storing them in a clay jar away from the air, but graft them while the buds are still dormant before they come into leaf.

Grafts made below ground level to the base of the vine are more reliable, because the soil takes a share in their nurture, but they fruit more slowly, just like cuttings that are planted in the ground. Grafts made above ground unite with difficulty, because they are caught by the wind, but they fruit more quickly. The stock on which we graft above ground level must be smooth and uniform and as thick as a thumb; rough edges from the saw should be smoothed off with a sharp pruning-knife. The scion should be pared on one side, to a length of two and a half fingers (as we see with the reeds that we write with) so that on one side the inner wood appears, undamaged, and on the other side the bark. The scion should be inserted, to the full length that has been stripped off, so that there is no gap between the stock and the scion, and filled up with plaster or clay to keep moisture out and keep the sap in. The trunk on the side of the cut should be fastened with a soft but unbreakable binding and then covered with sticky mud. Some mix cow dung with the mud.

Grafts made in high summer should be moistened with water by means of a sponge in late afternoon.

When a growing shoot has reached four fingers a stake should be placed alongside it and tied to it against the wind. When the growth has strengthened the tie should be cut with a pruning-knife so that it is no longer restricted and the sap from the trunk can be transmitted to the shoot.

Scions for grafting should be cut when the moon is waning: thus they will make stronger grafts.

Some graft not only in spring but also after the harvest, when the vine has thicker sap.

13. *Grafting by piercing.* Didymos.

I think grafting by piercing is the best method, because the grafted vine is not unproductive meanwhile but continues to bear its fruit, while the scion marries as it grows; the stock is not damaged by the piercing and is not compressed by binding. Grafting by piercing is done as follows. Pierce the trunk of the vine-stock with a so-called brace-and-bit,[1] bring towards it a new branch from the best neighbouring vine and insert it through the hole. Do not cut it from the parent plant. Thus it continues to be nourished by its original parent while it shares nourishment and grows together with the new stock. Within two years the scion will have united. At that stage, after they have united, the scion, still attached to its original parent, must be cut from it, while the stock, whatever is above the piercing, must be sawn off. From then onwards, allow the scion to be the leader.

14. *To make the same vine bear different fruits (grapes), both white and black or tawny.* Same author.

Take two cuttings of different varieties; split them down the middle, but be sure that the split does not go into an eye and that none of the pith is lost. The two kinds are to be set together and joined so that the eyes match one another and the two eyes become as one. Bind the two cuttings firmly together in papyrus, wrap them round with squill or with very sticky earth, and so plant them. Water them for 3 to 5 days, until the buds open.

15. *Keeping of grapes.*

Bunches of grapes gathered for storing over the winter should be cut after full moon, when the air is calm, about the fourth hour of the day when the dew is already dried off. Take care that all the grapes (the berries, that is) are sound: for this it is necessary to take the sharpest possible pruning-knife, so as to make the cut easily and without force. The bunches should be cut when they are at the point

---

1. Latin *terebra Gallica*, Greek *teretron to Gallikon*: cf. Columella, *On Agriculture* 4.29; Pliny, *Natural History* 17.116.

of ripeness, neither a little under-ripe nor just past their best. Some cut the bunches individually, while others cut the *oschai*, the leafy branches complete with their bunches; and then at once take out rotting, dried and unripe berries, if any, with scissors, so that they do not spoil the others. The cut of each bunch of grapes must be dipped in pitch melted over a fire. Then the bunches must be hung, each one separately and not touching, from the roof. Under them, in advance, spread chaff: lupin pods, if available, because these are bitterer and drier and they can keep the mice away; if lupin is not available, second choices would be the pods of broad bean, vetch or other pulses. If using cereal chaff, barley is preferable. If none of this is to be had, take dryish green leaves, cut them up small, and spread them underneath. Whole *oschai* should be stretched out under the roof, or hung, in the same way.

Some put the bunches in *siraion*, in grape syrup that is, for a short time.

Some put them up in pitched wooden boxes with dry sawdust of pine, fir or black poplar, or with millet flour.

Others dip them in boiling seawater, or if not available, brine, mixed with wine; then cool them and store them in barley chaff.

Some boil fig or vine ash in water, dip the grape bunches, cool them, and store them in the kinds of chaff already mentioned.

Bunches of grapes will also keep a very long time if hung up in grain stores, especially if the grain is stirred up. The dust rising from it, landing on the grapes, helps in some way to preserve them.

You can also keep grapes as follows: boil rain water until a third is left; then let it stand, to cool it; put it in a pitched vessel; then take bunches of ripe, rather large, grapes, removing unripe and rotten berries from them, and put them into the vessel. The water must cover them. Stop the mouth of the vessel carefully, sealing with gypsum, and put them away in a cold, dark place where they will not be near a fire. Even the water will be wine-like – useful for the sick as a wine substitute – and the grapes will remain perfect.

Some advise that when hanging grapes from the ceiling they should be tied not by the upper end, where the cut was made, but the lower end of the bunch, so that they air better, opening out as the berries bend backwards.

It is also good to hang them in a vat of must; as long as they do not touch the must or one another, they will remain in the condition they were in when picked.

You can store grapes by putting them, as soon as they are picked, undamaged and sound, into an earthenware vessel, stop the mouth of it carefully, and seal it with gypsum.

Likewise they will keep if dipped in potter's earth mixed with water to about the thickness of honey, hung, and then washed off when they are to be used.

Likewise they will keep if smeared with purslane juice and hung.

Bunches of grapes will keep for a whole year if you pick them a little early, dip them in hot water containing some alum and then quickly remove them.

Bunches of grapes will keep in honey.

All that is said here of grapes applies also to apples.

Book 5

1. *Soil suited to vines.* Florentinus.

A suitable ground for vines will have black soil, not too dense, and moist (with sweet water) at a certain depth. Soil of this kind, when it receives rain, does not filter it all through and lose it, nor keep it standing on the surface: water held on the surface rots the vines. The soil must be inspected at depth, because we often find black earth above and clayey below, or the opposite. Best is soil deposited by flowing rivers; hence we commend Egypt. To sum up, any black soil that is not too thick or sticky and contains moisture is relatively suitable for vine-growing.

2. *Vine varieties suited to various soils. Terrains suited to vines.* Same author.

In black, moist and irrigated soil, as just specified, white grape varieties should be planted, because these need more food from the soil: they are sturdy, compact in growth and demanding of nourishment. Clayey soil also, if it is not very light or fissured, takes white grape varieties. Dry, light and sandy soil does not suit such vines, but those with compact grapes and light[1] pith; black grape varieties are generally of this kind, producing fine, reliable and plentiful wine, as opposed to the white, which are more demanding of nourishment. Alone among white grapes the *Psithia*,[2] the *Kerkyraia*[3] and the so-called

---

1. Some mss. 'white'.
2. A group of varieties well known in classical times, yielding grapes that when semi-dried made good raisin wine (Dalby 2003 p. 166).
3. 'Corcyraean'; not recorded elsewhere as a variety.

Chloris[1] like light soils because they are relatively fatty. Varieties that are more moist must be planted in localities that are dry and subject to drought, drier varieties in cold and wet localities; in this way what is lacking in the plants will be supplied by the nature of the soil. In general it is not advisable to plant in fattier soils easily nourished varieties but those of opposite type. In black soil plant flourishing varieties capable of drawing from the soil all the nourishment they need. When luxuriant varieties are planted in fatty soil, they are not encouraged to ripen their fruit but to put out plenty of leaves; weak varieties planted in drier localities will bear weaker fruit. Thus, as explained, it is necessary to recognize and distinguish plants and soils and so blend their qualities. This is why some people transplant vines from mountain districts to plains and lowland plants to the mountains, claiming that the soil likes opposites.

The so-called *Mersites* is finer than all other varieties. This is the one that in Bithynia yields the wine called *Dendrogalenos* and, in other parts of the province, the *Tiarenos*; in Tion in Paphlagonia it yields the *Tianos*;[2] also the best known wine of Herakleia Pontike.[3] In general, wherever vines of this variety are planted, they produce a much better crop than others: the grapes are nicest for eating and nectar-like; bees browse it for their food; it is also very heavy-cropping, bearing bunches along the whole trunk; the bunches are round and the grapes translucent so that the pips and the membranes are visible; the stalks that support the bunches are generally robust and woody. It likes trees, and the height they give, and likes to be well stripped of leaves. The [must] from it is best pressed quickly.

The finest wine is that made from vines grown on dry and sloping terrain facing east and south.

It is better to plant tree-trained vines in plains, valleys and level terrain.

In every case the rule must be remembered and observed that the more suitable terrains for planting low-trained vines are hillsides,

1. 'Pale green'; not recorded elsewhere as a variety.
2. Tion or Tieon, east of Herakleia Pontike.
3. *Herakleotes*, elsewhere mentioned by Theophrastos, *On Odours* 52, who describes it as robust and with a good aroma (the robustness could be alleviated by blending).

gentle slopes, relatively high and relatively dry sites, which will have a milder and well-aired summer. Terrain extending along ridges or on mountain foothills requires low-trained and ground-trained vines, because on such sites anything earthy, arable and fertile is gradually, imperceptibly washed off and lost through erosion by rain. On the crests of mountains vines should not be planted: any moist earth will be eroded and leave the roots naked and without nourishment. On plains, level country and moist land tree-trained vines should be planted, particularly in warmer places where the winds are not too strong and will aerate them and nourish them where they are suspended on the trees; in cold places the strong winds injure tree-trained vines.

As to drinkability, without dispute the theriac vine produces better wine than all others; *Demokritos* testifies to healthiness and to wine quality. But its stem is light and weak.

3. *The nursery.* Didymos.

Nursery is the name for the spot where [vine] plants are put before they are planted out – where they are fed up, as the Bithynians say. They should be placed at a depth of not less than a foot; in that way the plant can easily be dug up with a fork, and it will be better warmed throughout by the sun.[1] The first buds and any extensive growth should be removed, so that its growth will serve to thicken it. This removal should be done with the hand, not with iron, because the touch of iron numbs the young vine.

Some plant out in the second, some in the third year. Vines planted out in the third year will be stronger.

The nursery should not be watered unless we are going to water the vineyard; the same practices adopted in the nursery should be followed in the vineyard.

4. *The lie of the land.* Demokritos.

Always pay attention to the nature of the land. If it is a hot district, we must plant northerly slopes [in vines]; if rather cold, southerly

---

1. Compare 5.12 'Depth of planting for vines'.

slopes; if moderate and temperate, easterly and westerly are better, and preferably the easterly if the *euros* is not troublesome. Sometimes westerly slopes will be preferable if they are at a distance from the sea and aired by the *zephyros*. In general north winds are wanted in warmer districts, south winds in chilly districts.

5. *Seaside and riverside districts*. Same author.

Districts near the sea are particularly suitable for vines, because of the warmth, and because moisture rising from the sea imperceptibly nourishes the plants. Winds off the sea are also particularly favourable to vines.

Most people think it is best not have a river as neighbour, still less marshland, because of the mist and the continual cold breezes to which such sites are subject. Another problem is that of rusts, which attack vines and seed crops and make the air unhealthy. Marsh meadows, therefore, should be given up, as far as that is possible.

It is important to note that vines subject to damage from such winds or mists or rusts will not be damaged if they are *dendritides*, that is, trained on trees.

6. *When to plant vines*. Cassianus.

Some advise that cuttings should be taken at the beginning of spring, but when *zephyros* is blowing, and planted immediately. Some instruct that cuttings should be taken and planted not at the very beginning of spring but when the plants are seen to be about to come into bud.

There are in fact various times for planting: some plant after the harvest when the leaves are falling from the vines, others at the beginning of spring; but I advise, having made the experiment, that in unirrigated districts all plants should preferably be put in in autumn, and most especially vines. In autumn the branches have been relieved of the strain of fruiting and of the weight of the grapes; they have revived and recovered their natural strength, and they have not yet been damaged by frost. They will therefore adapt to growing in the soil more readily, and particularly at that season, when it is natural for them to develop their roots. Therefore, as was said, in unirrigated districts one should plant in autumn, because the rains, throughout the winter, will compensate for the lack of surface water. I found myself doing this first on my Maratonymos estate and then copied it at other properties of mine. Those who saw and heard about it dismissed the idea at first. Finally, having realized that it was appropriate to the location, they learned from me and adopted it; it is now the usual practice in our district.[1]

One thing is clear: vines should not be planted after the spring equinox.

7. *How to predict what kind of wine a future vineyard will produce.* Diophanes.

I think it quite essential for the vintner to understand in advance what kind of wine will come from the field he is about to plant in vines. The test is made as follows. Dig a pit two feet deep in the field chosen as vineyard, take a clod from the dug earth, put it in a glass jar with clean rainwater, stir to make the water cloudy, allow it to stand long enough that the water appears clear to you through the glass; when it has reached that point, taste the water. Whatever taste it has, expect the wine to have a similar taste. If you find that it has an off smell, or that the taste is sharp, or salty, or pitchy, or otherwise not good, avoid that field. If it is good-smelling, pleasant and sweet, and altogether good, plant it with confidence.

8. *Selection of stems for cuttings; from what part of the vine they should be taken, and whether from young or ageing vines.* The Quintilii.

So that vines will bear fruit to their capacity it is necessary to note those that bear a good crop or a heavy crop, have many buds, and are unblemished; mark these, and at planting time take new plants from them: not from vines that are themselves newly planted, because these are weak, nor from ageing ones, because these are barren, but from vines in their first flourishing or a little further advanced. Cuttings should be taken not from the top, or from the lowest

---

1. Similarly on olives and other fruit trees at 10.2. The two passages are clearly by the same author, but whether it is Cassianus Bassus, as implied by the heading here, or Florentinus, as 10.2 implies, or another, is not certain.

part, but from the middle of the vine. Stems that are rough, rather flattened, ferule-like,[1] with few eyes, tapering, should be discarded; select those that are round, smooth, sturdy, with many eyes and with many offshoots.

Take the chosen cuttings with a part of last year's stem; as soon as you have cut them off, plant them, because they take better in the soil when just cut, before the air has got to them. If a short delay is necessary before planting, then as soon as you take the cuttings bury them in the soil, either free or loosely tied, so that the whole cutting can benefit from it – and the soil should be neither too dry nor too moist, preferably, in fact, the same place from which they were taken. If a longer delay is unavoidable, the cuttings should be put in a wine-vat with no liquid in it: spread some soil underneath first, then add more, so that they have the benefit of it all round them. The vat should be carefully sealed with mud so that no wind or air can enter. In this way the cuttings will remain undamaged for two months. With cuttings taken even further in advance some people insert them into a squill bulb or an edible bulb[2] and thus keep them. Those damaged and somewhat dried out by storage should be put in water for a whole night and day before planting. If the soil is rather dry, it is better to revive even healthy cuttings in water before planting. It is necessary to ensure that cuttings do not begin to shoot before planting, because they will then die.

From any stem the part that is best for planting is that between the first and the seventh eye. So a good cutting, one suitable for planting, starts from the first (that is, last year's) eye and includes seven. The remainder is useless, and those who cut longer stems into two or three parts, and plant them all, do no good.[3]

9. *How to plant vines; how to make them root more quickly; whether to plant upright or aslant.* Florentinus.

Those who plant vines must remember always to smear the roots and the tops of the stems beforehand with liquid cow dung: they say that

1. Hollow like a stem of giant fennel, *Ferula communis* L.
2. *Muscari comosum* (L.) Mill.
3. Repeated at 5.14, attributed to Florentinus and the Quintilii.

insects and grubs will smell it and not come near. Also sprinkle on *Quercus robur* acorns, broken down to bean size; to the acorn meal add vetch, broken and ground once, just crushed and split, and sprinkle both on to the ground where the vines are being planted. These contribute to rooting and also to the keeping quality of the wine and to heavy fruiting.[1] Some people dig in pulse pods, especially those of broad beans, with the plants; they warm them in winter and prevent damage by pests. Some add urine. In each planting hole you should throw in a handful of roasted grape pips, from black grapes if the plant is a white variety, from white grapes if it is a black variety. The cuttings can be planted upright, but aslant is better because they root more quickly. Holding the cutting either upright or aslant, place around it three or four stones of the size to fill the palm. Add to the heaped soil around it some manure, well trodden in; take care that none of the eyes on the underside are blinded; and add more stones, of similar size, to the soil that you are treading in. The manure that you are adding will warm and strengthen the plant; the grape pips make it put out roots more quickly; the stones prevent the open space being filled in completely, and also cool the roots in summer.

Sotion advises that the top of the base of the plant should be smeared with a very small quantity of cedar oil;[2] rotting will be prevented and pests, smelling the oil, will not approach.

Some do not disturb the soil but simply drive in a peg and then insert the cutting. I strongly disagree with this. Planting in fully dug earth is much better than planting using a peg, because this can blind eyes and twist the stem; in the usual method the stem is planted undamaged and undistorted.

10. *At what date in the lunar month to plant vines, and whether with the moon above or below the earth.* Anatolios.

Many old authors affirm that vines should be planted from the first day of the moon to the fourth. Some add that as planting is to be done on the first four days of the waxing moon, so pruning is to be done

1. Repeated at 5.24, attributed to Africanus.
2. Greek *kedria*, oil of *Cedrus libani* A.Rich. or of *Juniperus* spp.

on the first four days of its waning; others merely instruct planting while the moon is waxing. What is agreed is that vines should be put in when the moon is under the earth, and, likewise, wood should be cut when the moon is under the earth.[1]

Sotion says that vines, and indeed other trees, should be planted on the first two days of the lunar month, before the moon is visible to humans; all plants put in during these days will germinate well, he says. I have often planted when the moon was waning and not had reason to regret it. Sotion classes the 29th and 30th as moonless days.

Cuttings, whether to plant or to graft, should definitely be taken off when the moon is waning.

11. *What else to grow in vineyards.* Berytios.

Some plant broad beans and vetch in their vineyards because these can protect the vines from harm;[2] others plant gourds and melons.

Practice shows that it is best to grow nothing in vineyards. Other plants take nourishment from the vines, and the shade harms them.

More than anything else you must rule out cabbage;[3] it is dry by nature and has a natural antipathy to the vine, as is evident from the fact that when one is cooking cabbage and adds even a drop of wine, it will not cook and its colour is destroyed; and those who want to drink a lot of wine and not get drunk eat raw cabbage beforehand. If by chance vine and cabbage have been planted in close proximity, when the vine spreads and would otherwise approach the cabbage, it will spread unevenly and turn away owing to its antipathy.

I notice *Tarantinos* says that nothing at all should be grown between the rows of vines, as, taught by experience, I also advise.

12. *Depth of planting for vines.* Florentinus.

I consider that planting holes for vines should be not less than four feet deep. Those that are planted shallowly age more quickly and lose

1. 'Cutting wood' includes pruning and the taking of cuttings and scions.
2. Compare 5.31.
3. Greek *krambe*: *Brassica oleracea* L.

their fruit, because from less earth they get less nourishment, and they burn in summer. What is necessary is to dig and plant as deep as the sun's heat reaches, and it is known with confidence that the sun's heat does not reach deeper than the stated depth unless the soil is fissured. If you prepare your planting at less than the stated depth, you will have poor vines and they will age more quickly.

Take it that the first four feet of soil provide nourishment for plants; what lies below is barren. Planting to a depth of three feet is not so very bad.

13. *Whether to plant one or two cuttings in the planting hole.* Same author.

I think it is necessary in vineyards to plant two cuttings in place of one. If one fails, the other will survive. In nurseries it is probably not necessary to plant two together, because in nurseries the cuttings are planted more densely. It is possible there too, however.

When two cuttings have been planted together in the vineyard and have grown strong, the weaker must be taken out; the remaining one must be staked, whether it is to be left in its own place or transplanted. When two cuttings are left in one planting hole, the roots will be constricted and the plants will not get enough nourishment, like two babies suckled by the same nurse.

14. *The difference between layered vines and those from cuttings.* Didymos.

There seems to be a difference between layered vines and those from cuttings: layers have an assured growth, since they are already rooted, while cuttings attend first to rooting. Transplanting gives a better crop.[1] Layers will produce fruit in the second year or even before; plants grown from cuttings hardly fruit in the third or fourth year.

Those who cut the longer stems into two or three sections and plant them all are doing no good. Only the section from the first to the seventh eye is useful; the upper section is of no use, say *Florentinus* and *the Quintilii*.[2]

1. Relevant here only if 'transplanting' implies 'layering'. Duplicated at 5.24.
2. Repeated from 5.8, attributed to the Quintilii.

15. *Grape varieties should not be grown intermixed, particularly not white and black grapes.* Fronto.

Vines are not all of the same nature, nor of the same season; one will ripen quickly, another not. The fruit differs too, whether yellow, black or white; sweet or austere; light or heavy; suitable for keeping or not; some of the wine is better when aged, some is to be drunk on the spot. Each one differs in nature and in the care it requires. So they should not be intermixed, in case, by doing so, the poorer damages the better; and nothing is more injurious to wine than when early grapes are harvested along with later ones.

More than anything else it is necessary to ensure that white grapes are not trodden with black ones; better, then, if they are not grown together. The two have a certain natural antipathy.

16. *The vineyard should not have a single variety but several, planted separately.* Sotion.

The wisest farmers are those who plant three or four vine varieties in different areas of their vineyard. Depending on one variety causes trouble, whether it is that all the vines bear heavily or that they all fail. The reason for planting them separately and not intermixed is that vines have many differences, not only in colour but also in strength; and wine made from different varieties has very great differences.

17. *The differences between grape varieties.* Florentinus.

It is not the case that each grape variety yields the same wine wherever planted. The quality of the air has a great effect on wine quality, for good and bad. In general the *Aminnios* yields relatively acceptable wine everywhere, and particularly on sloping terrain either dry or moist, and especially when trained on trees.

A similarly pleasant wine is yielded by the vine that resembles the *Aminnios* but has small bunches and compact grapes; the Bithynians call it *Drosallis*, and some harvest it together with *Aminnios*.

Very fine and plentiful wine is yielded by a white grape which has rather large bunches and grows in the same dry districts, trained on trees; in Bithynia it is called *Leukothrakia*. It has very long bunches and grapes that are of even size, circular and fat, and reddish at the time of ripening; its stems, too, are red.

There is also a vine called *Bolene* in Bithynia, which ripens quickly and very early in the season. It bears big bunches almost a cubit long, with tender white grapes, translucent and round. Its unique feature is that it puts out three shoots from each eye, whereas others scarcely produce two from each eye. It must therefore be docked sharply when pruning, otherwise it will bear too heavily and quickly exhaust itself. This vine has good size, does not age quickly, is not badly affected by its environment, and withstands a range of climates. Its wine is quite good, perhaps because it is tree-trained, but not by nature long-lasting.

But the *Aminnios*, already mentioned, is no less heavy-fruiting than these, and must therefore be considered the best of all. *Varro* asserts that each *plethron* of the Aminnian grape produces 300 *amphorai* of wine.[1] It is possible to get more wine from each vine by leaving more shoots on it, because this variety likes to be pruned long and to be permitted a greater number of shoots. Therefore it is best to plant the *Aminnios* everywhere; if the soil has already been planted with different varieties, it can be grafted on to them. Grafting is no worse than planting; better still if the graft is layered in the second year.

We determine that a vine is heavy-fruiting not in the first or second year but after many years. The vine-dressers can often produce a heavy crop one year, or even two, by leaving more shoots on the plant. A heavy-fruiting vine will bear reliably even when a limited number of shoots are kept. In short, we should not regard as heavy-fruiting the vine that bears one bunch on each shoot, but the vine that produces more than one shoot from each eye and more than one bunch on each shoot.

18. *How to plant layers.* Anatolios.[2]

We plant the so-called *aporyx* as follows. Dig a trench one foot deep; bring the branch from the vine towards it (not cutting but bending it),

---

1. Varro in *Farming* does not make this assertion. He mentions the Aminnian variety only twice, on both occasions when quoting Cato, *On Farming*.
2. A repeat of some of the information at 4.3. The reason for the duplication may be that a different word for 'layer', *aporyx*, is used here; the compiler overlooked the fact that this is a synonym of *enrizon*.

place it in the trench and replace the soil, allowing part of the branch to show above the ground; in this way part of it is still attached to the vine, drawing nourishment from it as from a breast, while the rest is nourished in the earth, and, fed by these two mothers, it will root. *Aporyges*, thus planted, readily bear fruit and will be well-nourished, fed by their own and their mother's roots. In their third year they will plant out well.

19. *How to work the soil.* Sotion.

The field to be planted in vines must be cleared of everything, not just dug but ploughed several times; not only the roots are to be removed, but also stones, particularly the larger ones. Stones that are left on the surface, being heated by the sun in summer, will overheat the crowns of the vines, because solid bodies keep their heat; in winter, again, these stones will become cold, especially small ones, and will injure adjacent crowns. By contrast those that are deep in the soil, in the hot part of the day, will cool the roots.

The ground must be dug in such a way that what is above is turned underneath, and what is below is turned up. In this way, what is dry will enjoy the moisture above; what is damp and thick will have the warmth and lightness above.

An effort must be made to even out hollows, so far as possible, and not to allow any hollow places in a vineyard.

When trenching round the vines, after the first year, be sure consistently to remove the surface roots with a very sharp knife. Plants accustomed to root at random will be hindered from putting down deep roots.

20. *Trenching.* Same author.

We will trench, that is, dig around the vines, when they are two years old, to a depth of two feet and a breadth of three. In the case of tree-trained vines we will cut out intrusive tree-roots. While the vines are still tender they are oppressed and disturbed if approached by relatively big and strong roots; there must therefore be a considerable separation between the two plants, the vine and the tree.

21. *Care of vines.* Damegeron.

With a just-planted vine the strongest shoot must be cut off, not with a slanting cut, and not very near the eye but more than two fingers from it; not to the north but to the south, beginning the cut behind the eye so that the tear that runs from the cut will not harm the eye beneath. If moistness is a problem anoint the cut with boiled unsalted *amorge*.[1]

The plants[2] should be trenched round a second and even a third time. Some add dung. In the second year trench round them every six months.

It is necessary to remove carefully, by sawing, strong surface growth when the vines are beginning their third year; after the harvest, manure to a depth of one foot.

In wetter districts we trench round the vines but let the surface roots alone, so that, if the roots cannot run deep because the ground is saturated by moisture, they will be able to sustain the plant by running horizontally. Missing the force of the earth from below they will recover it on the surface.

22. *How many shoots to leave on a four-year vine; what vine-props to tie in to.* Same author.

In the fourth year of young vines it is enough for them to feed two shoots, and these should not have more than four eyes, of which the two nearest the crown should be blinded by scraping them off with a knife to prevent them budding; the upper two should be left to enlarge the plant.

At the beginning of spring, after pruning, insert a strong, straight vine-prop of a length of five to seven feet. It should be no thinner than the finest reed, so that it does not weigh down or shade the plant. A prop without bark is better, because beetles and other things that damage vines crawl into the bark and conceal themselves. Extend the plant along the prop and tie it in.

When the mature vine is six years old, pruning should allow it 3 or 4 shoulders depending on its strength, placing each shoot

---

1. *Amorge* of unsalted olives, cf. 2.10.
2. The text says 'eyes'. Owen translates 'plants' and I think he's right.

along a shoulder-prop that is strong enough to bear both the shoot and the fruit.

23. *Pruning.* Pamphilos.

Begin pruning in February or March, from 15th February to 20th March.

Some prune immediately after the vintage, saying that the vine is then lightened by losing its branches, whereas in spring its tears destroy its nourishment. But it is also the case that vines pruned in autumn come into bud more quickly in spring; and if the spring is cold, and hoar-frost falls, they will be burned. So it is better, in colder districts, to have a preliminary cut, not a full prune; that is, to leave clear eyes and shoots, which must then be pruned in the spring.

Begin pruning not in the early morning but when the frost has been melted by the sun and the shoot is warmed.

Pruning knives must be very sharp and clean-cutting.

24. *Good fruiting and good wine.* Africanus.

The vine will bear well if the vine-pruner wears an ivy wreath.

If you throw on to the places [reserved for] the vines some acorn broken to the size of beans, along with vetch lightly crushed and broken, it will promote heavy fruiting and superior wine.[1]

Shoots with plenty of eyes make a vine bear heavily.

Transplanting of vines promotes heavy fruiting and good wine.[2]

You will make vines fruit well if you plant liquorice[3] among them.

25. *When to dig mature vines; the benefits of digging.* Anatolios.

It is essential to dig before the buds open. If you dig after they open, when the grapes are coming and the leaves are growing, the

---

1. Repeated from 5.9, a chapter attributed to Florentinus.
2. Repeated from 5.14, where it is attributed to Didymos (but is only tangentially relevant).
3. Greek *glykyrriza*: *Glycyrrhiza glabra* L.

disturbance shakes the fruit and causes it to drop, so it is better to dig earlier. Plenty of digging and breaking up of the soil will render life and nourishment to the vine and produce a good crop. If you were unable to complete the work before the buds open it is better to postpone digging, completing it after the new growth has strengthened. Take great care when digging with a fork that the crown of the vine is not damaged by chipping or piercing; a wounded vine will become diseased and its fruit will fail.

26. *How to manure at the time of trenching.* Same author.

People in Libya and the East do not replace the soil immediately after trenching but leave the trenches all through the winter. Those in wetter regions fill them in again more quickly, covering the roots with soil *ekroias tas hodous.*[1] Some make a trench one foot deep, some deeper.

Mature vines are manured in the trench with ox, sheep or pig manure or that of other farm animals. Pigeon dung, being very hot, is good at making the vines grow quickly but is unsuitable for producing good wine. To each vine should be given 4 *kotylai* of whichever of these manures is selected. It should not be put to the trunk of the vine, but slightly away from it, so that the further roots share in the heat, and not directly on to bare roots because it would burn them.

If you are short of manure, bean pods or the pods of other pulses will serve instead; they also assist vines to resist frosts and protect them from destructive vermin. Grape pips also serve as manure; better still is old urine.

One-year-old vines should be trenched and manured moderately, likewise those of two years and up to the fifth year, that is, during the growing stage. In regions with hard winters it is better to do this for young vines in alternate years only. If ice forms in such places, it is also advisable to heap up earth towards the trunk.

The most workmanlike method of manuring would be to use in sandy soil sheep or goat dung, since these are evidently the gentlest,[2]

1. These three words make no sense to me.
2. It is assumed that sand is sharp.

and cow dung in white clay, which, being weak by nature, sufficiently relieves the relative sweetness and fattiness of this manure.

27. *Propping.* Didymos.

Some cut props in December and January, others in July and August. Some prop lower and some higher. *Aminnioi* should be propped one foot higher than other varieties, but not higher than six feet. In light, dry and sandy soil and in places troubled by strong winds, vines should be grown lower, but not lower than four feet. Props need to be sharpened to a point at both ends; the upper end only, not the lower which is sunk into the earth, should be dipped in boiling pitch. They should be set up straight, and not slanted towards one another, or they will make the vines slant like themselves.

28. *Thinning.* Sotion.

Unnecessary growths, while still tender, should be removed; this will give the vine more breathing space. They can be taken off by hand without harming the plant. Pruning and thinning are part of the same skill, and sometimes experts will take off a shoot that has some fruit while leaving one that has none. More growth should be taken off a young vine so that it will not be overloaded.

When the heat of the sun begins to lessen it is necessary to remove leaves so that all the grapes will be warmed by the sun and will ripen.

The vine should be dug even when it is still at the growing stage.

29. *Second thinning.* Paxamos.

With newly planted vines, as they shoot and after the flowering, remove unnecessary growth firmly but without force.

With vines that rot their fruit or ripen it with difficulty because of the moistness of the soil or excess of leaves, middle leaves should be thinned off 30 days before the harvest so that the winds can blow on them and cool the grapes. Top leaves should be left, so that they can ward off the sun from above and protect the fruit from the most extreme heat. However, if there is a lot of rain in late autumn, so that the grapes swell excessively, the top leaves must be removed as well so that the wine will not go vinegary. Some people in rather hot and dry districts shelter the grapes with brush and thorn because their own leaves are not enough.

The grower should walk round the vineyard frequently, straightening the props and levelling the yokes (yokes are the ties that fasten vines to their props), because they know that just as we become twisted if we let our bodies lean to one side, vines, too, are damaged if they lean and do not stand straight.

30. *To stop the vine producing* phtheires *or caterpillars and prevent damage by frost.* Africanus.

Rub the bark with bear fat and the vine will not produce *phtheires*.[1]

Or rub bear fat on the pruning-knives with which you cut your vines; but do it without anyone knowing, because knowledge of the treatment will destroy the benefit. Then neither *phtheires* nor frost will injure the vine.

Or rub the knives with garlic crushed in olive oil.

If you take the caterpillars[2] found on roses, boil them in oil and rub the knives with this, the vine will not be injured by any other creature or by frost.

Rub the knives with goat fat or with frog's blood.

Or rub the whetstone with ash in olive oil and then whet the knives.

Burn vine shoots, mix this with the sap of the vine, pour into the middle of the vineyard with some wine, and there will be no grubs.[3]

1. Literally 'lice'. 'Root louse' is now an alternative term for phylloxera (*Daktulosphaira vitifoliae* (Fitch, 1856)), but that species was unknown in early Europe. This *phtheir* might be, for example, *Panonychus ulmi* (Kock, 1836), a tiny red spider.
2. Greek *kampe*, here perhaps a rose sawfly such as *Allantus cinctus* (Linnaeus, 1758). The same name is given to an apple pest at 10.18, a vegetable pest at 12.8 and the cabbage white at 20.31; see also 15.1.
3. This chapter does not deal with *kampai* 'caterpillars' as promised; the topic of *skolekes* 'grubs' recurs at 5.48 (see note there), as does that of *kampai*.

31. *Preventing damage to vines from hoar-frost and rust.*[1] Diophanes.

Put out in the vineyard a series of heaps of dry dung, upwind of the vines. When you see hoar-frost spreading, set fire to the dung: the advance of the smoke will drive off the frost.

Vines that are easily scorched by hoar-frost should be pruned, and thus prompted to new growth, rather late; in that way they will blossom late. I think the *hippouris* vine,[2] for example, is relied on to suffer little from frost because it puts on new growth late, when the sun is already hot.

Some grow broad beans in the vineyard and rely on this to prevent damage to vines from hoar-frost.

32. *More on hoar-frost.*

If the vines are damaged by hoar-frost and it is clear that the fruit is lost, they must be cut back and pruned hard to retain their strength. They will then yield two years' harvest the following year.

From experience in Bithynia some assert that when frost is noted the vines should be dusted with tamarisk ash (or the ash of other wood if tamarisk is not available); the ash, settling on the buds, will prevent frost from lying on them.

33. *On rust.*[3] Berytios.

As soon as you see the rust in the air, preparing for attack, burn an ox's right horn and cow dung, up wind, and make plenty of smoke all around the field; ensure that the wind carries all the smoke towards the rust, because smoke will disperse the causal element in the air.

Apuleius says that three crabs, burned with cow dung or chaff and goat dung, will be a sufficient preventative.

If the rust has taken hold, you can stop the damage as follows. Chop the roots or leaves of squirting cucumber or colocynth,[4] steep

---

1. For rust see 5.33.
2. Otherwise unknown.
3. Greek *erysibe*: a fungal infection resembling that of *Phakopsora ampelopsidis* Dietel & P. Syd. 1898.
4. Greek *kolokynthis*: *Citrullus colocynthis* (L.) Schrad.

them in water, and sprinkle with this the plants that have been attacked by rust, before the sun rises. The ash of fig or oak, likewise steeped in water and sprinkled, will have the same effect.

Apuleius says that if you throw a branch of bay into the field the damage caused by rust will transfer to it.

It is important to know that everything rusts more at full moon, especially wheat, because the moon, being very hot and moist, rots the produce during the night.

Some people chop up a catfish and burn it, up wind, so that the smell reaches every part of the property.

A similar antipathy takes effect if a sealskin is pierced and stretched across your sieve and the seed is scattered through this when you are sowing. The same procedure will prevent hail falling, thanks to a natural antipathy.

34. *Treatment for vines that dry their fruit.* Vindanionius.

If the berry, when it reaches the size of a vetch seed, begins to dry out, then take off the whole dry part of the bunch, separating it from the healthy part or, better, including the healthy berries that are rather close to the dry ones, and then smear the cut with ash mixed with very sour vinegar. The ash from burning vine shoots is best. If you treat in this way the parts of the bunch that are sickening you will stop the damage. Rub the trunk with the same mixture.

Some sprinkle the lower parts of the crown, around the roots, with old and very sour urine. This treatment not only saves the crop but also makes the vine long-lived and flourishing.

35. *Vines that bear no fruit.* Demokritos.

Split the trunk with a chisel or auger, or, better, with an oak wedge. Put a stone into the split to keep the two sides apart, and pour in about 4 *kotylai* of old human urine, pouring it quickly over the whole trunk so that it also wets the roots; then throw on manure mixed with soil. When inserting the stone into the crown, dig away earth from around the roots. This treatment is suitably given in autumn.

36. *Star-struck vines.* Cassianus.

You can recognize star-struck vines by the very reddish colour of the leaves.[1] Treat this by piercing the crown all through with a gimlet and inserting an oak peg through the hole; or dig away shallowly from the root, insert a peg similarly, and replace the earth around it. This will cure the vine.

Some people irrigate such vines with seawater.

Others treat these vines, and also those damaged by any vine-dressers' tools, by coating them with olive oil boiled up with asphalt.

Some – in Bithynia, for example – have found by experience that star-struck vines can be treated by piercing the crown with a nail.

Others pour human urine on the crown and the roots.

37. *Diseased vines.* Damegeron.

Cure a diseased vine by spraying the trunk with the ash of vine shoots or of oak mixed with vinegar.

Also very helpful is human urine poured on the roots.

Some people cut diseased vines down to ground level, then heap up the surrounding earth lightly, mixing in a little manure. When new growth comes, clear off the weak and retain the strong. Next year, again, select the most suitable one of the remaining growth, removing the rest.

38. *Weeping vines.* Sotion.

Vines that produce plentiful tears are expelling what is undigested and never distributed to the whole body of the vine. We will scratch the trunk with a pruning-knife to make a wound (and if that achieves nothing we will scratch the thick part of the roots and make a kind of wound there). We will rub the wounds with *amorge*, boiled down to half and cooled. We will smear with mistletoe[2] the eye that lies below the cut: testing has shown this to be far better.

---

1. Perhaps a description of esca or *mal dell'esca*, thought to be caused by toxins from wood-rotting fungi.
2. Greek *ixos*: *Viscum album* L. Palladius, *Agriculture* 3.30 suggests that the correct reading might be *oxei* 'with vinegar'.

39. *Vines that shed their fruit.* Same author.

You will identify shedding vines by their whitish and dryish leaves and by their flat, strap-like, tender shoots. You will treat them by rubbing the crowns with ash mixed with very sour vinegar and particularly by spraying all round the crown. This ash, wetted, should be sprinkled over the whole vines.

Some people pour seawater on the roots. Others are keen to remove the tips of the grape bunches and so prevent shedding.

It is quite forgotten that *ryades*, vines that do not keep their fruit, are so named from the verb *rein* 'to flow, to drop'.

40. *Vines that run to wood.* Same author.[1]

Vines that run to wood – that have too much crest when they put out shoots – must be pruned long. If they persist we trench and bring in river-bed sand with a small proportion of ash.

Some place stones around the roots to cool the vine.

41. *Vines that rot their fruit.* Varro.

Some vines fruit normally but rot their grapes before they have swollen and ripened. You will cure these with purslane juice.[2]

Others mix barley meal with the purslane and coat the trunk with it.

Others treat half of each grape bunch with purslane juice.

Some put four *kotylai* [two pints] of old ash on the roots.

Or sand.

42. *Vines injured by the fork.* Same author.

When a vine is injured by the fork or some other implement, if the wound is below ground level, coat it with very light soil mixed with goat or sheep dung, and bind it; then hoe around the crown; and keep an eye on it. If the wound is at the root, mix light earth with dung, heap it over gently and hoe rather often, working around the trunk; avoid bending it and do not be too forceful.

1. Compare Theophrastos, *Plant Physiology* 3.14–15.
2. Greek *andrachne*: *Portulaca oleracea* L.

43. *How to find out before the vintage whether it will be plentiful and good, or poor.* Demokritos.

Take a grape, a berry that is, straight off the bunch with your fingers. If some moisture is expressed from it, this indicates a good vintage.

If there is plenty of wheat, some take it that juicy fruits will also yield well.

We can take it that the wine will be good and strong if there is plenty of rain during the spring; the same is indicated if there are rains when the grapes are the size of vetch seeds and still unripe. However, rain at vintage time will make the wine not only watery but also likely to turn to vinegar.

44. *Hedging.* Diophanes.

If you want to have a secure hedge, dig a trench one cubit deep, plant it with stakes, and stretch a rope along the trench. On the day before, get some split bitter vetch[1] seed ready, also fruits of bramble, Christ's thorn[2] and pyracantha[3] all dredged in thick honey. Your rope should be rubbed with these fruits of bramble and Christ's thorn, and the place sprinkled with the porridge. Leave it a short time. Then turn the earth back into the trench. In 28 days there will be shoots four palms high. Transplant them, no deeper than four palms, and within two months they will grow to more than a cubit high; eventually, growing interwoven to a great height, they will keep robbers out. Do this at the spring equinox.[4]

An easy way to make a hedge is to rub a rope with bramble fruit and dig it into the ground; chop thick reeds and plant them shallowly, placing them aslant and not upright, and adding in dung with the earth.

Some make a hedge as follows: they make slips from bramble stems, plant them on the line of the hedge one palm deep, and water them till they put out new growth.

1. Greek *orobos*: *Vicia ervilia* (L.) Willd.
2. Greek *paliouros*: *Paliurus spina-christi* Miller.
3. Greek *oxyakanthe*: *Pyracantha coccinea* M.J.Roemer.
4. Pliny, *Natural History* 17.62 cites Demokritos for this method of growing a myrtle hedge (compare 11.7), with a note that it can be done with brambles too.

Some, with their hands, rub a rope with ripe blackberries (the fruit of the bramble), dig it into the ground with dung, and water until they shoot.

Demokritos says that for fifteen days from the beginning of spring is the right time to plant a hedge in the following way. Take a rope that has been much used at sea and is too perished for other use. Rub it with bramble seed and the other previously-mentioned thorny plants and bitter vetch. Bury it in the trench, and water every day if possible. The hedge will then grow quickly and well, and it will be secure.

45. *When to harvest the grapes; signs that they are ripe.*[1]

It is not easy to determine when the grapes should be harvested. Some harvest before they are ripe, producing a wine that is light, weak, and will not keep. Others harvest late, not only damaging the vine because of the undue burden it has to bear, but also risking the quality of their wine if there should be hail or frost. There are tests for when to harvest, both from the taste of the fruit and from its appearance. Here are some indications.

Followers of *Demokritos* and *Africanus* say that the grape, once ripe, remains in proper condition for only six days and no more. When the pip no longer appears green but black, it is a sign that the fruit is ready.

Others do it by squeezing a grape. If the pip comes out naked, with none of the flesh around it, they judge the fruit to be ready for harvest; if the pip comes out with part of the flesh attached, the fruit is not ready.

Some take it as evidence that the harvest is ripe when the first of the fruits begin to wrinkle.

Others judge that the grapes are ripe in the following way. Where a bunch is most crowded they take out one grape, and after one or two days they look again at the bunch. If the place from which the grape was taken has kept its shape, the surrouding grapes not having increased in size, they advance the harvest. If the place from which

---

1. According to manuscript F, 'same author'.

the grape was taken has become smaller, the surrounding grapes having grown to fill it, they delay the harvest until growth stops.

46. *What house the moon must be in at vintage. Grapes must be harvested when the moon is waning and is under the earth.* Zoroaster.

It is necessary to harvest the grapes when the moon is in Cancer, Leo, Libra, Scorpio, Capricorn or Aquarius. When it is waning and is under the earth, work assiduously on the vintage.

47. *How to save unripened or otherwise spoiling grapes, and to treat the wine that will be made from them.* Leontinos.

All unripened or otherwise spoiled grapes should be separated from the rest of the crop, and their must should be treated as follows. Boil rainwater down to half. Take as much of this as equals a tenth part of the must, and pour it in. Then boil up the must and the water together, continuing until a tenth part has been boiled away.

Some do it in a different way. They add to the grapes water equal in volume to a third part of the expected must, then tread the grapes and boil the must, continuing until a third part has been boiled away.

48. *Treatment against pests that damage the vines.* Africanus.

You will destroy grubs[1] that are troubling the vines or making their nests in part of the vineyard if you smoke it by burning cow dung up wind.

Some fumigate the vineyard with galbanum,[2] or hartshorn, or goats' hoofs, or ivory dust, or lily root,[3] and in this way drive the creatures out.

You will also drive them out if you burn women's hair. This also cures miscarrying women and those whose womb rises;[4] these illnesses, too, are cured by fumigation with hair.

1. Greek *skolex*: here a borer beetle such as *Sinoxylon perforans* (Schrank, 1798).
2. Greek *chalbane*: resin of *Ferula galbaniflua* Boiss. & Buhse.
3. Greek *krinon*: *Lilium candidum* L.
4. 'Hysterical women', in the original sense and implication of the term.

Some fumigate with the peony plant,[1] or with the so-called burdock;[2] or else they grow these plants among the vines, and so expel the creatures.

Some boil [asafoetida] resin and olive oil and rub the vine trunks with this, beginning a little above the base.

To prevent caterpillars[3] ruining the vines, make garlic into a paste and rub the pruning-knives with it.

49. *Against* kantharides[4] *and larger pests that damage the crop.* Same author.

To prevent *kantharides* spoiling the vines, mix some of the beetles into oil and rub this on the whetstone with which you are to sharpen the pruning-knives.[5]

To drive larger insects off, some mix dogs' excrement with old urine and spray this all around the plants.

50. *A Democritean remedy, based on natural antipathy, to prevent vines, fruit trees, standing crops or anything else being infected by any pests, particularly larger creatures.* Demokritos.

Put no fewer than ten river or sea crabs into an earthenware vessel with water, seal it, and place it in the open air, in the sun, for ten days. Then sprinkle with this water whatever it is that you want to keep uninfected, every other day until it is fully grown. You will be surprised at the effect.[6]

51. Oinanthe. Florentinus.

Oinanthe is taken using a vine that gives good wine, and from the wild vine, and particularly from a tree-trained vine. It is taken at

1. Greek *paionia*: *Paeonia officinalis* L.
2. Greek *prosopitis*: *Arctium lappa* L.
3. Greek *kampe*: here a vine moth such as *Lobesia botrana* (Denis & Schiffermüller, 1775) or *Eupoecilia ambiguella* (Hübner, 1796).
4. A 'small beetle'; possibly a parasitic species such as *Pulvinaria vitis* Linnaeus, 1758.
5. Similarly 13.16.
6. Similarly 2.18 and 10.89. Likewise Palladius, *On Agriculture* 1.35.7 (and likewise credited to Demokritos).

flowering time: the bunches are picked and dried in the dark. The bunches are then put in a clean jar and equal quantities of aromatic old wine and of grape syrup are poured over them. It is carefully kneaded by hand and formed into cakes, which are stored.[1]

52. *Making raisins.* Same author.

Much has been said by early authors about the making of raisins. I have preferred to do it as follows. When the bunches have ripened, twist them on the shoot and leave them to shrivel on the vine. Then pick them and hang them in the dark. When the grapes are quite dry put them in a jar with sun-dried vine leaves underneath them. When the jar is full put more vine leaves on top, seal, and store in a very cold and smokeless room. Raisins prepared in this way will last a long time and will be very good to eat.

53. *Planting reeds.*

Reeds like sunny places and are nourished by the winds. In principle they grow from the 'bulbs', and that is the best way to propagate them. Also if the reed is laid down aslant it sends out shoots readily: in this case they should be set at a distance from one another, and laid down 3 or 4 fingers deep, with one or two eyes facing upwards. Those planted upright should have two joints, and should be planted at a depth of 12 fingers.

The time for planting, some say, is the beginning of spring, but since they are quickly injured by frost they should be planted in autumn in colder places. Reeds are cut in the same year, after the winter solstice, because they are known to continue growing until then.

Reeds that have been placed over smoke are said never to harbour the little creatures called *ips*,[2] which cause much damage to vines. They say that these creatures attack the vines from rotting reeds.

---

1. For its uses see 7.20, 7.25.
2. A borer, perhaps identical with the *skolex* 'grub' named at 2.48, perhaps different. Birdlime was used to prevent attacks by *ipes*, according to Theophrastos, *On Stones* 49.

Book 6

1. *The trough; the collecting vats for wine and oil.*
   Florentinus.

Having closed our discussion of the planting of vines we are now about to deal with the care and cure of wine, and we have thought it necessary to set out first how the trough and collecting vats are made ready.

The treading trough should be built at a suitable size for the expected quantity of fruit, so that the workers have space to move round, so that there is enough room for the grapes when harvested, so that if time is pressing more of them can be gathered at once, and so that the workers are not stifled by fumes rising[1] from the must.

The treading room must be cleaned of even the smallest amount of dust, especially its upper parts, so that nothing dirty and no creature bred there can fall into the wine and spoil it.

The trough [room] should be warm and well lit throughout.

The collecting vat should have a broad opening. After use it should be washed with hot seawater or brine and wiped dry with a sponge. It should be left unsealed so that it does not become mouldy. If mice ever fall into it they give a very bad odour; therefore a broad piece of wood should be put in it so that if ever a mouse does fall in it can climb out again.[2] When it is to be used once more it should be washed and sponged again and then aromatized with resin.

The collecting vat for oil,[3] by contrast, should be airtight.

1. *Anaphora* is used in two senses in this and the next sentence: 'rising fumes' from the must; 'upper parts or surfaces' of the treading room.
2. Compare 6.7.
3. So Cornarius, rightly; according to Liddell and Scott 1925–1940 this *elaiotropion* is the 'olive press'.

2. *The wine store; sinking the vats.* Same author.

The building housing the vats should have its window facing east and north in warm districts but facing south in colder districts. It should be a long way from the treading room and free of any bad smells.

The vats should be placed not touching one another but leaving a space of one foot between them, so that those in charge of the wine store have easy access to the further vats, and so that if [the wine in] one vat turns it will not take any others with it. Nothing catches quicker than wine, and particularly must.

The vats should be placed in a dry spot, because if the terrain produces weak, light and thin wine two-thirds of each vat is going to be buried, and if it produces strong and thick wine one half will be buried. Under each vat should be spread soft and perfectly dry sand, on top of this a layer of citronella,[1] and the gaps filled up with earth well baked in the sun. The sand and dry soil will draw all moisture to themselves, whether from the earth or from the vats, and will make the wine good. Its power can be demonstrated thus: fill a new basket with sand, pour sour wine into it, and what will filter through will be clean and odourless. If you have no sand, be sure to use soil that has previously been dried in the sun.

Nothing with a bad odour should ever be shut in the wine-store, whether animal skins, cheese, garlic, olive oil, figs, old tools; any such things will absorb moisture from the wine, swell, and give their bad odour back to the wine. The wine store must be set apart from pond, stable, privy, chaff-store, bakehouse and bathhouse. If trees ever grow around it they must be cut down, because the roots will soil the wine by winding around [the vats] and infecting them with the odour of the trees, particularly figs (wild figs even more so) and pomegranates.

If we live in country districts we should floor the wine-store with stone flags, standing clear of the soil, and place the vats on these flags with sand under them.

---

1. Greek *schoinos myrepsike*: one of several terms all probably denoting *Cymbopogon* species, including *C. Nardus* (L.) Rendle, citronella grass; *C. citratus* (DC. ex Nees) Stapf., lemon grass; *C. schoenanthus* L.; ginger-grass.

3. *Preparing vats.* Anatolios.

Not all earths are suitable for pottery. As potters' earth some prefer what has a red colour, others white, others again mix the two.

Some are satisfied, when testing whether a vat is well made, if it gives out a sharp and penetrating note when struck. But this is not enough. The client must be there at the manufacture, must verify that the clay is in best condition for working, and must not let the vat be put on the wheel before the clay has taken the shape that the vat will have when baked. Potters do not put all vats on the wheel, only the small ones; they build up the large ones to the required size while they are standing on the ground, in a room kept warm for as many days as necessary. Firing is also an important part of the manufacture: the fire must not be too low or too hot, but at the proper heat. Hence some people, avoiding this tiresome business of making new vats, use old ones, and this seriously diminishes the quality of their wine.

Of the vats made with a swollen belly, the best are the taller ones, and particularly those that have [wide] open mouths. The lips should be made to slope outwards, so that when we coat them with ash nothing falls into the vat; it rolls down the outside.

They must be pitched at once, while they are still warm.

Vats should not be large. In [smaller] ones that are not too narrow the wine does not bubble up too vigorously; the excess rises by itself and expels not only the odour but also the *anthos*.[1] Small containers help greatly with keeping and with wine quality. If we still have some big old vats, we should put the weaker and poorer [must] into them; the better should go into smaller vats.

4. *When and how to pitch.* Same author.

New vats should be pitched at once, straight from the kiln; old ones at the rising of Sirius. Some pitch every year; some do it every other year, but it is best to do it when the existing pitch becomes vinegary or runs off.

---

1. The surface yeast (Spanish *flor*).

5. *Testing pitch.* Didymos.

Early authors tell us that the best pitch is that of mount Ida, and next that of Pieria.

Some prefer Rhodian, some Bruttian.

In general it is better if clear.

Some test pitch as follows: they touch some flax fibre to it while it is boiling. Thick pitch will give off smoke and be better; thin pitch will be seen to be inferior.

Some people heat it, drop it into cold water, and test it not only by smell but also by taste.

Pitch that does not spit or bubble or make noises when boiled will be of best quality.

Finer pitch is sweeter to the taste, cleaner, smoother and good-smelling.

So boiled pitch is better than raw, and dry is better than wet.

The finest pitch is prepared as follows. Put it in an earthenware dish in the sun over a low fire; pour on to it some hot water filtered through vine ash, and stir the pitch. When it settles, it is drained off after 2 hours, and the same quantity of water is again added. Those who prepare a third each day, for three successive days, soaking up with a sponge the liquid that is given off, will as a result have pitch that is ideal for use.

Dry pitch is bitter. It is therefore better for use if boiled with wine, and better still if an aromatic is included.

They boil wet pitch down to a third, and in this way make use of it.

Some people add vine ash to it, and boil it off, and also add some wax along with the ash.

Some add wood-ash lye and old wine.

Some use wax alone, and they include some of the wax of Sardinia, because this has proved to be better for use: some melt in a quarter, some a sixth, and some a tenth. If we want to make the wine drier we must put in more wax.

Others, however, advise that no wax at all should be added to the pitch, because the wine will be astringent, and thus more readily turn vinegary.[1]

---

1. Compare 7.12, twenty-first section.

6. *Preparing pitch.* Same author.

In Italy they use the following recipe for pitching: 40 *mnai* pitch, 1 *mna* wax, 8 drams sal ammoniac, 4 drams manna-frankincense,[1] crushed, mixed in during the boiling, and pressed [into the inside surface]; then they rub on 8 scruples fine-pounded fenugreek, spreading it evenly.

Others take 1 *talanton* dry pitch, 15 *mnai* wax, 3 *litrai* vetch and wheat meal, same quantity of fenugreek roasted, chopped and sifted, aromatic reed,[2] 5 balls tejpat leaf;[3] they melt together the items that will melt, pound the dry items, and then rub on ½ *mna* hepatic aloes,[4] sifted. This pitching compound is the most approved. It improves weak wines, ensures that unstable ones will keep, and makes them aromatic.

7. *General instructions on pitching.* Florentinus.

It is best, for whatever type of pitching, to wash the pitch with lye and to mix with lentisk[5] or pine resin (or, if none, whatever kind you have) and some iris,[6] fenugreek[7] (which makes the wine stronger and heavier), cost,[8] cassia[9] and melilot or ginger-grass.[10]

---

1. Greek *manna libanotou* (see Pliny, *Natural History* 12.62; Galen, *On Substitutes* 19.734), small fragments of frankincense (*libanotos*: *Boswellia* spp.) cheaper than the large pieces.

2. Greek *kalamos aromatikos*: probably one of the *Cymbopogon* species (see p. 150 n. 1).

3. Greek *malabathron*: *Cinnamomum tamala* (Buch.-Ham.) T.Nees & Eberm. The *Periplus of the Erythraean Sea* 65 describes how the aromatic leaves were made up into balls by the producers in inland Southeast Asia.

4. Greek *aloe hepatitis*, a low grade of aloes, *aloe*: *Aloe perryi* Baker.

5. Greek *ritine schinine*, resin of *Pistacia lentiscus* L.

6. Greek *iris*: *Iris germanica* var. *florentina* (L.) Dykes.

7. *Trigonella foenum-graecum* L.

8. Greek *kostos*: *Saussurea lappa* C.B.Clarke, the spice costus or putchuk. The term was however later used for a garden plant, costmary (so named because of a similar aroma): see 11.27 and note.

9. Greek *kassia*: probably *Cinnamomum cassia* (Nees) Nees & Eberm. ex Blume and other species.

10. Greek *schoinou anthos*: probably *Cymbopogon schoenanthus* (L.), ginger-grass or camel's hay.

In general, carefully-grown wine requires a skilfully-blended pitch. For cheap wine is is enough to have good pitch and to add a moderate amount of iris and fenugreek and much less wax; if more is added it turns the wine, as we have already said.[1] The wax to be used is white, or, if not white, clean.

Wisely, some insert a straight reed or stick into the empty vats, so that if mosquitoes or other small creatures fall in they can use this to climb out.[2]

Better quality wine should not be put into newly pitched vats. Instead, fill them with wine that is turning; they will improve it.

Red wine can go into these; white wines should go into vats that were pitched two years earlier, or even more.

8. *Another useful method for pitching vats.* Same author.

2 *litrai* Cretan or Campanian hyssop;[3] 2 *litrai* Syrian rush;[4] 2 *litrai* Indian nard[5] or Celtic nard;[6] 1½ scruples good aloes; 1½ scruples Sicilian saffron;[7] 1 *litra* Illyrian iris,[8] for a quantity of ten standard amphoras.[9] After pitching the vats, sprinkle this on their sides and underlips, the pitch neither being cooled to coldness, nor so excessively hot that the compound is burned. Then pour in some aggressively young wine; taste it after a few days and you will think it good-smelling and old.

Re-pitch the vats each year, or at least every two years, using the same compound and the same quantity just specified.

---

1. Not exactly; compare the last section of 6.5.
2. 'Mosquitoes' is clearly an error in the text. The parallel passage at 6.1 has 'mice'.
3. Greek *hyssopos*: *Hyssopus officinalis* L., cultivated in both these regions for medicinal purposes.
4. Greek *schoinos syriake*: probably one of the *Cymbopogon* species (see p. 150 n. 1).
5. Greek *nardos Indike*: *Nardostachys jatamansi* D.Don (DC.), spikenard.
6. Greek *nardos Keltike*: *Valeriana celtica* L.
7. Greek *krokos*: *Crocus sativus* L. as grown in Sicily for the spice trade.
8. Greek *iris Illyrike*: *Iris pumila* L.
9. The quantities are too large; the text is doubtful at this point.

9. *Aromatizing the vats.* Varro.

After pitching, some anoint the vats shortly before filling them with must. Some do this to the lip only, some the lid as well. The mixture is pitch, grape syrup and seawater.

Others add liquid pitch and salt to the grape syrup, and anoint the lips of the vats with a sponge.

Others merely anoint the lids with *amorge*.

10. *Equipment for the vintage.* Didymos.

The treading-troughs must be opened up 20 days in advance to air them, washed down with seawater, and fumigated.

11. *Duties of those responsible for the* kanthelia; *treading the grapes; how the treading team should work in the troughs.* Apuleius.

Those responsible for the big baskets (the so-called *kanthelia*) should pick out leaves, any unripe grapes that get in, and any dry grapes they find. The treaders, too, should pick out any such things missed by the people responsible for the baskets. Leaves that are pressed with the grapes make the wine more astringent and likely to spoil. Unripe and dry grapes cause serious harm.

As soon as the bunches from the baskets are emptied on to the troughs the team whose task this is must press them with their feet, treading every grape equally; they must turn over the trodden mass of grapes, so that much of the liquid runs into the collecting vat. After a second treading they must stop, the grapes now being warm and not too juicy, and put them under the press. If they are warm and tender they will press better, but if grapes going into the press are too juicy it will be necessary to apply weight to break their skins.

The treaders must clean their feet very carefully before entering the trough. When they are in the trough none of them must eat or drink. They must not keep going in and out; if any of them do need to go out, they must not do so barefoot. They must be clothed, and wear an undergarment, because of the perspiration. A good aroma around the troughs must be ensured by means of frankincense or another aromatic.

Stemphyla, incidentally, means not only olive stones (as some think) but also grapes [after pressing]. If you hear the word, think of the two senses: sometimes grapes, sometimes olive stones.

12. *How the vats are filled with must after treading is completed.* Diophanes.

Before being filled with must the vats should be sponged out with strong brine and smoked with frankincense. They should not be filled too full nor left too empty; it is necessary to judge how much the must will rise as it ferments, so that it does not overflow; so that the foam will come up to the lip, and nothing but scum is expelled. It is necessary to skim the must in the vats frequently for five days, with the hands and with ladles, removing the foam and whatever else is superfluous. Take all skimmings out of the vat-room and discard them at a distance. If much of this remains, it will turn and will breed flies; a bad odour will result, and from both causes the wine will turn sour. Thus it is necessary to aromatize pressing-vats, and particularly wine-stores, with incense.

13. *Making the so-called* thamna *from grapes taken straight from the trough after treading.* Anatolios.

The pressings, the grapes that is, must be taken immediately after the must has flowed from them, put in a vat, and trodden down. The wine made from them, locally known as *thamna*, is a pleasant enough drink for the farm workers, while the grapes that finally remain provide adequate food for animals.

As soon as the grapes have been taken from the trough, it and the floor beneath must be swept clean, sponged down with seawater or brine, and fumigated. Any liquid that remains always turns vinegary, spoils the grapes that are to be trodden next day, and produces little flies,[1] which are a sign of turned wine.

---

1. Greek *konops*: here meaning vinegar fly, *Drosophila melanogaster* Meigen, 1830 and relatives.

14. *Preventing must from overflowing.* Florentinus.

We hang a garland of pennyroyal[1] or horse-mint or oregano[2] around the shoulders of the vessels.

Some [...] the inside of the vats near the lips; others smear the lips on the inside with lard as used for conserving; others use cows' milk cheese. This is the best for keeping the fermenting must inside the vat.

15. *Settling must rapidly for use.* Same author.

Add a *kotyle* of mild vinegar to a *metretes* of must. After 3 days it will be clear.

You will find in book III of *Diophanes* the best methods for rapidly settling must.

16. *How to have must throughout the year; testing whether it is watered.* Same author.

Before pressing the grapes, take the must that runs freely from them (some call it *prochyma*) and put it, that same day, into a vessel pitched inside and out, so that it is half full; then seal it carefully with gypsum. The must will remain very sweet for a long time.

It will keep even longer if the vessel is sealed with a skin and is put into a well for 30 days. It will not ferment and will remain as must.

If you tread the grapes lightly, so that they are not pressed fully, the juice you get will also be good for keeping.

Others put the must into old vessels previously containing old wine.

Others put a jar, pitched inside and out as described above,[3] into a well so that only the lips are above water; this has been found excellent in practice.

Others bury the vessel in wet sand; others cover it with grape pips and then heap the wet sand over it.

1. Greek *glechon*: *Mentha pulegium* L.
2. Greek *origanon*: *Origanum vulgare* L.
3. Compare 6.6–8.

Others put the must in an unpitched container, pound [and add] Alexandrian natron,[1] and store in the dark.

A test for whether must contains water is described in the next chapter.

17. *Testing whether must contains water.*[2] Sotion.

Drop some *achrades*, that is, very sour little pears, into the must. If it contains water they will sink to the bottom; if it does not, they will float.

18. *Using gypsum.* Didymos.

Put the gypsum into a flat vessel and pour on enough must to cover the gypsum; stir it well and then let it stand so that the thicker part of the gypsum sinks to the bottom. Pour off the must above it, until, when you stop stirring, no part of the gypsum separates out.

19. *Helping must that is turning sour.* Demokritos.

To one *amphora* add 2 *kotylai* of raisins, soaked till they swell and then squeezed out.

Or strain through river sand, as mentioned above.[3]

Or add 4 drams red dye.[4]

1. Egyptian natron was a lower grade, according to Dioscorides, *Materia Medica* 5.113. On its production see Pliny, *Natural History* 31.109.
2. See also 7.8.
3. Compare the third section of 6.2.
4. Greek *sandyx*, usually a dye made from lead or iron.

Book 7

1. *How grape harvests differ.* The Quintilii.

Valley land produces abundant, poor quality wine. From the hills it is better: the grapes are ripened by the wind, the general temperament of the air, and, most of all, the strength of the sun. The sun makes the grapes not only stronger, but also sweeter, if it heats them enough. The moon alone, being hot and wet, ripens the grapes. Night alone makes them sweet. But they need plenty of sun so that the wine will keep better, will reach its peak more quickly, and will breathe.

Grapes from hot districts make better-keeping wine; those from other parts, or where the country is somewhat wild, make dilute and weak wine.

If the vine bears few grapes, the wine they produce will be more powerful, as if all the nourishment and power is lavished on a smaller quantity of fruit.

2. *What kind of wines should be in the open air, and what kind under a roof.* Same authors.

Stronger wine should be placed in the open air, but with walls to shield it from midday and afternoon sun. Lighter wines should be placed under a roof. The windows should be made rather high, facing north and east.

3. *The difference between young and old wine, and between wine from white and black grapes.* Diophanes.

Wine from black grapes will be relatively strong, from white grapes moderate, from tawny grapes a little easier to drink than from black.

Young wine is coldest; old wine hottest, strongest and most aromatic, because time consumes the watery element in it.

4. *How to cure and stabilize the wine from grapes that have absorbed much water before picking, also from grapes similarly watered after harvesting.* Demokritos.

If because of a wet summer the grapes, while on the vine, have absorbed a lot of water, or if by chance after picking, owing to a sudden downpour, they are much wetter than they should be, we still have to tread them. So, if you find that the must produced by treading is rather weak (and you will learn this by tasting), then after it has gone into the vats and has begun its fermentation, we rack it immediately into other vats; all the solid matter will remain at the bottom owing to its weight. Then add salt to the quantity of 3 *kotylai* for 10 *metretai*.

Some deal with this better by boiling the wine until it is reduced by a twentieth and adding one hundredth part of gypsum.

The Spartans leave their wine on the fire until a fifth has boiled away, and use it after four years.

5. *Opening the vats, and what precautions to take at this time.* Zoroaster.

It is important, when opening the wine vats, to pay attention to the rising of the stars,[1] because that is when the wine stirs. It must not be touched with the hands. If you open it during the day, shield it from the sun so that no ray falls on it. If you are to open it at night (as necessity often dictates) shield it from the light of the moon.

6. *Racking wine; when to rack wines; the quality of wine that has been replaced in the same vat.* Same author.

Wines should be racked in a north wind, never in a south wind. Weaker wines should be racked in spring, stronger wines in summer, those produced in dry districts after the winter solstice.

Wine racked at full moon turns to vinegar.

---

1. 'The stars' are the Pleiades, as explained at 7.10.

It is necessary to understand that wine when taken off its nourishing lees becomes finer and weaker; so keep in mind that in winter it must be warmed, in summer it must be cooled.

Rack when the moon is waxing and is under the earth.

Sotion says that it is best to rack during the days before the moon, that is, on the first and second days of the lunar month, before the moon appears to humans.

When transferring wine into small vessels it is necessary to attend to the risings of stars: the lees stir at these risings, and also when the rose flowers and when the vine shoots.

The wise – and *Hesiod* in particular – advise that when the vat is opened the wine from the top and from the bottom should be used freely, the wine from the middle should be retained: it is stronger, more likely to keep, and suitable for ageing. The wine near the top of the vat, because it mixes with the air, has breathed and is weaker; that from the bottom quickly turns because it is near the lees. *Drink up when the vat is begun and when it ends. Guard what comes from the middle*, says Hesiod.[1]

When wine is racked into jars they should not be filled to the lip, but to just below the shoulder, so that the wine is not stifled but has some breathing space.

The emptied vats must be washed immediately with brine, or with vine ash, or with Kimolian earth[2] or clay.

7. *When and how to taste wine.* Florentinus.

Some taste wines when the wind is northerly, because wines are then unstirred and uncloudy. But experts prefer to taste when the wind is southerly, because that stirs up the wine and demonstrates its qualities. One should not taste on an empty stomach, which dulls the taste; nor after a drinking session, nor after heavy eating. One should not taste after eating bitter or very salty food or food that will affect the taste, but after eating as little as possible of some digestible food. Buyers, of course, should be offered a tasting when the wind is in the north.

1. Hesiod, *Works and Days* 368–369.
2. A white clay used in baths and in medicine: see Strabo, *Geography* 10.5.1.

Some, wishing to deceive buyers, keep an empty tasting-cup which they have soaked in the finest old aromatic wine; its qualities linger, and seem to belong to the wine that is served afterwards, and so those tasting are tricked. Other dealers, more dishonest still, put out cheese and nuts in their wineries, so that visitors are tempted to eat, and the accuracy of their sense of taste is ruined. I set this down not for us to imitate, but to avoid being deceived ourselves.

The farmer should taste his wine frequently, both the new and the old, or he may not notice when it is about to go.

8. *Testing wine and must for water.*[1] Demokritos.

The landlord often needs to entrust wine and must to supervisors and staff. The buyer often needs to test whether wine is pure. Some drop an apple into the wine-jar, but wild pears are better; some use a locust, others a cricket. If these things float, the wine is pure; if they sink it contains water.

Some dip in oil a reed or bit of wood or papyrus or salad leaf or some other dry vegetable substance, dry it off, drop it into the wine, then pull whatever it was out again. If there is water in the wine, there will be drops of water on the oil.

Some have a simpler way. They put some of the wine into a new, unwetted jug and put it aside for two days. If there is water in the wine, it will permeate the jug.

Some warm the wine, put it in a new jug and place it in the open air; if there is water in the wine, it will turn to vinegar.

Some put wine into the so-called quicklime or *titanos*. If there is water in it it will penetrate the quicklime; if it is pure it will set the quicklime.

Some pour wine into a frying-pan containing hot oil. If there is water in the wine it will bubble noisily and spit.

Some dip a new sponge in oil, block the mouth of the wine-jar [with it] and turn it round; if there is water in the wine it will seep out through the sponge. We use the same mothod for testing oil.

1. See also 6.17.

9. *Separating wine from water.* Africanus.

Put alum water into the wine-jar. Then block the mouth of the vessel with a sponge dipped in oil. Tilt it so that it begins to spill out. It is the water that will run out.

10. *At what time of year wines usually turn.* Paxamos.

All wines, as a rule, will turn at around the setting of the Pleiades[1] and the winter solstice; or when the vine flowers, and about the summer solstice and the burning of Sirius,[2] and, in general, around the major seasonal signs;[3] and after heat and cold, in heavy rains or persistent winds or violent thunder; or at the time when the roses flower; or after persistent lightning.

11. *How to ensure that wines are not turned by thunder and lightning.* Zoroaster.

Iron placed on the lids of the wine-vats will ward off the injury done by thunder and lightning.

Some place a bay branch there owing to the antipathy.

12. *Precautions to ensure that wine stabilizes and does not turn.* Fronto.

Roasted salt dropped into the wine stops it turning and prevents too-vigorous fermentation and excessive foaming.

Sweet almonds added to black wine stabilize it.

Raisins, the pips removed and soaked in must or grape syrup with sand, make wine fatty and stable. Some prefer grapes that have dried naturally on the vine, and in fact use these exclusively.

Adding gypsum initially makes wine sourer, but in time the sourness dissipates, while the benefit of adding gypsum persists.

Fenugreek, dried in the sun, chopped and mixed with the wine, stabilizes it and prevents it from turning.

---

1. They set at dawn in early November (1.1, 1.9, 2.14, 3.13), in the evening in mid April (1.9).
2. From 19th, 20th or 24th July (1.8, 1.9, 2.15).
3. Partly repeated at 7.15.

Turning wines that are taken off their own foul lees and put on to the sediment from good wine will be stabilized.

Some people light torches, quench them in the must, and in this way ensure that the wine will not turn.

Some roast cedar-cones[1] and oak galls[2] and drop them in the wine to stabilize it.

Some burn the stone called *porinon*[3] and put it in the wine.

Others combine the ash from burning vine shoots with ground fennel seed[4] and mix these into the wine.

Some take wines that are just turning, rack them into newly pitched jars, and move them into another room. If they were injured by warmth they move them into a cooler place; if by moisture and cold, they move them into a warm and dry place.

Some burn oak wood or acorns and drop some of the ash into the wine.

Some mix milk and honey and put it in the must.

Some burn shellfish shells, break them as small as possible, and put some of this in the wine.

Others burn up olive stones, quench them with grape syrup [or] aromatic old wine, chop them up and pour them into the wine.

We stabilize wine by dropping vine roots into the must. Clay (particularly if dried), dropped in after the fermentation, clarifies wines by carrying the cloudiness down to the lees, and gives them a good aroma, because it is sweet (hence the creatures that feed on it in winter survive). The clay therefore replaces the sweetness of the must and stabilizes it.

Virgin olive oil,[5] added with grape syrup, makes wines more stable and makes weaker wines stronger.

Black and white hellebore, added in small quantity, clarifies wine, stabilizes it, and is good for those who drink it.

1. Greek *kedrou karpos* (and later *kedrou prisma*): cone of *Cedrus libani* A.Rich., rich in tannin and with antiseptic properties.
2. Galls caused by the wasp *Andricus kollari* (Hartig, 1843), nowadays exported from Syria and known in the trade as Aleppo galls; rich in tannin.
3. 'A kind of marble, like Parian, but lighter' (Theophrastos, *On Stones* 7).
4. Greek *marathron*: *Foeniculum vulgare* Mill.
5. Greek *elaion stakton*, free-flow olive oil (the only occurrence of this phrase).

Black chickpeas,[1] roasted briefly, ground and mixed in, stabilize wine and make it diuretic.

Grape syrup mixed with wine stabilizes it.

Wax in the pitching of the vat makes wine more astringent.[2]

Linseed mixed with grape syrup or must stabilizes wine.

White vetch flour stops wine.

Bruttian pitch, as found in the bottoms of wine-vats, crushed and sieved into the wine, stabilizes wines.

Pine resin, and particularly terebinth resin,[3] stops wines.

Crushed alum makes wine astringent and stable and stops it turning to vinegar.

13. *A wonderful preparation to stabilize wines, called 'panacea'.* Damegeron.

Have ready the following items. 2 scruples aloes, 2 scruples frankincense, 2 scruples amomum,[4] 4 scruples melilot, 1 scruple cassia, 2 scruples spikenard,[5] 4 scruples tejpat, 2 scruples myrrh.[6] Bind all of these in a linen cloth. Into each vat, after the wine has gone in and has settled, add one spoonful,[7] and stir with a rooted reed for 3 days.

Some people spice their wines as follows. They add 3 scruples saffron, which gives it a good colour; 4 drams male frankincense, sifted, which makes it austere;[8] 1 ball of tejpat, which makes it aromatic. Chop and sift each of these, mix them, sift again, and add two spoonfuls for each *amphora*, while the wine is settling and has

---

1. Greek *erebinthos melas*: presumably the black chickpea known today, which differs chemically from the commoner white varieties (see Rossi and others 1984).

2. Compare 6.5, fifteenth section.

3. Greek *retine terebinthine*, from the tree called *terebinthos*: *Pistacia atlantica* Desf.

4. Greek *amomon*: perhaps *Amomum subulatum* Roxb.

5. Greek *nardou stachys*: *Nardostachys jatamansi* D.Don (DC.)

6. Greek *smyrna*: *Commiphora* spp.

7. According to pseudo-Galen, *On Weights and Measures* 62, one *kochliarion* or spoonful equated to three scruples in weight or to one-eighth of a ladle (or fluid ounce) in volume.

8. See introduction, p. 17.

not yet begun to ferment. With all your wines, be sure to spice them while they are settling.

Others spice their wines as follows. Take equal quantities of cardamom,[1] Illyrian iris, cassia, spikenard, melilot, *xylobalsamon*,[2] Alexandrian rush,[3] cost, Celtic nard; chop, sieve and add to the wine.

Some boil must down to a third and mix it with the wine.

Some add gypsum.

14. *An infallible verse to ensure that wine never turns.* Africanus.

The wine will never be able to turn if you write on the jar, or on the vats, the following divine words: *Taste and know that the Lord is good.*[4] You will do well also to write this on an apple and throw the apple into the wine.

15. *Signs and predictions that wine will turn or will be stable.* Sotion.

When the wine has gone into the vat, after a certain time it should be emptied without disturbance into another vessel, leaving the lees in the vat, which should be sealed carefully. Then check several times by smell whether the lees undergo any souring, whether flies are produced, or anything of the kind. If this happens, expect the wine to turn. If nothing of the kind is observed, the wine will keep.

Some people take a reed that is hollow throughout and put it into the vat, all the way to the bottom, while keeping the thumb over the upper end; then take the thumb off, inhale the odour of the lees at the bottom of the vat, and suck some of the lees into the mouth. By the state of the lees they judge how the wine will be.

Some boil up a little of the wine, cool it, and taste it; by the quality of this they are confident of knowing what the quality of the

---

1. Greek *kardamomon*: *Elettaria cardamomum* (L.) Maton.

2. *Commiphora opobalsamum* Engl.

3. Greek *schoinos Alexandrine*: probably one of the *Cymbopogon* species (see p. 150 n. 1).

4. The word for 'good' is *chrestos*; hence it is possible to understand the words to mean 'Taste and know that Christ is the Lord'.

rest of the wine will be. The sample for tasting must come from the middle of the vessel.

Others find evidence in the lids of the wine-vessels. They uncover the vat and taste the liquid on the underside of the lid, judging that the wine will be like it: a wine-like taste means excellent wine; a watery taste means wine that will not keep.

Some test by the taste of the wine itself. If it is austere from the beginning, it will keep; if it is loose-flavoured, the contrary.

It is possible to test wine by the *anthos* floating on its surface. If it develops a flat, soft, purplish *anthos*, the wine will keep rather well; if the *anthos* is glutinous it is not good; a black or yellow *anthos* floating on the wine shows that it will be weak; white *anthos* shows that it will be stable. A net of *anthos* like a spider's web shows that it will turn to vinegar straight away.

If at harvest you see a snake coiled around the vine, take it that the wine will turn to vinegar.

If when the wine is being trodden or is going into the vats it is thick and sticky, as you can tell by touch, the wine will keep rather well; if it is thin and weak, it will turn easily.

Wines that are already austere when they are still at the stage of must will keep better and will eventually be pleasanter to drink; those that are initially sweet and raw will last only a short time.

When wine is turning the vessel will be warm to the touch; if it is stable the vessel will be cold.

If the lid of the vat is always found to be dry, the wine will keep particularly well; if it is moist, this means turning to vinegar.

If in spring wine is warm to the taste, it will turn quickly; if it is cold, it will stabilize.

If the wine has an odour of honey vinegar, you should realize that this is the fault of the vat, and move the wine to a new vessel.

Some people test as follows whether the wine is stable. They dip their hands in the wine; then, when their hands have cooled, they decide by the odour. If it is rather vinegary, this indicates that the wine is turning.

Others pour some of the wine into a narrow-mouthed vessel, stop it tightly, submerge it in water for three days, then take it out and test it.

Others pour some of the wine into sand, filter it through, and if its flavour does not alter, regard its quality as proved.

Wines usually turn at the solstices and when the vine begins to shoot;[1] this is when they need to be tested.

Others test their wine as follows. They make leaves of lead, tin or copper three fingers long and three wide, stick them – perfectly clean – [inside] the lid of each vat with wax, and then replace the lids on the vats. After forty days they open the vats. If they find that the wines have *anthos* and have a sweet and good smell, and the metal leaves are quite clean, they conclude that the wines are sound. But if the wine is unstable they would find the lead leaf whitened, with patches resembling white lead. A tin leaf, if the wine was unstable, would have a black sweat on its surface, and this sweat would be acid. A copper leaf, if the wine was stable, would be clean and bright, but if the wine was on the turn it would be foul-smelling, with bubbles.

Some people mix pearl barley with the wine, let it stand, and taste it.

Others, while boiling some of the wine, drop into it celery seed, barley bran, bay leaves and shoots of a black vine, then cool it, taste it, and judge accordingly.

16. *Treating wine that has begun to turn to vinegar.* Tarantinos.

Fill a new jug with pure water, seal it carefully, drop it into the vat and then put the lid on the vat, leaving a little air space. After three days you will find the wine cured and the water smelling [of vinegar].[2] Do this until the wine is fully cured.

Others pour a fiftieth part of goat's milk into the wine, cover the wine for five days, then transfer it to another container and cover it for ten days. The wine will not turn.

17. *Stabilizing wine for export by sea.* Diophanes.

Filter *amorge* through linen and boil it down to half its quantity; pour [with] Attic honey into the bottom of the amphora [*keramion*]

1. Abridged from 7.10.
2. Similarly at 7.26.

before it is filled with wine. The wine will then last for the longest possible time.

18. *How to manage grapes so that the wine they yield will be sweet.* Didymos.

Some people in Bithynia make sweet wine as follows. Thirty days before the vintage they twist the stem that bears the bunches of grapes, and take off all the leaves, so that the sun's rays will remove all the water and make the wine sweet (just as we do when cooking must).[1] The reason for twisting the stems is to cut off the moisture and nourishment of the vine from the bunches and to ensure they get no water from it.

Some people, after stripping the leaves from the bunches of grapes, when the grapes begin to shrivel, pick them off bunch by bunch and put them out in the sun, so that they dry completely into raisins; then, gathering them up in the heat of the sun, they move them to the trough, leave them there for the rest of the day and the whole of the following night, and tread them at dawn.

19. *How to produce sweet wine from the must.* Same author.

If you want the wine you have trodden to be sweet, then after putting it in the vats you must leave them uncovered for three days and then put on the lids so that they do not quite meet the lips but leave a small opening; use sticks or reeds or the like to keep it open. After the fifth day put the lids on fully, sealing them with ash mixed with water, but leaving little vents. After the seventh day, seal up these vents. If you want the wine even sweeter, leave the vats uncovered for five days, and then replace the lids as described.

20. *To make wine aromatic and pleasant to the taste.* Pamphilos.

Collect a few ripe myrtle berries, dry them, chop them, add them [...] *kabos* called *choinix*, and leave for ten days; then open and use.[2]

---

1. I.e. in the making of grape syrup.
2. Some words are missing: there is no mention of wine. *Choinix* is a dry measure.

You can make your wine aromatic each day by steeping perfect apples in water, removing them, and mixing the water with the wine. The apples will also be good to eat.

Oinanthe,[1] particularly that from tree-trained vines, taken at flowering time and added to the wine, makes it aromatic.

Wax, burned in the vat, gives aroma; the wine must be put in after the burning.

Rubbing the leaves of stone pine or *strobilos*,[2] Aleppo pine[3] and cypress on the lip of the vat, then stirring the must, makes the wine very aromatic.

If you want your wine to have the aroma of incense, or apple, or some other substance, put one of these items [into the jar] before you are to fill it with wine; fasten it, and leave it; remove the substance before it spoils or alters in aroma, and put in the wine. Seal it, and use it.

The following are substances that give a good aroma: southernwood, bitter almonds, potter's earth, hazelwort leaves,[4] camel's thorn roots,[5] asparagus flower,[6] cedar cone, fenugreek flour. Put these into either baskets or bouquets and hang them at the top of the vessel containing the wine so as not to touch the liquid. When they have transferred their aroma, remove them – in all cases before they spoil or alter.

21. *Making white wine black and black wine white.* Varro.

Mix 8 drams of rough salt to 10 *kotylai* of wine.

The same effect is obtained by adding whey to the wine.

If you burn vine stems and add the ash to the wine-jar, stir it, and leave it 40 days, the wine will be white. White wine will turn black if you add the ash from burning black wine stems.

---

1. See 5.51.
2. Greek *peuke* (*strobilos*, added as a synonym in the text, is often the term for the cone and its edible kernel): *Pinus pinea* L. In chapter 24 the term *pitys karpimos* 'fruiting pine' is used for this species.
3. Greek *pitys*: *Pinus halepensis* Mill.
4. Greek *asaron*: *Asarum europaeum* L.
5. Greek *aspalathos*: *Alhagi maurorum* Medik.
6. Greek *asparagos*: *Asparagus officinalis* L.

22. *To clarify wine.* Fronto.

Drop the white of three eggs into a pitcher, beat till they foam; also add white salt and some of the wine, mix till very white; then fill with wine. Do this with each wine-jar; then store.

23. *To make wine go further in mixing, so that a smaller quantity will serve more people.* Paxamos.

Grate dried roots of marshmallow into the wine, stir it, and use it.

24. *To make aggressively young wine old.* Damegeron.

Take bitter almonds, wormwood, the needles of stone pine, fenugreek; roast, grind, and mix in, allowing 1 *kyathos* per *amphora*. This makes wines keep and makes them seem old.

You can make wines seem old by taking two jars containing old wine, just emptied; break off and discard the ears and lips and the projections of the base, which did not absorb any wine, but retain the rest, with the old wine lees. Smash them up, sift them, and add half a *modion* to each *amphora*. Stir the wine, seal it, and leave it fifteen days; then open and use it, and you will think it is ten-year-old wine. After emptying that wine-jar, pour the lees into a new jug; bake them, break them up again, and use as before.[1] This use of potsherds is better than any of the previously-mentioned aromatics.

Some make their wines seem old in the following way. They take 1 scruple melilot, 3 scruples liquorice, same quantity Celtic nard, 2 scruples hepatic aloes; grind, sift, add to the wine, and use it.

25. *So that wine does not have* anthos. Sotion.

Sprinkle dried *oinanthe* over the wine; or mix vetch flour with the wine. If the *oinanthe* and flour sink, transfer the wine into another vessel.

---

1. Adopting the text suggested by the Syriac version (the Greek texts vary and make little sense).

26. *To stop moistness in wine.* Apuleius.

Pour in 4 *kotylai* of garum; add pomegranate leaves. This cures moistness.[1]

You will cure a bad odour as follows: take greasy torches, light them, and plunge them in the wine.

Some stop up a vessel containing water and submerge it in the wine-vat. After three days the wine will be pure and the water will have the bad odour.[2]

Some burn up potsherds and drop them in; others submerge hot barley bread in the wine in a basket; others mix in the whey from fresh cheese; others put in willow wood, and in this way remove all the badness of the wine.

27. *Curing wine spoiled by vermin venom.* Demokritos.

Warm bread dropped in, or an iron ring, will remove the venom.

28. *Settling wine that is full of lees or cloudy.* Anatolios.

Some people add, to each *metretes*, one *kotyle* of *amorge* boiled down to a third; this immediately settles it.

29. *To spoil wine.* Africanus.

Chew cabbage leaves and drop the juice into the wine.

30. *So as not to smell of wine after drinking.* Same author.

Chew *iris troglodytis*.[3]

31. *So as not to be drunk after drinking a lot of wine.* Same author.

Bake and eat a goat lung.

---

1. In terms of the four humours, water is wet; wine is dry. Moistness is therefore a fault in wine.
2. Similarly at 7.16.
3. If this is the 'African iris' mentioned by Pliny, *Natural History* 21.41, it was the largest and bitterest kind.

Before other food eat 5 or 7 bitter almonds, or raw cabbage, and you will not get drunk.

A drinker will not get drunk if wearing a wreath of *chamaipitys* branches.[1]

Or, at the first cup, recite the following Homeric line: *Three times, from the mountains of Ida, Zeus wise in counsel thundered.*[2]

32. *How to stop the craving for wine.* Demokritos.

Collect the *ichor* that runs from the vine-shoots when they are cut; secretly give it to the addict to drink along with wine, and the craving for wine will cease.

33. *To restore sobriety in drunkards.* Berytios.

A good drink of vinegar makes drunkards sober.
   Eating cabbage leaves.
   Honey-soaked pastries.
   Cakes.
   Also, questions and discussions concerning ancient history.
   And wreaths of many flowers worn on the head.

34. *Aside from wine, certain other beverages are also intoxicating.* Leontinos.

Among intoxicating beverages wine comes first; second, surprising as it seems, water; third, the drinks made from wheat and barley, mostly favoured by barbarians; fourth, the drink made from emmer and from oats. Those from broomcorn millet and from foxtail millet[3] are also intoxicating.

Old people, and all those with cold constitutions, get drunk easily. Women, because of their temperaments, get drunk less easily than men, but still do so after a certain quantity of wine.

---

1. Greek *chamaipitys*: ground-pine, *Ajuga iva* (L.) Schreber, or yellow bugle, *A. chamaepitys* (L.) Schreber.
2. *Iliad* 8.170.
3. Greek *elymos*: *Setaria italica* (L.) P. Beauv.

35. *Making wine without grapes.* Sotion.

The fresh fruit of the myrtle and cornel,[1] ground and pressed, make a wine. Wine can also be made from the segments of pomegranates, clean [of pith], the seeds removed, and pressed.

Some people make wine from fresh figs, as follows. They fill an earthenware vessel, formerly used for wine, half full of figs, then fill it up with pure water. They taste it frequently, and when the taste becomes wine-like they strain it off and use it.

36. *An infallible preparation for wine that maintains health until old age.* Vindanionius.

4 drams best iris, 1 *tryblion* fennel seed, same quantity of flour, 1 dram pepper, 2 drams Trogodytic myrrh,[2] 1½ drams hartwort,[3] 1½ drams spignel,[4] 2 drams celery; grind; add a sufficient quantity of aromatic white wine, mix and form into cakes, wrap tightly in linen, put in a vessel, pour in best quality wine, and seal. Open after four days: drink one wine-cup before food. Anyone who uses this regularly will keep healthy. It is better mixed with must.

37. *Strained wines.*

Put the strainer in pure brine, or in seawater mixed with drinking water, for 2 days, then steep it in wine. When it is to be used, drain it, then rub its lips with ground almond or walnut.

Some mix their strained wines with anise,[5] soot, gypsum, grape syrup, honey, lees of good wine, or bitter vetch flour.

---

1. Greek *kranon*: *Cornus mas* L.
2. Best quality myrrh, from what is now northern Somalia (see Lionel Casson, *The Periplus Maris Erythraei* [Princeton, 1989] pp. 118–120).
3. Greek *seseli*: *Tordylium apulum* L.
4. Greek *meon*: *Meum athamanticum* Jacquin.
5. Greek *anison*: *Pimpinella anisum* L.

Book 8

1. *Recipes for medicinal wines.*

The mixing and preparation of medicinal wines to cure different ailments, as tested and approved by many early authors. These preparations contain no drugs, only natural ingredients such as rose petals, dill, wormwood, pennyroyal and the like. Whichever it is must be ground, fastened in a bouquet, and put into the wine, as specified below.

2. *Rose wine.*

Fasten together one part each of dried mountain rose petals, anise, saffron and honey,[1] and add to the wine.

3. *Dill wine.*

Put the dill seed in a linen bouquet, and let it drop into the wine. This wine is soporific, diuretic and digestive.

4. *Anise wine.*

Put the anise seed in the wine: it cures dysuria and helps the bowels.

5. *Pear wine.*

Put pears in: this wine stops diarrhoea.[2]

---

1. The honey must be added separately (unless there is something more seriously wrong with the text). In the recipe given by Palladius, *Agriculture* 6.13, rose petals are steeped in wine for 30 days, after which honey is added.
2. Cf. Dioscorides, *Materia Medica* 5.24.

6. *Hazelwort wine.*

This wine is diuretic; it restores those who are dropsical, jaundiced, liverish, sciatic, or suffering from tertian fever; it cures tremors.

7. *Pennyroyal wine.*

Pennyroyal has to be boiled in wine until a third [of the liquid] is left. This wine is an antidote to animal stings and is helpful against winter colds.

8. *Bay wine.*

This wine is extremely hot and diuretic. It helps with coughs, chestiness[1] and colic; it is useful to older people, and against worms and earache; it helps hysterical women.

9. *Fennel wine.*

This wine encourages the appetite, restores the stomach, and is diuretic.

10. *Fleabane wine.*

This wine is useful to those who are sciatic and stomachic, and is an antidote against venomous creatures.

11. *Verjuice wine.*[2]

This wine is good for the stomach and is suitable for those suffering from paralysis, narcosis, trembling, blackouts, kidney troubles, colic and pestilential diseases.

12. *Parsley wine.*

This wine strengthens the stomach, causes belching, and awakens the appetite; it is also diuretic and very soporific.

---

1. Greek *thorakes*, literally 'chests'. In other sources this is not the name of an illness.
2. Greek *omphakites*, flavoured with unripe grapes.

13. *Rue wine.*

This wine is hot and is an antidote against noxious drugs and venomous creatures.

14. *Fenugreek wine.*

This wine, made with the addition of ground fenugreek, is very useful to the liver.

15. *Hyssop wine.*

This wine clears the chest, effects digestion (because it is hot) and soothes the bowels.

16. *Celery wine.*

Grind celery seed and add to the wine; this helps urination and belching and with pains in the nerves and hypochondria.

17. *Quince wine.*

Put very aromatic quinces into an earthenware vessel, pour on wine, seal and leave for three days; use on the fourth.

18. *To make a purging wine.*

After trenching, grind the roots of black hellebore; then clear off the roots of the vines, scatter the ground hellebore around them, and re-bury them.[1]

19. *A wine able to draw down a woman's milk and to prevent her sickening.*

Gather thyme when it flowers, dry and pound it; put 4 *choinikes* in an earthenware vessel, add a *metretes* of white wine; seal the vessel for 40 days.

---

1. This method differs entirely from the others in book 8. It can be compared with similar practices described at 4.8.

20. *A wine against dysentery and diarrhoea.*

Take 30 slightly unripe pomegranates, crush them, put them into an earthenware vessel, add 3 *choes* of austere black wine. Use after 30 days.

21. *Vermouth.*

Pound 8 drams of wormwood, preferably Pontic;[1] put in a linen bag, not too fine-meshed, and insert in an amphora. Some cut the quantity by half; many add cassia. Then pour must in until it is full; leave one air-vent in case it bubbles over. Make as many amphoras as you like in this way. Use vermouth for pain in the liver and hypochondria, for indigestion and pain in the stomach. It ejects intestinal worms.[2]

22. *Making Aminaean wine.*[3] Didymos.

Some put wine of Aminaean-like grapes in amphoras that have contained Italian wine, and bury them out in the open. Some also add a few bitter almonds and a little tejpat and grape syrup.

Others, aloes 2 dr., amomum 3 dr., cost 4 dr., tejpat leaf 4 dr., melilot 9 dr., spikenard 2 dr., cinnamon 3 dr.: these quantities are for 7 *amphorai* of wine.

Others again, 4 dr. each of myrrh, cassia, saffron; and some use [aromatic] reed instead of myrrh.

23. *Making Thasian wine.*[4] Florentinus.

We dry ripe grapes in bunches in the sun for 5 days; on the 6th at midday we put them, still warm, into must, with seawater which has been boiled down to half, then remove them and put them in the trough and press them; then, after a night and a day, we put [the must] in vessels. When it has fermented and cleared, we add a 25th part of grape syrup; after the spring equinox we rack into smaller jars.

---

1. Greek *apsinthion pontikon*: *Artemisia pontica* L.
2. Hence the English name 'wormwood'.
3. *Aminnia* (variously spelt) was a grape variety or group of varieties and was at some periods rated the best. These are recipes for imitating the typical flavour.
4. Properly the wine of the Aegean island of Thasos. This is a recipe for imitating the flavour.

24. *Making Coan wine.*[1] Berytios.

Some boil 3 parts must and one part seawater down to two-thirds.

Others mix 1 *kotyle* salt, 3 *kotylai* grape syrup, about 1 *kotyle* must, 1 *kotyle* bitter vetch flour, 100 dr. melilot, 16 dr. apples,[2] 16 dr. Celtic nard, into 2 *metretai* white wine.

25. *Honey wine.*

Put Attic honey in an earthenware vessel and set it in hot ashes to drive off the scum; and after it has heated add 4 pints wine to 1 pint honey; then put the honey wine in well-pitched jars and hang in them linen bags containing 12 scruples pounded dried cost. Cover with linen and store in the loft.

Some pound 12 scruples tejpat leaf and fennel to the honey wine, and after 15 days find it surprisingly good; when kept longer, incomparable.

Others make honey wine thus: they mix myrrh 6 scruples, cassia 12 scruples, cost 2 scruples, spikenard 4 scruples, pepper 4 scruples, Attic honey 6 pints, wine 24 pints and stand in the sun from the rising of Sirius[3] for 40 days. Some people call this 'nectar'.

26. Oinomeli *from must.*

[Boil][4] the must until about half remains. To ten pints must mix one pint Attic honey, put in an earthenware vessel, seal it with gypsum and store it in the dark.

It is necessary to know that honey wine made from must is windy and not easy on the stomach; but it is good for the bowels.

27. *Preparing* hydromelon.

Take 32 best quality apples, chop them small, remove the pips with a reed, put them into 8 pints best honey and leave for 8 months.

---

1. Originally the wine of the Aegean island of Cos, distinctive because it included seawater. It was already widely imitated at the time of Cato, who gives a recipe (Cato, *On Farming* 112). See Dalby 2003 pp. 89–90.
2. An error.
3. See introduction.
4. The manuscripts say 'Let the must stand until ...'

Mix with 12 pints old rainwater and put out in the sun during the burning of Sirius, protecting from rain and dew.

Others have a better method for making *hydromelon*, as follows. Crush the finest fully-ripe apples, press juice from them and mix 4 pints of this juice, 8 pints finest skimmed honey, 12 pints rainwater; put out in the sun; heat over a moderate fire; use.

Some, at Beroia for example, use a bain-marie, so that the mixture is heated by the water rather than the fire.

28. *Preparing hydromel.*

Take old rainwater (or otherwise water boiled down to a third), mix with a sufficient quantity of honey; put in a jar, leaving an air-vent, and store in the dark for 10 days; then use. It will be better when aged. Expert physicians, aware that this consists only of honey and water, use it in treating the sick.

Others mix pure snow with honey, pound it and store it. This is a medicine for the feverish; they call it *chionomeli*, 'snow honey'.

29. *Preparing rhodomel.*

Take fine rose petals (mountain roses if available), remove the bases of the petals, press them in a basin. Take 2 pints of the juice to 1 pint honey; skim the honey, add the juice, put in a jar, stir vigorously, and store in a dry place.

30. *Preparing celery wine.*

12 scruples celery seed (some take 16 scruples), 6 scruples rue seed or fresh rue leaves, 1 pint skimmed honey, 4 or 5 pints wine: mix all this and store 15 days.

31. *Making* konditon.[1] Demokritos.

Washed, dried, finely ground peppercorns, 8 scruples. Attic honey, 1 pint. Old white wine, 4 or 5 pints.

---

1. Latin *conditum.* See Dalby 2003 p. 95.

32. *Making the best grape syrup.* Leontinos.

Take 50 pints of the best must and 100 pints of the best wine, boil down to a third, and skim. You will make a high quality product.

33. *Making a different vinegar; how to make wine into vinegar.* Varro.

Take a root of beet, pound it and put it in the wine; after three hours it will be vinegar. You can restore it, if you want, by adding a cabbage root.

34. *Making vinegar without wine.* Same author.

Put in a jar some juicy peaches, sprinkle on roasted barley, and leave to work for [...] days,[1] then strain and use.

You can also make vinegar without wine as follows. Put in a jar fresh figs and roasted barley and the flesh of citrons and stir vigorously. When they have fermented, strain and use.

Make vinegar without wine as follows. Boil together gypsum and seawater, then add river water, and use after filtering.

35. *Vinegar to promote digestion and good health.* Sotion.

Put 8 drams squill and 1 or 2 pints vinegar in a vessel, with one part each of pepper, mint and cassia, also juniper berries; use after a time.

36. *Preparing sweet vinegar.* Same author.

Take a jar of very sour vinegar and an equal quantity of good must from treading. Mix together, seal with pitch, leave for 30 days, then use.

Some make rather sweet vinegar as follows. Take one *metretes* of must that runs off from the treading and two *metretai* vinegar; heat them together till a third has boiled away.

---

1. The number is missing from the text.

Some take 2 *metretai* must, 1 *metretes* vinegar, 3 *metretai* boiled drinking water; heat them together till a third of the whole volume has boiled away and two thirds remain.

37. *Preparing sour vinegar.* Same author.

Dry grape pips for two days, and then add them to must, along with a few unripe grapes; you will make it sour. Use after 7 days.

Or add feverfew:[1] this will sour it.

You will also turn it sour if you take a fourth or a fifth part from vinegar, boil it over the fire, then put it back with the rest and store it in the sun for 8 days.

To make vinegar very sour and good to the taste people add old roots of dog's-tooth grass to it, and raisins, and bruised leaves of the wild pear, and bramble root, and whey.

Also adding to vinegar red-hot embers of burned oak, and liquor from cooking chickpeas, and red-hot potsherds, makes it sour.

38. *To keep sour vinegar.* Apuleius.

Mix broad beans with some lemon;[2] put it in a jar.

39. *Making pepper vinegar.* Same author.

Put whole peppercorns in a linen bouquet and hang them in the vinegar for 8 days; then use.

40. *Testing whether vinegar contains water.* Same author.

Add natron to the vinegar. If it bubbles as if boiling, take it that it contains water.

41. *Stretching vinegar.* Demokritos.

Take a known quantity of vinegar, for example one *metretes*. Boil seawater down to half its volume and take one *metretes* of this. Mix the two together; store in a jar.

---

1. Greek *pyrethron*: *Tanacetum parthenium* (L.) Schultz-Bip.
2. Greek *oxy kitron* 'sour citron': *Citrus limon* (L.) Burm.f.

Some people steep and then strain barley grains; they take one *metretes* of the liquor with one *metretes* vinegar, stir them together, add a sufficient quantity of salt, roasted and still hot; stop the jar and put it aside for 20 days.

Some take figs that have been rained on and have rotted on the tree, put them in water and let them rot down together, and thus produce vinegar.

42. *Making squill vinegar.* Pythagoras.[1]

Put in an earthenware jar 36 pints of the best and sharpest vinegar. Take inner layers of white squill, cut small and dried in the sun for 30 days; steep this in the vinegar for 12 days. Then strain off the vinegar, store it, use it as required. Squill vinegar is just as effective as squill wine.

---

1. It cannot be shown that Pythagoras wrote anything at all, certainly not recipes for squill vinegar, but it is true that according to another source (pseudo-Galen, *On Accessible Remedies*: Galen vol. 14 p. 567 Kühn) Pythagoras took to using squill vinegar at the age of fifty and lived to 117.

Book 9

1. *The myth of the olive tree.*

They say the olive tree came to human knowledge in this way. In
the beginning the whole earth was covered by water, and the first
land to appear was where Athens stands. Athena and Poseidon fell
in love with the spot and competed to build a city there and name
it after themselves. In order to resolve the dispute Zeus said that
whichever gave the finest gift to the city would be the possessor of
it. Poseidon then adorned Athens with harbours and shipyards.
Athena gave an olive tree, flourishing and heavy with fruit; she was
crowned with its leaves in the sight of all as the victor, and they
named the city Athens in her honour. Poseidon, defeated, went
back to his usual sphere.

This is why the supervisors of the games present a garland of wild
olive to the winners of competitions.

Those who write the name of Athena on an olive leaf and bind
the leaf to their head with a thread have alleviated and sometimes
actually cured headaches.

2. *Planting and care of olive trees; olive-growing the best of pursuits.* Florentinus.

The produce of olive trees is more indispensable than any other; no
other can be stored for such a long time. Those who give their time
to farming must therefore pay the greatest attention to olive-growing.
The produce of olives renders safe and solid profit; the fruit of the
olive also offers the greatest benefit to a healthy life.

The turning leaves of the olive foretell the summer solstice, as do those of the linden,[1] elm and white poplar.

Consider that the olive is thriving if it bears fruit not along the shoots but at their extremities.

The olive is pure; it wants each of its harvesters to be pure, and to swear that he has come from no other bed than that of his own wife. Thus it will also fruit better next year. They say that in Anazarba in Cilicia virgin children tend the olives, and for this reason their olives bear better than any elsewhere.

3. *Suitable air for olives; layout of orchards.* Same author.

Hot, dry air is suitable to olives: this can be seen in Libya and Cilicia and the olive orchards there. A contribution to the suitability of the air is made by the sloping and elevated configuration of the land. Trees in such locations produce excellent oil because excessive burning of the sun is cooled by the winds – so much so that 'pressed-unripe' oil[2] is produced. Olive trees in the plains, less stirred by the winds and more severely burned by continual sun, produce a thick oil. In general it is to be noted that the winds have effect not only on plants but on everything; strong and violent winds are in opposition to all plants; temperate and mild winds favour all plants, but particularly olives. You will find especially flourishing those olive plantations that the breath of the wind is able to enter, the spaces between them being broad so that the wind can blow through easily. This, then, is why we said that sloping and hilly sites are very suitable to olives; they welcome gentle winds, which do not go to waste but penetrate each tree alike, nourishing them and awakening the growth of the plant.

4. *When to plant olives and in what soils.* Same author.

Olives should be planted between the setting of the Hyades and the winter solstice, that is, from 15th November to 20th December. The

---

1. Greek *philyra*: *Tilia* spp., e.g. *Tilia platyphyllos* Scop.
2. Greek *omotribes*. According to Galen this was identical with *omphakinon*, the speciality oil from unripe olives whose making is described at 9.19: compare Theophrastos, *On Odours* 15; Dioscorides, *Materia Medica* 1.30; Galen, *On Compound Medicines by Type* [vol. 13 p. 382 Kühn].

olive can also be planted in spring, because the two seasons resemble one another in humidity and in warmth. Autumn has soil still warm from the [summer] sun and moisture from the rains that follow the harvest; spring has moisture from the preceding rains and gains warmth from the approaching sun.

A moister soil produces healthier and fattier olive trees; this soil should therefore be chosen for preference. Second after this is white clay; third, hard clay. We do not recommend rich soil, nor red soil, because it is hot and burns the plants. 'Sunken'[1] soil is much more to be avoided. It bears fruit that lacks fattiness; the product is therefore watery. But thin soil is suitable, as Attica proves.

5. *The nursery.* Didymos.

It is simpler to put the plants in their own ground, avoiding the delay caused by moving them from nurseries. However, since trees transplanted from nurseries have a more certain growth, we shall set out the nursery method. As we have often said,[2] the nursery must resemble in all respects the eventual plantation, not only in quality and layout but also in its presentation to the weather, so that the olives when eventually planted out are not disoriented.

Take into your nurseries [shoots] from young and well-fruiting trees *en oun metro pachei*,[3] not growing out of the trunk but higher up, from among new shoots and young branches. The proper length is a cubit, and the bark must not be damaged by the cut: this has to be watched very carefully. The cut should be smoothed off all round with a sharp pruning-knife to keep the plant perfect and clean. The lower end of the cutting should be coated with cow dung mixed with ash. We set it in the ground so that it projects by four fingers, and the ground at this point should be made concave so as as to gather the rain. As already explained, care must be taken that the cutting is not placed upside down.[4] We will then stick a reed in the ground

1. A term comparable to 'carious', used of soil by Cato, *On Farming* 5.6 and Columella, *Farming* 2.4.5.
2. E.g. 2.48.
3. These four words cannot be translated. An earlier version of the text probably recommended what thickness the shoots should be.
4. Not said earlier but repeated later, at 9.11.

beside it so that those hoeing the ground will see where the cutting is. The plants in the nurseries should be shaken every month for seven months. Growing in the nursery may be worthwhile for up to three years; in year four, however, prune superfluous branches and take the new trees to their eventual plantation, moving along with them some of their own soil with which they have been nourished. This growing of new olives from cuttings is the better method.

Some, however, take off growth that happens to come up from the lowest parts of the trees. In Syria these suckers are called *gorphia*. They are planted in the nurseries, and then transplanted when they seem to be ready for it. Some, instead of using nurseries, have put them in their final location at once, and have succeeded; but it is preferable to start them in nurseries, where, since they are watered, they soon begin rapid growth, and are then easily transplanted.

6. *Planting holes for olives.* Same author.

To make an olive plantation the area where they are to be planted must be cleared, plants of all other kinds removed, and a wall or fence built around it. Dig planting holes preferably the year before planting, so that the soil will be loosened by the sun, the winds and the rains, to allow the plants to put down roots. If we are in a hurry to plant, then burn dry sticks and reeds, and whatever else burns well, in the planting hole for several days, two months or at the very least one month beforehand. The depth of the planting-holes must be three cubits, or not less than two and a half. They should be 50 cubits apart, so that the crowns air and the intervening ground breathes. Those who have no interest in inter-cropping plant closer together, but ensuring that the trees will not shade one another.

7. *Selecting new olive trees.* Same author.

New olive trees should be selected as follows: they should have come from appropriate locations, from young trees that fruit consistently each year; they should have the thickness of a *stelechos* or greater;[1] they should be smooth and straight.

---

1. *Stelechos* 'trunk' is perhaps an error here; it is not normally a measure of thickness.

8. *Making olive trees heavy-fruiting.* Africanus.

Bore a hole right through the crown with an auger. Take 2 young shoots from other heavy-fruiting olive trees; push the tips of the shoots into each end of the hole until they emerge on the other side, grasp them and pull them firmly through. When they are wedged, cut off the extra, that is, whatever of the shoots remains on the outside; coat the holes on each side with mud mixed with chaff. The tree will now bear heavily and will be a *good olive tree.*[1]

9. *Care of mature olive trees.* Sotion.

We have given sufficient instruction on the planting and rearing of olives. It is now necessary to discuss the care of mature olive trees.

Do the digging, the trenching that is, at the same season specified for young trees.[2] The depth and the breadth of ground composted, the amount of manure and the height to which the soil is raised, must depend on the size of the crowns, on the nature of the soil and of the trees. Less manure should be added, and at intervals of several years, and dug in more thinly, to soils that are moist and more suited to growing; otherwise the trees will be forced into growth and the fruit will be damaged in blossom. In drier soils and those less favourable to growth, more manure should be given, more frequently, and the soil raised higher around the crowns, so that the manure promotes growth and the tree is protected by soil from the sun's burning.

Prune mature olive trees (like other trees) in autumn, after the setting of the Pleiades.[3] At this season trees appear to be firmer and stronger: first, the moist element in them has been taken into the shoots and to feed the fruit; second, remaining moisture has been dried up by the heat of the sun; third, the winter rains have not yet arrived. For all these reasons, trees are strongest in autumn and this is the ideal season for pruning them, especially olives. Before pruning it is necessary to manure: the benefit of the manure will then balance the damage of the pruning. The crowns, when pruned, suffer owing to the cuts; if manured they recover and are readier to put on growth.

1. *Epistle to the Romans* 11.24. The instruction is repeated at 9.10.
2. Not stated clearly in preceding text: in the spring, perhaps (cf. 3.6).
3. See introduction.

Dry wood and what grows from the middle must be pruned off to allow it air. Remove fronds that overlay others; plan a more open tree. Distorted shoots, and particularly those of excessive length, must be cut off, likewise those whose strength develops at too great a height: they will by their nature be less productive, which is why farmers all agree that olive trees ought not to rise higher than ten cubits. Growth above this height is easily damaged, the branches being susceptible to violent winds and the blossom liable to be shaken off prematurely. Many, therefore, train the fronds of newly planted olives down to the ground, forcing the tree to be more limited in its growth and more ground-seeking. Enough has now been said of the pruning of mature olives, a process to be carried out every three to four years.

Suckers growing up from the crown must be taken off while they are still tender, every year, so that the tree does not put effort into them.

10. *How to make olive trees flourish and fruit heavily, and how to treat them when sick.* The Quintilii.

You will make olive trees finer, more flourishing and very heavy-cropping if after trenching round them you put to the roots *amorge* from unsalted olives mixed half-and-half with drinking water, 2 *kotylai* to each tree; or one or two baskets of bean shucks – in proportion to the size of the tree – or a similar quantity of clayey soil mixed with cow dung or seaweed. No less effective is old human urine poured on to the trunk. After this application it is necessary to heap soil around the tree, to a height of two palms above the roots, making the surrounding ground concave to catch rainwater. It is best to carry out this treatment during the burning of Sirius.[1] It is better also to irrigate at this period, especially if there is a drought.

You will make unproductive trees heavy-cropping if you do as follows. Measuring about the height of a cubit from the base, bore into the trunk with an auger on the south-facing side, making a hole the size of a big finger right through the trunk. Take two olive stems from another tree, one that is still fruiting well, and put them into the hole from either end, so that each stem passes through to the

1. See introduction.

opposite side; grasp the ends and pull them firmly through. When the hole is plugged at both ends in this way, cut off the protruding stems and smear the ends of the holes with mud mixed with chaff. You should choose the olive stems, as described, depending on how you want the olives to be;[1] and you will get better oil if you choose stems from a good oil-producing tree. You should take the stems from the south side of the tree.

Olive trees that run to wood – those that produce plenty of leaf and very little fruit – are treated thus: drive into the roots a stake of wild olive, or pine, or oak, or a stone.

Trees that bear plenty of fruit but do not ripen it, and those that drop their blossom, are cured thus. Trench around the base of the trunk and put to it two baskets of seaweed for a large tree, less for a smaller one; then mix *amorge* with drinking water and pour 4 *choes* to the base of each tree. If you have no seaweed, use *amorge* alone.

We gave a general description of the treatment for maggots that spoil the fruit, and other environmental damage, in our book on vines.[2] If you find that the roots are drying out and are sick, you must realize that grubs that originate in the rootstock are to blame. There are several ways to get rid of them, as already explained; one in particular is to plant squill around the tree.

11. *Olives are planted in many different ways.*[3] Leontinos.

Keep in mind that the plant will sometimes be entirely buried in the soil, while sometimes it will be partly covered and partly visible. Those that are to be wholly buried need not be marked in any way when chosen. Those that are to be partly uncovered must be planted with their original orientation, facing east, south or west, so that the air will not disorient them.

If there are no rains, plants must be watered, twice and three times if possible. Into the hole, on each side of the plant and long enough to emerge from the soil, insert two smooth straight lengths

1. The text says 'depending on how you want the holes to be'. Cornarius's Latin translation rightly substitutes 'olives' for 'holes'. This instruction is repeated from 9.8.
2. Book 5, especially chapters 48–50.
3. This chapter has some overlaps with 9.5.

of wood, or reeds, or branches, tied together. When the plant has been trodden in, these can be removed and the space they leave can be filled with small stones or shards, topped with a larger stone; thus rainwater will reach the roots.

They should be planted as soon as taken, and during rainy weather.

The planting of olives is done in various ways. Some plant *skytalai* 'billets'; they take rather thick branches, saw them into lengths of one cubit, and plant these. Some plant *charakes* 'slips', as follows: they saw the thick branches into lengths of two cubits, then put a flattish stone into the bottom of the planting hole, stand the cutting upright on this and earth it up. Others plant the finest of the *paraphyades* 'suckers' that grow beside the trunk; and others trim these suckers with a pruning knife while they are still growing from the base of the trunk, afterwards putting them in their planting holes at the setting of Arcturus.[1] Others plant *tropaia*, as they are called, as follows: they cut lengths of 4 or 5 cubits [from suckers] growing from the base of the trunk, mark them with red earth to show how they lay to east or south, and put them in planting holes with every precaution; this kind of planting, when successful, takes faster and bears fruit more quickly. Some plant from trunks, as follows: they cut the trunks themselves into segments, put into the planting holes these segments with bark at the top, earth them over (with manure mixed in) one palm deep, and leave them. And some chop out sections from the earthward part of the trunk, with the bark, four palms long; then they put a stone in the bottom of the planting hole, and around it 3 or 4 of the sections upright, and earth them over one palm deep.

In whatever way the planting is done, the sections planted must be trimmed with a saw, and the bark must be carefully protected from tearing. The cut must be smoothed with a sharp pruning knife without harming the bark. Then we smear the lower part of the scion with mud mixed with ash.

Be careful not to plant the scion upside down; to plant upside down is to torture the plant.

Manure must be put into the planting holes.

1. Presumably not the morning setting on 7 June (1.8) but the evening setting.

12. *So that olive trees do not shed their fruit.* Demokritos.

An olive tree will not shed its fruit if you take a broad bean with a worm in it, stop the worm-hole with wax, take out a sod of earth from the roots, drop the bean in and fill in the earth.

13. *Pruning olives.* Varro.

The olive tree should be pruned after it has fruited. Do not suppose that by removing certain branches you will reduce the next harvest. You will have much more fruit from the new shoots.

14. *The olive-grape.* Africanus.

It is proper not to omit the sympathy of the olive for the vine, as described by *Florentinus* in book 11 of his *Georgics*. He says that if someone grafts an olive on to a vine it will grow olives as well as grapes, and he claims to have seen a tree of this kind in Marius Maximus's orchard.[1] He tasted the fruit and had the impression that he was tasting pressed grapes and pressed olives at the same time. Florentinus adds that plants of this kind grow in north Africa and are called *uvoliva* in their own language.[2] Props must be arranged sufficiently strong to carry the weight of the olive (if we were to graft the other way round, props would not be needed). Piercing the vine at ground level, we insert the olive scion; thus it can take up sweetness from the vine along with richness and nourishment from the soil. We will get more benefit from it afterwards, without overloading the vine, if we take cuttings from the olive and plant them out; even when they root for themselves they will preserve the mixture. The fruit is called *elaiostaphylos* 'olive-grape'.

15. *Manure suitable for olive trees.* Didymos.

All manure except human is suited to the olive tree. Manure should not be put directly to the roots, but a little further away from the trunk.

---

1. This is presumably the Marius Maximus who was consul in 223, author of a series of Imperial biographies that were among the sources of the surviving *Historia Augusta*.
2. 'Their own language' is Latin, in which *uvoliva* would mean 'grape-olive'.

Olives should be manured every two or three years: the cultivator should by all means add manure to the planting hole and mix it with the soil.

16. *Cleft-grafting olives.* Florentinus.

Some olives have thin bark, some have thick. Those with thick and moist bark should be grafted to the bark; those with thin and dry bark should be grafted to the wood. The season for this grafting is from 22nd May until the new moon of June. Grafted olives need to be watered frequently because of their dryness.

Some people graft directly on to the roots that emerge from the soil.

17. *How and when to select and harvest olives.* Paxamos.

The ideal time for making ordinary olive oil[1] is when more than half the fruit has turned black. Then the gathering must be hurried on, before the frosts come; the work will then be easier and the yield more plentiful. The fruit must be gathered in fine weather, not in rain. When wet the stems are weaker and easily bruised; therefore even after a mere shower the branches should not be disturbed or the fruit picked until the moisture has dispersed from the fruit.

If there is mud, rush mats or something else of that kind should be put down, and failing that the olives should be rinsed in warm water: this not only cleans them but increases the yield, so that even if they are not muddy it is still good to rinse them in warm water.

Wisely, some people shake the branches with their hands to dislodge the fruit, not using sticks on the tree. Otherwise the tree does not fruit so well next year. The fruit itself is damaged by violent treatment; if it falls on to stones or rough clods it picks up some quality of the soil, and makes the oil earthy. Therefore step-ladders must be used, with planks resting on them; the harvesters can stand on these and pick the fruit.

1. As opposed to unripe or green olive oil, described at 9.19.

18. *How to make oil without olives.* Damegeron.

Oil can be made from the fruit of the terebinth, ground in the mill like olives and pressed. The cake serves as food for pigs, and for burning.

Oil can also be made from sesame.

Also from walnuts: the shells must be removed before the nuts are pressed.

19. *Making unripe olive oil.* Apuleius.

As may be seen from the name, unripe olive oil is made from unripe berries.[1]

When you see them begin to turn colour, tell the children or the workers to collect them from the trees by hand, being careful not to drop any. Pick as many each day as can be worked on overnight or on the following day. After picking, spread them out on rush or cane matting so that the watery element in them can be exuded and so that they are not damaged by one another's heat. Remove any leaves or twigs: if these remain they will reduce the keeping quality of the oil. In the evening take the olives, sprinkle them with salt, put them in the mill (which must be clean) and mill them gently by hand. The olive stones must not be smashed, because the *ichor* from them will infect the oil. Turn the millstone gently and lightly so that only the flesh and skin of the olives are crushed. After milling take the crushed olives in small tubs to the press and add wickerwork mats (willow contributes significantly to the oil); then press, employing light weight and no force. The oil that flows first, after light pressure, is pleasantest and smoothest; collect it in clean vessels and keep it separate. Then press the olives remaining under the press with a little more force, and again keep [the oil] separate; it will be not quite so good as the first but better than what follows. As soon as these first two products have run off add a little salt and natron to them and stir with an olive-wood stick; then leave them alone till they have settled, and you will find the watery element, that is, the *amorge*, lying underneath and the oiliest part floating

---

1. In Latin this would have read: 'As may be seen from the name, green olive oil is made from green olives.' In other words, 'green' referred literally not to the oil but to the olives: a sensible point to make. In Greek the point is lost.

on top. This must be taken off, separating it from the *amorge*, and stored in a glass vessel. Glass is best for storing olive oil because it is cold by nature; by its nature, olive oil likes cold. If you have no glass vessels, put the oil in new earthenware vessels whose insides have been covered with gypsum or *amorge*. Store them in a north-facing, dry room. Oil likes to rest in a dry and cold place; warmth and moisture are in opposition to oil.

20. *Making aromatic oil.* Diophanes.

Take 8 pints of grape juice, or must as it is called,[1] 2 pints olive oil, and a good quantity of pounded iris bulbs, tied in a bunch, and put in a jar for 10 days. After this, strain off and use the oil. The wine will be suitable for women to drink.

21. *How to make olive oil clean.* Tarantinos.

Roast salt over a fire and, while still hot, drop into the oil.

Pine cones, burned and dropped in while still fiery hot, have the same effect; also citron root dropped in; also roasted lees of oil.

22. *Treating rancid oil.* Same author.

Boil white wax in good olive oil, and add it while still liquid.

Roast salt and add it while still very hot.

It is worth knowing that any olive oil keeps better in an underground room; also that fire or sun will clean any olive oil, or boiling water if placed in the oil in a bronze or otherwise unbreakable vessel.

Rancid olive oil is also cured by adding anise seed. If you add the anise in advance it will not go rancid.

23. *Treating bad-smelling olive oil.* Same author.

Crush green olives without the stones and put them in the jar of olive oil while the sun is hot. If you have no olives, crush fresh olive fronds and put them in them instead. Some people use both – fastening

---

1. In the text the Latin word *mustum* is added as gloss to the Greek *gleukos* 'must'.

them together in a bouquet – and add ground salt. The bouquet must be removed after three days and the oil stirred. After it has settled, transfer it to a new jar.

Other people bake old bricks and put them in while still red-hot.

Others break up dry barley loaves, wrap them in very loose linen bags, and add them. They do this two or three times, and finally add salt crystals, afterwards transferring the oil to a new jar.

Others rub melilot in oil and add it to the oil for a night and a day.

24. *Settling cloudy olive oil.* Same author.

Put the oil in a wide-mouthed vessel and place it in hot sun; roast fine salt and sprinkle it in; when it has settled, rack off the oil.

You can clean dirty oil as follows. Grind olive bark and twigs with salt, fasten it all in a bouquet and hang in the oil jar.

25. *If a mouse or other creature falls into the oil and spoils its aroma.* Demokritos.

Tie up a handful of coriander[1] and hang it in the oil. If the bad aroma persists, change the coriander.

Some people dry the coriander in the dark, pound it, and add it to the oil.

Others dry fenugreek in the sun and add it to the vessel.

It is better to burn olive wood and then douse the embers in the oil.

Other people remove the pips from raisins, pound the raisins and add them; then after 10 days remove and squeeze out the raisins, stir the oil, and rack it into another vessel.

Others grind the raisins (without removing the pips) in a mortar and add them to the oil.

26. *Imitating Spanish olive oil.* Damegeron.

Take oil that is clear of all *amorge*, and boiling fast; add to it three volumes of water, not too hot, with a little salt ground and dissolved.

---

1. The whole plant, green or dry.

Stir together until fully mixed. Leave aside for an interval, until the water, like *amorge*, settles out underneath. Then remove the oil by skimming it with the device already described, the *konche*.[1] Mix it again, with cold water, and skim it off again clear. Then, when the oil has settled, mix in the juice of ground fresh olive leaves, so that it absorbs some of their sourness and bitterness. Use after three days, or even on the same day.

Others put unripe olive oil (or oil that is otherwise of high quality) in a mortar and smear [...].[2] When wanted, they use this in place of Spanish.

27. *Imitating Istrian olive oil.* Sotion.

To unripe olive oil (or oil that is otherwise of high quality) add dried elecampane,[3] bay leaves, dried *kypeiros*,[4] all ground together into a powder and sifted through a sieve, with roasted ground salt. Mix in vigorously. Leave for three days or more, sealing on the third day. This is the so-called 'Liburnian oil': the Istrians themselves [...].

28. *Very fine conserved olives.* Florentinus.

Taking large perfect olives, picked by hand, cut them round with a sharp reed and put them in a new jar, not yet pitched, sprinkling on top a very little salt, and when it has dissolved have ready another jar, with honey if available, if not, *hepsema* and a citron leaf, and put the olives into this marinade so that it covers them. Some add fennel seed, caraway,[5] celery seed and dill[6] to this marinade, and make a quite remarkable olive conserve, which is unfamiliar to many.

1. Not described earlier.
2. Something is missing. Possibly the alternative method was to grind olive leaves with some of this good quality oil and then to flavour ordinary oil with the mixture, omitting the elaborate manoeuvres with hot oil and hot water.
3. *Innoula* (a Latin loanword, the Greek term being *helenion*): *Inula helenium* L.
4. Probably one of the *Cyperus* species; perhaps tiger-nut, *C. esculentus* L.
5. Greek *karnabadion*: *Carum carvi* L.
6. Greek *anethon*: *Anethum graveolens* L.

29. *Conserve in* oxymeli.[1] Same author.

Take long ones with their stalks, best quality of course, black and unbruised, wash in cold water and dry on wicker mats; then put them in a bowl and pour olive oil on them and sprinkle on fine salt, one *choinix* to 9 *choinikes* of olives; move them gently with the hands but do not let them bruise; then put them in a jar, pour in *oxymeli* so that it covers them, top with fennel fronds, and store.

30. *Conserve in must.* Same author.

Picking white olives they marinate them in seawater for 6 days. Then they put them in a jar and pour fresh must in, but they do not completely fill it or the must would overflow in fermenting; after fermentation they seal it. Others put in a handful of salt before the must, and then the olives, and seal when it has fermented.

31. *Conserve of olives with grape pressings.* Didymos.

Take fresh grape pressings, before they have dried out, and add to a jar alternately with olives; then seal.

32. *Bruised olives.* Same author.

Take relatively unblemished olives, before they turn in colour. Bruise them on a wooden surface and put them in hot water. Then put them in a basket, press them down, and add salt not finely ground. Next day fill a jar with them, adding a handful of salt and covering with fronds of fennel.

Others, after bruising, remove the stones, sprinkle with ground salt, cumin[2] and fronds of fennel, then add good quality must and seal.

1. A mixture of honey and vinegar (Dalby 2003 p. 180). Dioskourides, *Materia Medica* 5.14 gives a recipe: take 5 *kotylai* wine vinegar, 1 *mna* sea salt, 10 *mnai* liquid honey, 10 *kotylai* water; mix and boil until one-tenth has boiled away; cool and store.
2. Greek *kyminon*: *Cuminum cyminum L.*

33. Kolymbades. Same author.

For *kolymbades* take large olives with their stalks, when full-grown and about to turn dark, and take care they do not bruise one another by being carried in too large a jar. Wash them, a few at a time, in cold water and put them for a day in wicker baskets in the shade to dry, turning them carefully so that they dry evenly. Then put in the bottom [of a jar] a handful of crushed salt and 4 *choes* of 'second brine'[1] with 3 *kotylai* vinegar and add 20 *choinikes* of olives, and when the jar is full, agitate it. The liquid should reach the top; add fennel fronds and seal. We advise that the brine be put in first so that the olives will not be bruised as they are added.

Others, picking [olives] with their stalks, put them in a jar containing seawater and leave for 5 or 6 days, take them out, and put them in jars of brine and seal. This is all done before the winter solstice.

1. As Cornarius saw, this is the Latin *muria*, a fishy brine or stock, a lighter variant of the *garos* for which instructions are given at 20.46.

Book 10

1. *The pleasure garden.* Florentinus.

If you want a garden you must choose a suitable location. It should be among the farm buildings if there is room; if not, then close to them, not only so that those within have the pleasure of seeing the garden, but also so that the air about it, drawing on what rises from the plants, will make the property healthy. It should be entirely surrounded by a wall or other enclosure. Do not plant it at random or in a confused way, relying, so to speak, on the contrasts between the plants to lend beauty. Instead, put in each kind in its own place, so that the smaller are not overpowered or deprived of nourishment by the larger. Fill the spaces between the trees with roses, lilies, violets and crocus, plants that are the most pleasant and inviting in appearance, aroma and use – and are also useful to bees.

Plants should be taken from mature and healthy trees. Note that plants grown from seed are as a rule the worst of all. Suckers of each kind are better, and better still are grafts. Their fruit is not only finer but also more plentiful, and they are the first to begin fruiting.

2. *At what season and in which part of the month to plant trees.* Same author.

The autumn season is more suited to planting, and particularly in waterless places, because new plants are watered throughout the winter. Plant, therefore, from when the rains come, immediately after the setting of the Pleiades,[1] until the winter solstice – that is, from 7th or 11th November until 20th December.

1. Between 2nd and 11th November (1.1, 1.9, 2.14, 3.13).

All the learned writers on farming, without exception, have chosen this autumn season as the suitable time for planting (so *the Quintilii* say) but plant in spring what you did not get around to planting in autumn.

I myself, practising what experience has taught me, have gained the greatest profit from vineyards planted at this season on the Maratonymos estate and on other nearby properties of mine. I have also planted in autumn a great many autumn-fruiting shelled-fruit trees,[1] and others, and have noticed the benefit. People in our country generally, observing our success there, no longer plant exclusively in spring in accordance with the old practice but for preference in autumn, following my instruction.[2] Although the experience suffices, I think it necessary to explain the logic of my decision to plant in autumn. Take it that nature cannot do two contradictory things at the same time. While putting resources into one, it perforce disregards the other. In plant growth, for example, at certain times nature will foster the upper parts of the plant; at other times it will nourish the lower part (I mean, the roots). Now, clearly, in spring it is nourishing the upper parts of the plant, producing flowers and leaf buds; in autumn, by contrast, nature is not nourishing the upper parts – the leaves are shed – but it is nourishing the roots. Evidently we should choose for planting the season in which nature is putting resources into the roots.

All trees, just like vines, must be planted when the moon is under the earth. If a tree is planted when the moon is waxing it will grow rapidly; if when waning, it will be low-growing but stronger.

3. *Which trees are to be grown from seed, which from cuttings; which from slips, and which from branches.* Didymos.

Trees are propagated in various ways. Certain kinds are usefully grown from seed, others from quicksets (so-called suckers), others from hardwood cuttings, others again from softwood cuttings.[3] It is essential to get clear the methods for propagating each tree.

1. For definition see 10.74.
2. Similarly on vines at 5.6, again with mention of 'the Maratonymos estate'.
3. I don't know what distinction is intended between these: no difference is made between them in the following list.

From seed are grown pistachio, hazel, almond, chestnut, peach, plum, stone pine, date, cypress, bay, apple, maple, fir, Aleppo pine. These are better when transplanted. From quicksets or suckers are grown apple and similar trees such as cherry, jujube, hazel, *chamaidaphne*,[1] myrtle, medlar; quicksets or suckers are so called because they grow alongside the tree and are taken off it with a certain amount of root.[2] Quicksets and suckers must be transplanted. From slips and cuttings are grown almond, pear, mulberry,[3] citron, apple, olive, quince, black poplar, white poplar, ivy, jujube, myrtle, chestnut. These, too, are finer when transplanted. Those capable of growing from suckers and also from slips and cuttings are: fig, mulberry, citron, pomegranate, olive, sycamore fig,[4] white poplar, *kentromyrsine*,[5] quince. Those that will only grow from slips and cuttings (not from quicksets, because the roots do not send up suckers) are these: vine, willow, box, tree-medick. Those that will grow from seed and from quicksets are these: apricot, plum, almond, date, pistachio.[6]

4. *Growing dates.* Leontinos.

Dig a planting hole two cubits deep and at least equally wide. Fill it with the same earth mixed with goat manure, but leave it unfilled to a depth of half a cubit. In the middle arrange the date stone on the ground in such a way that the sharp point faces east. Earth up with soil mixed with manure and salt, and water daily until it shoots. Some transplant it, some leave it where it is.

Since it likes salty soil, it should be trenched round once a year and salt dug in. They will quickly gain size in this way.

1. Possibly *Ruscus hypoglossum* L., large butcher's broom.
2. The two words are *moscheuma* 'sucker', literally 'calf', and *paraspas* for which I use 'quickset', literally 'torn from alongside'.
3. Greek *sykaminos*: *Morus nigra* L.
4. Greek *sykomoron*: *Ficus sycomorus* L.
5. Possibly *Ruscus aculeatus* L., butcher's broom.
6. The list includes decorative shrubs and trees alongside fruit trees. It is a mess; evidently it has invited additions by successive compilers. Among evident errors is the listing of apple (*mêlea*) among plants grown from seed. I have wondered whether 'manna ash' (*melia*) is meant, but if one began to emend this chapter one would never stop.

They flourish better if watered with the lees of old wine.[1]

Stones of dates should not be planted directly in the earth but in a planter, and then transplanted.[2]

One date palm loves another date palm; loves it bitterly, in fact. To be precise, the female palm loves the male, so *Florentinus* says in his *Georgika*, and her desire is only soothed by the presence of her beloved. The tree may be observed to stoop, and to bow her head, and to fail to produce fruit. The farmer is aware of this: it is evident that she is in love, but it is not clear with which tree. He therefore touches many trees, returns to the one that is in love, and touches her with his hand. She appears to respond as if to a kiss and indicates the tree with which she is in love by nodding her spathes or, as one may say, her 'arms': she looks towards it and turns herself wholly, as if in eagerness, towards it. Satisfaction for the female is found when the farmer then touches the male and brings its 'arms' close to the female; in particular he takes the flower from the spathe of the male and places it in the 'brain' of the female. This satisfies her love, and the female tree now flourishes and bears the finest fruit.[3]

5. *How to make date palms fruit plentifully.* Demokritos.

Their fruit does well when the empty sheaths, called *helikes*, are taken [from the male] when in flower, dried and placed at the top of the [female] trunk, like wild figs in fig trees.

6. *Use of palm stems in weaving.* Didymos.

The trees grow tall and flourishing when old wine lees are filtered and poured on to the roots; adding salt also helps.[4] To produce leaf stems that are white and suitable for mats and baskets, we should take them from the leaves while they are still green and store them under cover for 4 days. Thereafter we can allow them to be moistened

---

1. Repeated at 10.6.
2. This sentence contradicts the earlier instruction and for 'stone' uses the term *ostoun*, literally 'bone', rather than *pyren*. It is presumably from a different source.
3. For earlier, less elaborate versions of this see Pliny, *Natural History* 13.34–35; Achilles Tatius, *Leucippe and Clitophon* 1.17.
4. Cf. 10.4

by nocturnal dew and dried by the daytime sun until they have turned white.

7. *When to plant citrons, their care, and how to make them produce red fruit.* Florentinus.

The citron is to be planted between autumn and the spring equinox. It likes abundant water. Alone among trees this kind is helped by the south wind; it is harmed by the north wind. When the fruits swell, most of them should be taken off and only a few left.

It should be planted against a wall to give it protection on its northern side. It is covered during winter in rush mats, or, better, gourd stems, because this species has a natural antipathy that wards off the frost; therefore burn the woodier and thicker stems of gourd and sprinkle the ash around the roots.

If before the citron fruit grows to its full size you insert it in a pottery or glass vessel, as it swells it will be moulded by the vessel, and will grow to the vessel's size, as if competing with it. The vessel should have a piercing or vent.

If bud-grafted, it must be understood, the citron bears no fruit; it should therefore be grafted on wood, like the vine.

If you want to produce black citrons, graft an apple branch on the citron tree, and vice versa: when citron is grafted on to apple, the reverse occurs.

If you cover the fruits with kneaded gypsum you will keep them sound throughout.[1]

If this tree is touched by frost, being naturally rather tender, it will burn and be killed. Some wealthy luxury-lovers plant citron trees against the wall in verandas facing south, and water them generously. In summer they leave the verandas open to the sky, allowing the plants to be warmed by the sun; when winter approaches they roof them over.

If you want to produce red citrons, graft them on mulberry, and vice versa; the citrons will be red and it will bear both kinds of fruit.

Citron is also grafted on pomegranate.

---

1. Repeated at 10.10.

8. *More on growing citrons.* Anatolios.

Some grow citrons not only from cuttings but from layers. They bend down the sprig, fix into the ground two sections of the branch, earth it over, and the new shoot grows from underground, so to speak.

Some take short slips of citron that cannot be bent to the ground and plant them upside down, thick part uppermost, thin part fixed in the ground, adding the ash from the melon-bed.[1]

9. *How to make citrons take the form of any kind of bird, or of a human face or that of any animal.* Africanus.

You can make this fruit take the shape of a human face, or that of another animal, in the following way. Form the shape, cover it with gypsum or clay and let this dry, then split it into two with some sharp implement, producing front and back moulds that will fit together. Dry them and bake them like pottery. When the fruit is half the required size, put the moulds around it and tie them together carefully so that the growth of the fruit will not force them apart; whether it is pear, apple, pomegranate or citron it will take the shape of the moulds. In short, fruits will take the shape of animals if they are inserted in moulds and allowed to grow.

10. *Keeping and storing citrons.* Sotion.

If you cover citron fruit carefully with well-kneaded gypsum you will keep them sound and intact throughout the year.

Citrons stored under barley grains do not go rotten.

11. *Planting pistachios.* Diophanes.

Take the nut unshelled – that is, with the whole shell intact – and plant it as described.

Didymos in his *Georgika* says pistachio is to be grafted on almond.

---

1. I.e. from burning off melons, watermelons and gourds at the end of the season.

12. *More on planting pistachios.*[1] Damegeron.

Pistachios are sown around 1st April, male and female plants united by nature, the male with its back to the *zephyros* because in this way they will bear fruit most plentifully. They are cleft-grafted at the same time of year, on their own kind and on terebinth; I think also on almond.

Paxamos says that a planting hole must be made in advance in well-dug land that gets plenty of sun. Vigorous new suckers must be taken from trees and bound together; they must be placed in the hole, in the second lunar month, fastened together from ground level to where they branch, and the hole must be manured, earthed up, and trenched round, with care given to watering them for 8 days, and during this same period they must remain tied together. When the trees are three years old, dig out the planting hole completely around the root, manure it, settle the tree lower than before, and earth it up, so that even when it is a large and strong tree it will not be blown over by the wind.

13. *Planting and care of peaches.*[2] Florentinus.

Peaches like wet places, or those that are regularly irrigated: this gives larger fruit.

Some take off the majority of the *persika* leaving few on the tree.

The tree grows well if we plant the stone as soon as we eat the fruit, leaving a little of the flesh around it.

It is known that peach trees age quickly; they should therefore be grafted on plum or bitter almond or sloe.[3]

Brabilos is the proper name of the tree that grows from the 'bone' of a *persikon*.

1. There is some confusion, but two practices are described. In the first section, ascribed to Damegeron, one male tree pollinates several female trees with the help of the prevailing wind. In the second section, ascribed to Paxamos, male and female trees (the sex being known because they are grown from suckers) are planted together.
2. Medieval Greek *dorakinon*: *Persica vulgaris* Mill. This chapter exemplifies changes in vocabulary: in earlier Greek *persikon* meant 'peach' and *brabilos* meant 'sloe', but these words later became obsolete and the meaning of *brabilos* was forgotten, hence the erroneous guesswork of the last sentence.
3. Greek *brabilos*: *Prunus spinosa* L.

14. *Making* persika *carry writing.* Demokritos.

We can produce a *persikon* with writing on it as follows. After eating a peach, soak the stone for two or three days. Then open it; take the kernel found inside; write whatever you wish, with a bronze stylus, shallowly on the skin; then wrap it in papyrus and sow it. Whatever you write on the kernel you will find written on the fruit.

Some also do this with the almond.

15. *Making peaches red.* Same author.

You will produce red peaches if you plant roses under the trees.

You can produce red fruit in another way. If you bury the stone of the *persikon*, dig it up after 7 days (during which time it will have opened naturally) and pour cinnabar[1] inside it, then rebury it and look after it carefully, you will get red *persika* from it.

If in the same way you choose to pour a different dye into the stone you will produce fruit of that colour.

16. *Making peaches stoneless.* Africanus.

Bore into the middle of the trunk, penetrating through the inner wood, and insert a slip of willow or dogwood[2] into it.

17. *Grafting peaches.* Didymos.

The peach is grafted on plum, on almond and on plane; from the latter red peaches are produced.

18. *The season for planting apples and their general care.* Anatolios.

Apples can be planted in two seasons, spring and autumn. In dry districts it is better to plant in autumn after the first rains. Apples like cold, moist, rich locations.

---

1. Greek *kinnabari*, a red dye for which ancient sources suggest at least three origins, two mineral, one vegetable: the latter, afterwards called 'dragon's blood', is the plant *Dracaena cinnabari* Balf.f., native to Socotra.
2. Greek *kraneia*: *Cornus mas* L.

They will not be attacked by grubs if squill is planted around them. You can treat a tree that has grubs if you pour pig manure, mixed with human urine, around the roots. The apple tree likes urine a great deal and should be watered with it frequently. Some add goat manure to the urine and pour old lees of wine on to the roots, thus producing sweeter fruit.

You can treat a sick apple tree by watering it for six days, at sunset, with donkey manure mixed with water, [continuing this treatment][1] at rather frequent intervals until it shoots.

If you want the tree to bear abundant fruit and not to shed it, cut off the wide mouth of a lead pipe and tie or fasten this around the trunk at a height of one foot. When the fruit begins to swell remove this band. Do this every year and it will flourish.

To prevent the fruit rotting on the tree and being attacked by caterpillars,[2] smear the gall of a green lizard around the trunk.

The healthiest seedling apples should be taken and planted in planting holes, leaving only the extremity showing; the roots should be smeared with ox gall before planting, because such a plant is very quickly attacked by grubs.

Troublesome grubs should be dug out with a bronze spike: remove the bark until the creature is caught, and smear the wounds with dung.

19. *How to make apples red.* Berytios.

Water the tree with urine and the fruit will turn red.

Some produce red apples as follows. They fix stakes in the ground, bend down the fruit-bearing branches (without breaking them), tie them to the stakes and fill pits or other receptacles around them with water. They claim that when at dawn the sun's rays strike the water they release warm vapour and also are reflected on to the fruit, producing a good red colour.

---

1. This has to be understood, unless something more is missing; otherwise 'for six days at sunset' and 'at rather frequent intervals until it shoots' are contradictory.
2. Greek *kampe*. The instruction can be compared with another at 10.23, probably intended against pear midge. I don't know what apple pests would be dissuaded by this method, except perhaps ants and aphids, but these cannot be called *kampai*.

Some grow roses under the trees and in this way produce red fruit.

20. *Grafting apples.* Diophanes.

The apple is grafted on any wild pear, and on quince; the finest apples grow on quince stock, the kind the Athenians call *melimela*. Apples can also be grafted on plane; this produces red apples.

Didymos in his *Georgika* says that apples are suitably grafted on plum,[1] and that apple grafted on citron bears fruit almost all through the year.

21. *Keeping apples.* Apuleius.

Apples, if harvested at their peak, keep a very long time, but they must be picked by hand to avoid bruising. Each singly must be wrapped in seaweed, in algae that is, so as to be completely covered, and put into unfired earthenware pots, with seaweed between the apples so that they do not touch one another, and the pots sealed. These must be stored in a cool loft well away from smoke and bad smells. If seaweed is not available each apple can be put in a separate small unfired earthenware pot, sealed and stored. Some cover each apple in potter's clay, dry it, and store.

Apples are kept sound if walnut leaves are spread under them: this contributes a great deal to their colour and their flavour. You will do better if you wrap each apple separately in walnut leaves and store it.

You will keep apples if you put them inside waxed pots, seal these carefully, and store them.

Apples keep without rotting if stored in barley.

You will also keep apples as follows. Take an unpitched earthenware vessel, pierced at the bottom, fill it with clean, freshly hand-picked apples, stop it well with *myakanthe*[2] or the like, hang it in any kind of tree, leave all winter, and the fruit will remain just as when it was put away: I found this by experience.

1. The same information is ascribed to Diophanes at 10.73.
2. Possibly butcher's broom, *Ruscus aculeatus* L.

Apples are also kept as follows. Wrap up each apple in dried fig leaves, then cover them in white potter's clay, dry in the sun and store; they will remain as when put away.

Apples keep if put into grape must – protected by the lees – and they also protect the wine and make it more aromatic, to everyone's surprise. If put into a new jar, and the jar placed in a wine-vat so that it floats, and the vat sealed, they will stay fresh and the wine will be aromatic.

Also they are put into chests with clean hanks of wool and kept in that way.[1]

Winter apples are best kept in seed, as are grapes (as we have already explained).[2]

Smear the apple tops with the bile of green lizards and they will not rot.

22. *The planting of pears, their care, and how to prevent grittiness in the fruit.* The Quintilii.

Remove everything stony from the holes before planting; add sieved earth to the planting hole, and water. If the tree is already planted, uncover the roots deeply, remove everything stony, sieve the soil you have removed, replace it adding manure; then, after earthing up, give some water.

Pears as a group like cold and damp places.

They are grown not only from seedlings but also from cuttings; if you are going to plant out seedlings they should be three years old, never less than two. Some take the best suckers from the base of the trunk and plant them just like olive suckers. Some choose the finest, most vigorous shoots from higher on the tree, and plant those with success.

---

1. Some manuscripts repeat this and the previous section at 10.28 below as means of keeping quinces.
2. There are similar ideas at 4.15, but nothing identical. 'Seed' probably means cereal seed, as occasionally elsewhere in Byzantine texts; if the instruction is translated from Latin, it may mean emmer seed in particular, as Latin *semen* sometimes does.

23. *More on growing pears.* Diophanes.

Pears as a group like cool, damp, lush country; but there are many kinds, and they demand various methods of planting. The large kinds, both long and round-fruited, that ripen their fruit on the tree, need planting early. The rest should be planted between midwinter and the middle of spring.

They are planted on ground that is well-aired and inclined to east or north. They are set from seedlings as well as cuttings; the seedlings must be at least two years old [when planted out]. Plant them out in earth mixed with dung. More successful, however, are those who graft rather than grow from seed. They get seedling wild pears or other suitable stocks from healthy terrain, plant as above, and then, when the plants have taken, graft or rind-graft on to them whatever kind of pear they choose.

If you want to make the pear sweet, and make it crop more heavily, split the trunk at ground level, drive in a peg of oak or Valonia oak, and earth it up. At blossom time you can cure it if unhealthy by pouring lees of old wine on the roots, and watering for 15 days, then earthing them up. By pouring on wine lees you will make the fruit sweeter even if the tree is not unhealthy.

The fruit will not be attacked by grubs[1] if the roots at planting are smeared with ox gall.

24. *Cleft-grafting pears.* Tarantinos.

Pear is cleft-grafted on pomegranate, and on quince, and on almond, and on terebinth, and on mulberry. If grafted on mulberry it produces red pears.

25. *Keeping pears.* Demokritos.

Tip the stalks of the pears with pitch and hang them up.

Others put the pears in a new earthenware vessel, pour in grape syrup or must or wine to fill the vessel, and store.

Others have buried them in sawdust and kept them in that way.

Some put them up in dried walnut leaves.

1. Perhaps pear midge, *Contarinia pyrivora* (Riley, 1886).

Others put them in a new earthenware vessel containing a little salt: they pour in grape syrup or must or wine, add the pears, seal the vessel and store it.

Some put them up in grape pips from [the making of] sweet wine, separating each from the next.

26. *Growing quinces.* Didymos.

Quinces are planted at the same season and in the same way already described for cherries.

27. *Making quinces take a particular shape.* Demokritos.

Quinces will take the shape of living things if you allow them to grow into moulds.[1]

28. *Keeping quinces.* Same author.

Quinces keep if put into grape must – protected by the lees – and they also protect the wine and make it more aromatic, to everyone's surprise. If put into a new jar, and the jar placed in a wine-vat so that it floats, and the vat sealed, they will stay fresh and the wine will be aromatic.

Also they are put into chests with clean hanks of wool.[2]

Quinces are also kept for a very long time if buried in sawdust, because they are dried by the sawdust and so preserved.

They are also put stored in chaff and kept in good condition.

They should not be kept in the same room where other fruits are stored: their sourness and odour infects the stored fruit, especially grapes.

Some wrap up the quinces in leaves, cover them carefully in clay mixed with hair, or potter's earth, dry in the sun, and store. When needed, they chip off the clay and find the quinces in the same condition in which they were stored. The same should be done with apples; the previous instructions for quinces can also be followed for apples.

Quinces are also kept in barley; also in grape must.

1. A fuller explanation is given at 10.9, on citrons.
2. Compare 10.21 on apples.

29. *Planting, treatment, and general care of pomegranates*. Florentinus.

The pomegranate likes warm air and is planted in dry ground. Where you plant them you should plant squill along with them.

[Fruits] will stay fresh on the tree till spring if when they have ripened you twist their stems, that is, turn them once or twice, and put dry gourds or turnips around each, so that they will not get wet or be eaten by birds.

You will cure sick trees by covering the trunk, at root level, with seaweed thrown up on the shore, and watering assiduously.

Diophanes in his *Georgika* says that pomegranates grow red if the roots of the trees are watered with bathing lye.[1]

Demokritos says that pomegranate and myrtle like one another and do well if planted side by side; their roots tend to intertwine even if they are not particularly close together.

30. *So that pomegranates will not split*. Africanus.

Before planting, put pebbles into the planting hole.[2] If dealing with trees that are already planted, plant squill bulbs around them; through antipathy these will not allow the pomegranates to split.

Likewise if you plant them upside down, [their fruits] will not split.

31. *Growing seedless pomegranates*. Same author.

If you take out, as with grape vines, a large part of the inner wood, and heap earth against the split trunk, and after an interval cut off the tree's strong new shoots, it will produce seedless fruit.[3]

---

1. Repeated at 10.33.
2. 'Three pebbles' according to Columella, *On Trees* 23.2.
3. Needham cites Seneca, *Letters to Lucilius* 85.5: 'The wise man is called imperturbable in the same way that some pomegranates are called seedless: not that there is no hardness of seed in them, just that there is less.'

32. *Pomegranate fronds ward off vermin.* Same author.

Pomegranate fronds are said to keep vermin away; this is why they are chosen as mats for picnics,[1] for safety's sake.

33. *Making pomegrates redder.* Didymos.

If you want to produce a red pomegranate, irrigate the tree with water mixed with lye from bathing.[2]

34. *How to make a sour pomegranate sweet.* Paxamos.

Dig around the roots of the tree, smear them with pigs' manure, earth up, and sprinkle with human urine. You will find more about this in my other *Georgika*, book three, chapter 27.

35. *Making pomegranates bear plentiful fruit.* Demokritos.

Grind purslane and spurge together finely and smear around the base of the trunk.

36. *How to tell, after picking a pomegranate, how many segments it contains.* Africanus.

Open one of the fruits and count the segments in it. Be sure that each fruit will contain the same number. Whether they are small or large, this does not correspond to a larger or smaller number of segments but to whether they are individually larger or smaller.

37. *Grafting pomegranates.* Florentinus.

The pomegranate is grafted differently from other trees. They choose a stem that is easily bent, so that it will touch the ground, graft on to this as with other trees, and secure the graft with ties. Then they bend the stem to the ground, so as to bury not the grafted part, but the part below the join, and fix it there firmly so that it will stay in the ground until the graft takes. It is necessary to understand that with

---

1. Greek *stibades*, matting or bedding, typically arranged in a semicircle, for outdoor dining.
2. Repeated from 10.29.

other trees we take scions before they bud, but with pomegranates after they bud.

As was said above, pomegranate especially likes myrtle. *Didymos* mentions this in *Georgika* and adds, of course, that if pomegranate is grafted on myrtle, or myrtle on pomegranate, they will bear much larger fruit.

Pomegranate is suitably grafted on myrtle and on willow.

Citron is grafted on pomegranate, so *Didymos* says in *Georgika*.

38. *Keeping and storing pomegranates.* Berytios.

Pomegranates that you are to keep for winter must be carried gently and not bruised, because this lays them open to rotting. Choosing undamaged fruits, dip the cut stalks in boiled pitch and hang them up.

Others dip the pomegranates, then let them cool and hang them.

A wine is made from pomegranates. It is very good to drink.

Others wrap each fruit in dry brush and rushes, carefully cover them completely in gypsum, so that if they swell they will not split the covering, and leave them on the tree. This can also be done with apples.

Others put them in oak sawdust, pouring on vinegar.

Some heat up seawater, or boil brine, dip the pomegranates in this, then cool them in the sun and hang them. When about to use them they steep them in water for 2 days.

Some, [intending] that the pomegranates stay on the tree for a while, put each fruit into earthenware newly made, close it and secure it so that they do not knock against the stem or each other; they get sound fruit that lasts a long time.

Pomegranates keep for a long time if they are dipped in clean hot water and immediately taken out.

Pomegranates should be stored in dry sand or in a heap of grain, in the dark, until they shrivel.

39. *Growing plums.* Pamphilos.

Plums like dry soil. They grow like sloes. They are cleft-grafted, at the same season and on the same days as sloes, on their own kind and on apple.

40. *Keeping plums.* Same author.

They are put into vessels; some pour new wine[1] on to them, others sweet wine, fill them up, close them, and leave them.

41. *Planting cherries.* Florentinus.

Cherries are grown and cleft-grafted in the same way as apples and pears. This tree likes cold and moist locations. It responds well to grafting; the cherry tree does not give fine or sweet fruit unless grafted.

If you graft black grape on to cherry, it will produce grapes in spring.

42. *Keeping cherries.* Florentinus.

If cherries are taken from the tree before sunrise and put in a container in the bottom of which savory[2] has been placed, then the cherries, then more savory, and then sweet honey vinegar is added, they will keep.

They also keep on rush.[3]

43. *Growing jujubes.*[4] Vindanionius.

The jujube is also grown from cuttings taken from the centre of the tree, so *Didymos* says in *Georgika*.

44. *Keeping jujubes.* Same author.

Jujubes keep when stored in honey vinegar, with rush leaves placed below and above them.

45. *The season for planting figs and their care.* Didymos.

Figs are planted at two seasons of the year, spring and autumn. Of all trees fig does best when planted in spring, because it is a tender

1. Meaning 'must'.
2. Greek *thrymbe* (and later *thymbra*): *Satureja hortensis* L.
3. Does this mean on rush mats? Or stored between layers of rush leaves, as with jujubes at 10.44?
4. Greek *zizyphon*: *Zizyphus jujuba* Mill.

plant, quickly damaged by ice and wind and therefore best planted in spring after the frosts.

I have been very successful after planting figs during July, transplanting them and irrigating them. I have had big, fruit-bearing trees and have succeeded from repeated experiments after planting not only in spring but in July.

Figs should be planted in rather warm locations and in fatty soil, not irrigated. Excessive water injures the natural health of figs and makes them rot easily.

There is another way to grow them. If one soaks figs, rubs them on to a rope, puts this in the ground and waters it, many plants will grow. These must be transplanted.

If you plant seedling figs, they must be placed inside a squill bulb.

Some soak the seedling in brine before planting it. It is better, whether planting a seedling or a cutting, to plunge it in ox dung.

Others throw in quicklime after planting. It does the plant no harm.

It is necessary to understand that fig trees fruit more heavily as they age.

Some put ash to the roots, others put red ochre.

If you don't want the fig tree to grow high, plant the layer upside down.

Fig trees also grow very well from seed.[1]

46. *To ensure when planting figs that they will be free of maggots.* Same author.

Figs will not develop maggots if you insert the about-to-be-planted cutting in a squill bulb. You will clear existing maggots if you sprinkle caustic soda on the roots and on cavities in the trunk.

---

1. Greek *kenchramis* 'fig seed', a classical word that was forgotten by the time of the *Geoponika*. The compiler may not have realized that this section merely repeats what is said earlier in the chapter.

47. *Producing figs with writing.* Demokritos.

Write whatever you choose on the eye of the fig tree when it is about to come into leaf, and it will produce figs with the writing on them.

48. *To ensure that a fig tree does not shed its fruit.* Same author.

The fig will not shed its fruit if you take mulberries and smear the base of the trunk with them.

It also will not shed its fruit if you cover the roots with salt and seaweed, or if you smear the trunk with red ochre at full moon.

Or hang wild fig fruits around it. For this reason some graft a branch [of wild fig] on to each tree, so that they will not have to take trouble over this each year.

The fig keeps its fruit if around the Pleiades[1] you trench around the tree and pour into the crown *amorge* mixed half-and-half with water.

49. *To tame a wild fig.* Africanus.

You will tame a wild fig if you cut off the branches, soak in wine mixed with oil, and irrigate for seven days.[2]

50. *Scab on fig trees.* Leontinos.

You will cure a scabby fig-tree if you plant a squill bulb beside the roots, or if you mix red earth with water and smear it around the trunk.

51. *To produce laxative figs; to produce early figs.* *From* Demokritos.

When you plant the fig tree, put to the extremities of the roots pounded black hellebore and spurge, and you will have figs that are laxative.

---

1. Presumably the dawn setting of the Pleiades, between 2nd and 11th November (1.1, 1.9, 2.14, 3.13).
2. The text is too brief to be clear. Needham takes it that you soak the cut branches in wine mixed with oil and then irrigate the tree with this; Owen takes it that you soak the branchless stump in wine mixed with oil and then water it for seven days. Perhaps, after all, it does not matter.

Figs ripen earlier than normal if you add a mixture of pigeon dung, pepper and olive oil.[1]

Florentinus says in *Georgika* that figs will come early and will be theriac if the fruit is anointed with the theriac medicine.

If you want to eat figs before the season, mix pigeon dung and pepper with olive oil and smear it on the early fruit.

52. *Cleft-grafting fig trees.* Leontinos.

Fig is cleft-grafted on mulberry and on plane.

The fig tree is grafted not only in spring, like other trees, but also through the summer until the winter solstice, so *Florentinus* says.

53. *To produce figs that are white on one side and black or red on the other.* Africanus.

Take different cuttings [i.e. of differently coloured figs], and initially tie together shoots of the same age; put them in a planting hole, manure and water them. When they bud, tie them together again at each eye so that they will become a single trunk; after two years, if you wish, plant them on, and you will have two-coloured figs.

Some do this more effectively as follows. They tie together two seedlings from different figs, plant them in a pot, and then plant them on.

54. *How dried figs, called* ischades, *are kept without going mouldy.* Paxamos

Dried figs can be kept without going mouldy if you drop three dried figs into raw pitch; put one at the bottom of the jar, fill it half way with dried figs, then put in the second pitched fig, then fill it full, with the third pitched fig on the top.

They keep well for a very long time if you put them in a basket and hang them in a clay oven after the bread has been taken out, then put them in a new jar unpitched.

---

1. The prescription is repeated below: there the mixture is to be smeared on to the early fruits, *olynthoi* (which often fail to ripen).

[Drying figs.]

Figs must be picked with the pedicle by which they are attached to the tree, sprinkled with brine boiled with olive oil, and put out in the sun; then packed in a jar, sealed with mud.

Give them one night's dew, then place them in the jar.

55. *On* olynthoi *or unripe figs.* Africanus.

The early figs will not drop if you grind a *choinix* of salt, pour it around the root, and heap soil over it.

56. *How figs can be kept as fresh as if still on the tree.* Same author.

Figs cannot remain on the tree after ripening, like other fruit; they fall of their own accord if not picked. However, it is possible to keep them fresh, as if still on the tree, by the following method. When you are about to close the wine vats, take a new earthenware pot or other vessel, but not round: it must have a square bottom. Pick some figs, slightly underripe, with the pedicles or navels, that is, the stem by which they are attached to the tree. Put them gently in the pot, not touching one another. Close it carefully and put it in the wine vat so that it floats. Then cover the vat. The figs will keep in the condition in which you stored them, as long as the wine does not turn to vinegar.

Figs can also be kept fresh as follows. From the sides of young gourds take away sections of rind; dig out chambers, as it were, and place one fig in each; cover them with the removed rind; hang them in a dark place, protecting them against fire and smoke. The figs must be picked with their pedicles, as before; they last longer when undamaged.

Some place figs in honey in such a way that they are not touched by one another or by the vessel, then close and store the vessel.

Others carefully place a cup made of glass or some other transparent material upside down over the fruit, seal it all round with wax so as to leave no vent; it will keep unspoiled.

57. *When to plant* Thasia;[1] *their care and grafting.*
Florentinus.

It is better to plant almonds in autumn, until the winter solstice. Planting them in spring is not easy because this species buds very early.

Almonds like relatively warm locations; hence they appear particularly suited to islands.

The almond should also be cleft-grafted in autumn because it shows so early in spring. Those who graft almonds must take scions from the middle of the tree, not from the top.[2]

Almonds are also grown from seed, from self-sown seedlings and from quicksets or suckers. Some have taken the most flourishing new branch from the top of the tree, planted it, and succeeded very well. When we are to plant almonds from seed, we must take fresh seeds and initially steep them in dung mixed with water. Some steep the seeds in hydromel for one night beforehand. The seed when planted must be placed upright, the mousetail towards the ground, the woody and bare end upwards.

Some say the tree grows better if a ferule[3] has been previously placed in the planting hole.

58. *When to harvest almonds.* Same author.

When the rind is ready to split, gather them, shell them and wash them in brine, which both whitens them and makes them sound. Dry them in the sun and store them.

If they are stored in chaff they are easier to shell.

59. *Making bitter almonds sweet.* Africanus.

You will make sweet what was previously bitter if you hollow out the trunk in a square shape to a height of one palm and take the sap each year until it becomes sweet.

---

1. *Thasion*, as the following text proves, is a rare alternative name for the sweet almond (cf. Diphilos of Siphnos quoted at *Epitome of Athenaios* 54b), typical produce of the Greek island of Thasos. The term is also used at 10.76.
2. Similarly at 10.62, where the instruction is attributed to Paxamos.
3. Greek *narthex*: *Ferula communis* L., giant fennel.

Some use a better method: they dig around the tree, put pigs' dung to it, add urine, then heap up with earth and irrigate each year until it becomes sweet. If they are cut out [as in the previous method], every tree drops its fruit.

You will make a previously harsh and bitter almond tender and sweet if you remove the soil around the crown as far as the topmost roots and irrigate it frequently with hot water during the period before it blossoms.[1]

60. *Producing almonds with writing.* Demokritos.

Break open the almond neatly, keeping the kernel undamaged. Open it, write whatever you wish on the kernel, fasten it together with papyrus; plant it, plastering it round with mud and pigs' dung, and cover it with soil.

61. *Making a barren almond tree bear fruit.* Same author.

You will make a barren tree produce fruit if you lay bare the roots in winter. If it still produces leaves but no fruit, bore into the part of the trunk that is nearest the ground, knock a peg of oily torchwood into the hole, pour on human urine, and heap up the earth against it.

62. *Cleft-grafting almonds.* Paxamos.

Almonds are cleft-grafted at the end of autumn, using new branches not growing from the top of the crown but emerging half way up.[2]

63. *When to plant chestnuts.* Damegeron.

The sweet chestnut, called *Dios balanos* by some, likes sandy soil and cold locations.

It is grown from cloning and from seed, but the cloning methods are less risky, and will produce fruit after two years. It is planted from the equinox onwards, not only from *skytala* and new branches, but

---

1. Compare Theophrastos, *History of Plants* 2.7.7.
2. Similarly in the third section of 10.57.

also from suckers that have roots, like the olive.[1] It is sown not like the almond and walnut, but with the mousetail upwards.

64. *When to plant walnuts; their care.* Same author.

Walnuts are planted at the same season as almonds. They are grown from seed, quicksets and suckers. They like locations that are dry and rather cold than warm.

If you intend to grow walnut from seed you will do better to steep the seed for five days in a vessel containing fresh child's urine and then sow it.

Walnuts will be fine-fleshed and digestible – and you will achieve this with almonds too – if you frequently pour ash around the crown and the roots.

The walnut grows more quickly when frequently planted on, and especially if one drives a copper nail or peg into the tree deep enough to reach the heartwood.

If one drills through the heartwood with an auger, making a hole right through the tree, and then drives an elm-wood peg of suitable diameter all the way through, the harsh and masculine qualities [of the fruit] will be turned to digestibility.

The walnut tree will not shed its fruit if you apply around it mullein root[2] and discarded grape pips.

65. *Cleft-grafting walnuts.* Same author.

Some authors on farming say that the walnut cannot be grafted on a different kind, and that similarly other resinous trees will not take a scion of another kind and cannot be grafted on another. This is not true, as experience has often shown. Thus I have often cleft-grafted and crown-grafted pistachio on to *terminthos*, which local people call terebinth, a particularly resinous kind, and had large trees from it – so it can be said that apart from its own kind terebinth definitely accepts pistachio – and I have often successfully cleft-grafted and crown-grafted walnut. It may not take easily, but one should not give up after the first unsuccessful attempt.

1. For the terminology used here compare 9.11 on olives.
2. Greek *phlomos*: *Verbascum* spp., e.g. *Verbascum nigrum* L. Repeated at 10.87.

Some cleft-graft the walnut as follows. When a seedling has reached its second and third year, they take off the plant, cleft-graft on the root as one does on wood, and grow on.

Others choose, a year in advance, a new branch of walnut as a scion, and twist and bend it. This injury will give the scion rather generous heartwood; it will more easily withstand the knife and will take when grafted.

66. *To make trees bear walnuts without rinds.* Africanus.

You will produce naked walnuts, without rinds, if you remove the shell of a walnut while keeping the kernel undamaged, wrap the kernel in wool or in fresh grape or plane leaves (so that although naked it will not be eaten by ants) and sow it.

Florentinus says the same happens with almonds and with other *akrodrya* that have an outer rind if they are sown by this method.

67. *To dry up a walnut or any other tree.* Demokritos.

Before eating, chew some uncooked lentils, the seeds that is; after chewing, when you have [the pulp] in your mouth, bite on any branch of a walnut tree that is in blossom; it will dry up.

Or drive a red-hot nail into the root of any tree.

Or drill into it with an auger and insert a peg of tamarisk wood.

Or dig around it and throw on the roots dittany,[1] or broad beans, or a menstrual towel.

68. *The Pontic nut or hazelnut.* Didymos.

The hazel, too, is put in at the same season as the almond and walnut. It likes clayey and well-watered places.

There is a round and a more oval kind. The round kind, if put in at the same time as the oval, shoots more quickly.

69. *On mulberries and how to make them white.* Berytios.

White poplar on which mulberry is cleft-grafted or bud-grafted will produce white mulberries.

1. Greek *diktamnon*: *Origanum dictamnus* L.

Mulberries in a glass jar keep longest.[1]

It is planted at two periods, in autumn and in spring, and mostly from new branches, like figs. It grows best if the ground around it is frequently hoed, not at great depth, but as far as the upper roots.

Mulberries can be grown from seed if one firstly breaks up the fruit, then picks out the seeds, sows them and waters them; but it does better from a layer or a slip. It is cleft-grafted on chestnut and Valonia oak.[2]

70. *On keeping and storing mulberries.*
Same author.

Mulberries last longest when carefully placed in a glass vessel which is then filled up with the juice of the same fruit and covered.[3]

71. *Planting medlars.* Didymos.

The medlar is planted, in the same way as the quince, from 23rd March.

72. *Planting cornels.* Anatolios.

Cornels are planted like olives, but in rainy places, between 24th December and 29th January.

73. *Explanations of the names of fruits and nuts.*
Demokritos.

The authors of the farming books, being highly educated, did not use our everyday names of fruits. They use terms like 'royal nut', or again 'Pontic nut', or maybe 'Zeus's acorn'. I think we need to explain what is a royal nut, what is a Pontic nut, and likewise with the other terms that they used. Royal nut is what we call simply *karyon* 'walnut'. 'Pontic nut' is our *leptokaryon* 'hazelnut'. 'Zeus's acorn' is *kastanon* 'chestnut'. 'Cuckoo-apple' is what we call *damaskenon* 'plum'. The

1. Repeated with more detail at 10.70.
2. Greek *phegos*: *Quercus macrolepis* Kotschy.
3. Expanded from 10.69.

'Armenian apple' is the *berikokkon* 'apricot'. The *terminthos* is what we call *terebinthos* 'terebinth'.[1]

74. *The difference between* opora *and* akrodrya. Same author.

Opora is the name for whatever fruit has green[2] flesh, such as peaches, apples, pears, plums and all that have no woody exterior. *Akrodrya* is the name for whatever has an external rind, such as pomegranates, pistachios, chestnuts, and all that have a woody exterior.

75. *When and how to graft trees.* Florentinus.

There are three methods of grafting, one specifically called cleft-grafting, another crown-grafting, and a third bud-grafting.[3] Thick-barked and sappy trees, whose bark takes up much moisture from the ground, such as the fig, chestnut and olive, are suitably grafted into the bark. Before grafting it is necessary to prepare a small wedge from hard wood, which must be inserted a little way between the bark and the wood so that the bark remains unbroken (it is essential to ensure this); then gently remove the wedge and immediately insert the scion. This method is called crown-grafting. Thin-barked and dry trees, those whose moisture is not in the bark but in the heartwood, such as citron and vine and the like, are grafted by splitting across the wood and inserting the scion. This method is called cleft-grafting. In both the above methods the scion must be cut precisely so that neither the scion nor the stock exudes moisture. Scions should be cut with sharp knives from the northerly side of

1. Even if by 'Demokritos' we understand not the early philosopher but the Hellenistic author whose works went under this name, the attribution is false. The terms *berikokkon* and *damaskenon* were not used in Greek before Roman times. This text was written later than, or from a standpoint different from, the reference to the names of terebinth at 10.65.
2. Greek *chloodes*, green more in freshness than in colour.
3. Translation is made no easier by the fact that there are two terms for crown-grafting, *enthematismos* and *emphyllismos*; to keep them distinct I have translated the former 'rind-grafting'. Thus there are four terms in all. What is worse, three of them are sometimes used for 'grafting' in general (for example, in this first sentence 'grafting' and 'cleft-grafting' both render *enkentrismos*).

healthy, full-grown, heavily fruiting trees; they should be tender, smooth, with frequent eyes, with two or three top buds but a single stem at the base; they should be as thick as the little finger, and of the previous year, because scions of the same year are ready to grow but bear no fruit. Scions should be pared with a sharp knife at the base on one side, like a writing-reed, while taking care not to split the heartwood. The pared scion should be of the same size as the split and opening into which it is to be set: on the scion the paring should be two fingers long, and on the stock the split should be two fingers deep. After grafting nothing must be removed from the scion: it must be left as it is. The area of the graft should be plastered with clayey mud: red earth is ineffective because it burns out the stock.

Grafting is advantageous to the extent that even when a tree is grafted on its own kind it will be better nourished and finer.

Scions must be taken when the moon is waning, ten or more days before grafting, and put away in a vessel that is securely covered to exclude the air. The scions when taken must still be 'lowing'; when grafting takes place the stock must be eager to grow, which is why scions must be taken ten or more days in advance.

Here is the reason why scions must not be grafted as soon as they are taken.[1] If the scion is inserted in the stock while still living and swollen, it unavoidably withers a little before they can unite. The result is that a gap develops between the scion and the stock; air gets into the intervening space and prevents the union from taking place. But if the scions are put away in some vessel for several days before grafting, the effect now occurs in the vessel and no longer takes place after grafting; no gap develops in the join, air does not get in, and they quickly unite.

Scions should be grafted when the south wind is blowing, not the north wind. And, of course, rain is conducive to cleft-grafting but unhelpful to crown-grafting.

---

1. This is the second of two reasons; they are based on different principles. The previous paragraph shows how the lunar calendar dictates times for cutting scions and grafting them (while implying an analogy with the mating of cattle). The present paragraph gives a physiological reason why there must be an interval between cutting and grafting.

One needs to know that cleft-grafting works between the autumn equinox and the winter solstice, and [again] after *zephyros* blows (that is, after 7th February) until the summer solstice. But some say the best time for cleft-grafting is immediately after the rising of Sirius[1] and again in summer after the burning of Sirius.[2]

If being stored for an interval, scions should be placed in a vessel and stuck into mud. The vessel should be sealed carefully so that the air does not reach its contents.

76. *Crown-grafting and cleft-grafting; what stocks will take what slips in crown and cleft-grafting.* Diophanes.

Fig is rind-grafted on mulberry and plane. Mulberry is rind-grafted on chestnut, Valonia oak, apple, terebinth, wild pears, elm, white poplar (which produces white fruit). Pears are rind-grafted on pomegranates, quinces, mulberries, almond and terebinth. If you rind-graft pears on mulberry you will have red pears. Apples are cleft-grafted on all kinds of wild pear; also on quinces, and this produces the finest apples, called *melimela* at Athens; also on plum (and plum on apple); also on plane, which produces red apples. Walnut is cleft-grafted on arbutus alone. Pomegranates are rind-grafted on willow. Bay is cleft-grafted on manna ash. Peach[3] is grafted on plum and on almond. Plums are cleft-grafted on all kinds of wild pear, on quinces and on apples. Chestnut is cleft-grafted on walnut, oak, and Valonia oak. Cherry is cleft-grafted on terebinth and peach,[4] and peach on cherry. Quinces are cleft-grafted on pyracantha. Myrtle is rind-grafted on willow. Apricot[5] is grafted on plum and on almond.

The citron, with its thin bark, does not take grafts easily. It is cleft-grafted on itself, and on apples. I have often done this, but, after sprouting, it has withered and died. I believe, if it took, it would

---

1. Presumably not the morning rising in late July (1.8, 1.9, 2.15) but the evening rising of Sirius.
2. After the forty days beginning 19th, 20th or 24th July (1.8, 1.9, 2.15).
3. *Dorakinon*, not a word that Diophanes would have known.
4. *Persikon*, the older name for peach.
5. Here *berikokkon*, not a word that Diophanes would have known.

produce the fruits called *kitromela*.[1] If you can rind-graft citron on mulberry you will get red citrons.[2] Quince and wild fig will take any tree that you want to cleft-graft or rind-graft on them.

Citron is cleft-grafted successfully on pomegranate, as *Didymos* says in his *Georgika*.

Florentinus in his *Georgika* says that vine cleft-grafts well on cherry, and will bear grapes in spring.

Olive cleft-grafted on grape bears the 'olive-grape'.[3]

Aromatic pears are successfully grafted on apples, as I have learned by experiment.

77. *When and how to bud-graft.* Didymos.

Bud-grafting is suitably carried out before the summer solstice. I have performed bud-grafting around the spring equinox on fine days, when the trees are beginning to bud, and succeeded very well.

The tree on which you are to graft must be cleared of growth, that is, suckers and leafage, leaving only the better and more tender new branches. Then, taking from a tree that fruits well a perfect shoot of this year's growth, an eye from it, carefully cut out, is grafted on to the stock of the other. The bark alone must be neatly stripped away; the woody part must be kept undamaged and untouched. This is quite essential. It is good when the eye of the graft falls exactly on the eye of the stock – when placed there it unites completely – but it is possible to place the graft not in place of an eye but on any other smooth part of the stock. The barks of the two trees must be of the same thickness. When union has taken place cut off immediately what is above the graft so that the nourishment goes not to this but to the grafted bud. When the grafts have developed three leaves the ties should be removed.

Often instead of removing the eye from the bud of this year's growth I have grafted the bud itself, leaving the eye untouched in the bud, stripping away the bark from the section behind the eye and cutting away a certain part of the wood as in a writing-reed, and

1. Perhaps lemons.
2. Cf. 10.7.
3. Described fully at 9.14.

so grafting the eye with the remaining part of the wood; I have got better trees from this type of crown-grafting.

Even the less promising of grafts will bear double the quantity of fruit.[1]

78. *When to prune trees.* Leontinos.

Fruit trees and bushes, and also nut trees, should be pruned immediately after the fruit has been gathered. Everything unhealthy and superfluous should be removed, using very sharp pruning knives.

New trees should be left with no more than a single [main shoot].

Suckers should be removed from trunks. Trees should grow smooth and straight, with, at the top, three or four undamaged new shoots well separated from one another. Thus the plant is shaped while it is still young and tender.

79. *Star-struck trees.* Demokritos.

Star-struck trees will revive if watered with myrrh.

80. *To keep birds off a tree.* Same author.

Rub your pruning-knife with garlic, or hang garlic in the tree.

81. *Care of young trees.* Varro.

Young trees planted in the autumn should be left undisturbed until spring. When spring sets in they should be hoed four times with forks. Begin to hoe those planted in the spring when you are sure they have taken; the same for those that are transplanted. In the first year they should be watered in the summer and unwanted growth removed, not with an iron blade but by hand, if they are rather luxuriant and if it will come away easily. If not, it is better to leave them than to use iron on young plants: the touch of iron numbs them. It is necessary to fix stakes to support them. Young fruit trees should be manured in January, but not directly on the roots, because it overheats them.

---

1. Unusual use of *aristera*. Owen understands it in the opposite sense.

82. *To make all trees fruit more heavily.* Africanus.

Rub purslane and spurge, mixed and well pounded together, around the trunk.

All trees will produce more plentiful fruit if you smear their roots with pigeon dung.

83. *To make a barren tree produce fruit.* Zoroaster.

You must roll up your sleeves, tighten your belt, take your axe or hatchet, and approach the tree in anger with the intention of cutting it down. Someone must then approach you and plead with you not to chop it down, promising that it will produce a crop. You must appear to be persuaded and spare the tree. It will fruit well from then onwards.

Also broad bean shucks scattered around the base of the trunk cause a tree to fruit.[1]

84. *Treatment of trees, curing every malady.* Paxamos.

For each tree a special and distinct treatment is appropriate; however, I will not pass over the treatment that is given to trees in general. I will set it out plainly. If you want all trees to remain healthy and flourishing, dig around the roots and water them and the base of the trunk with human or animal urine; if the rains have failed, irrigate with water too.

It has the same result if you mix *amorge* with water half and half, and pour that around each tree.[2]

Some, when planting, smear the roots with bull's bile; plants thus treated remain healthy.

Some smear the trunks of new plants with the juice of the weed called *polypremnos*,[3] and thus keep them healthy and get the greatest quantity of fruit from them.

In general, as *Didymos* says in his *Georgika*, every tree is helped if broad bean shucks, or those of other pulses, or cereal husks, are put dry [to the roots].[4]

1. Repeated at 10.84.
2. Compare Cato, *On Farming* 36.
3. Unidentified (literally 'many trunks').
4. Repeated from 10.83.

85. *How one can transplant large trees and those that are carrying fruit.* Anatolios.

After making very deep planting holes, cutting the green growth all round, keeping the bigger branches untrimmed and the roots undamaged, they plant the trunk upright with plenty of its original soil and with manure, letting it retain whatever was its original incline. They place on either side of it an earthenware pot with a hole in the base, through which they can water the roots directly, and they cover them so that the openings will not become blocked. The transplanting is best done before the setting of the Pleiades. In placing the tree it must retain its original orientation as to east and west.

86. *How one can keep seeds for a period and then grow them.* Pamphilos.

Since plants often shrivel when kept for a period, they can be kept as seeds in the following way. When the fruit has ripened on the tree, they take it and cover it in ash so that it dries up in the dark; afterwards they make a planting hole, put the fruit in it and water it daily until it shoots. When it is two or three years old they move it with the roots and earth it up, leaving only the tops showing.

Some believe that growing from seed is a cheap method. One needs to know that every seed will produce the original kind except olive: this produces not the olive but the *kotinos*, that is, wild olive.

87. *To prevent trees shedding their fruit.* Sotion.

If darnel, the so-called *zizanion*, as found in the wheat, is taken from the ground in large quantity with the roots when it begins to weep, arranged in the form of a wreath and placed around the trunk, the tree will be fruitful and will not shed its fruit.

When the plant called mullein is put around the walnut tree, the latter will not shed its fruit.[1]

It will not shed so much fruit if the crab, that is, the *pagouros*, is put around it.[2]

1. Repeated from 10.64.
2. Compare 2.43 and 10.89.

Likewise if you put lead around the trunk as a wreath it will not shed its fruit but bear heavily.

Plants do not throw off their fruit if you dig around the root, pierce it, insert a dogwood peg, then earth it up.

Some bare the tenderest and biggest roots, split them, insert a hard flint, bind it in, then earth them up again.

Didymos in *Georgika* says that one also saves the fruit by writing the Homeric line *He was bound in a bronze jar for thirteen months.*[1]

It keeps the fruit if one finds a naturally pierced stone and puts it on a new branch of the tree.

It also keeps the fruit if you write the following and neatly tie it to the tree: *And he shall be as the wood planted by the springs of the waters, which shall give its fruit in its season, and its leaf shall not drop.*[2]

The germander plant,[3] hung [in the tree], keeps the fruit.

88. *Treatment of trees that lose their blossom or shed their leaves.* The Quintilii.

Trees that shed their leaves or lose their blossom should be treated as follows. Trench around the roots and add bean shucks mixed with water to the quantity of eight *choes* for a large tree, not less than two *choes* for a small one. Sick trees will be cured by this method and will remain healthy in the future.

89. *A natural Demokritean method to prevent animals damaging plants and seeds.* Demokritos.

Throw at least 10 *karkinoi* or *pagouroi*, in other words sea or freshwater crabs, into water [in a vessel]; leave them eight days, then cover and put them in the open air to dry in the sun for 10 days. Sprinkle with this water for 8 days any plants you wish to protect, and you will be surprised at the effect.[4]

The same effect is produced by dogs' dung mixed with the most foul-smelling urine and sprinkled over.

1. *Iliad* 5.387. The subject is the god Ares.
2. *Psalms* 1.3.
3. Greek *polion*: *Teucrium polium* L.
4. Similarly 2.18 and 5.50. Likewise Palladius, *On Agriculture* 1.35.7 (and likewise credited to Demokritos).

90. *Avoiding damage to trees and vines by grubs and other pests.* Florentinus.

Rub the roots with Lemnian red lead and oregano diluted with water, and plant squill around the tree.

If you drive in pine stakes around the trees, the grubs will be killed.

You will keep safe from grubs each tree that you manure with pigs' dung moistened with donkey urine, so *Didymos* says in *Georgika*. The same author says that if you anoint the roots with bull's bile the tree will not age quickly and will not produce grubs.

Trees will not produce grubs if you bare the roots and smear them all round with pigeon dung.

Book II

1. *What trees are evergreen, never shedding their leaves in winter.*

Trees that are evergreen, never losing their leaves in winter, 14 in total: date palm, citron, stone pine, bay, olive, cypress, carob,[1] Aleppo pine, holly oak, box,[2] myrtle, cedar, willow and juniper.

2. *Story of the bay tree.*

Daphne was the very beautiful daughter of the river Ladon.[3] Apollo wanted to make love to her, chased her, and caught her. They say that she prayed to mother Earth, who saved her. Earth immediately put forth a plant in her place: Apollo saw this and was astonished. He named the tree *daphne* after the girl, took a shoot from it and wore it as a wreath. Thereafter the plant became a symbol of prophecy. Also relevant is what follows:

The girl is called *Sophrone* 'Chastity'; chastity evidently confers the ability to prophesy.

The ancients made the bay tree sacred to Apollo because the plant is full of fire, and Apollo is fire: he is the sun. Hence he is the enemy of demons, and where there is bay, demons stay away.

Also those who burn this plant when divining seem to find the power of prophecy.

---

1. Greek *keratea*: *Ceratonia siliqua* L.
2. Greek *pyxos*: *Buxus sempervirens* L.
3. For this versions of the story of Daphne see, for example, Nonnos, *Dionysiaka* 42.387 ff. According to Ovid, *Metamorphoses* 1.452 ff., Daphne was the daughter of the Thessalian river Peneus.

They also say about the bay tree that it is health-giving; hence its leaves are given by the people to their magistrates on the first of January, along with dried figs.

No epilepsy and no demon will trouble a place where there is bay, just as lightning will not strike where there is a fig tree.

Also the name Daphne is applied to the Palace,[1] because of the discovery of *daphne*, bay, at Rome: they say that Latinus, son of Kirke, brother of Telegonos, father-in-law of Aeneas, when founding the acropolis before Aeneas arrived, found bay growing there. 'Acropolis' was the name given by the ancients to the encampments of kings, because, for security, they were built at the highest point of cities.

3. *Propagating bay with grafts, seeds and suckers.* Quintilius.

Quintilius advises cleft-grafting bay on itself, on sorb and on manna ash.

Diophanes says that the seed of bay should be gathered around 1st December; it is sown after 15th March. Suckers are taken off in October and planted out. The Romans call this plant 'noble'; it is suitable for hedging vineyards.

4. *Story of the cypress.*

Cypresses have two names, *Charites* 'Graces' for the pleasure they give because they are sweet and pleasing and resemble hair, *kyparissoi* because they conceive and grow shoots and fruits at the same time. They were the children of Eteokles. Dancing like goddesses they missed their footing and fell into a well. Earth took pity on the girls' suffering and sent up beautiful plants in their likeness to be their memorial and to give pleasure to mortals.[2]

5. *Planting cypress.* Didymos.

Cypress seed is gathered after 1st September and is sown in vegetable beds between 24th October and [the beginning of] winter. After

---

1. The Great Palace at Constantinople, of which one wing was named Daphne.
2. A story that Eteokles, king of Orchomenos, initiated the worship of the Graces (but not that he was their father) is told by Pausanias, *Guide to Greece* 9.34–38.

sowing the cypresses, intersperse some slender barley, because often the cypress will grow vigorously during the first year and reach the same height as the barley. Then transplant it. Self-sown seedlings from fallen cypress seed are transplanted in the same way.[1]

Demokritos says that cypress should be planted in a hedge so that it can serve two purposes, pleasure and protection.

It prefers damp and shady places.

The male cypress has no seed.

6. *Story of the myrtle.*

Myrsine was a child of Attike, more beautiful than all the other girls, stronger than all the boys. She was dear to the goddess Athena, spent her time in wrestling rings and the race tracks, and wreathed the young competitors and winners with bay. Some of the losers, who had come to hate her, murdered her out of jealousy, but this did not end Athena's love for her. *Myrsine*, the myrtle, now that she has changed her nature, remains as dear to the goddess as is the olive; but the fruit she bears is not olives but myrtle-berries.

7. *Planting myrtle.* Florentinus.

It is good to plant myrtles at all elevated sites: it will give the place a good aroma.

Some plant from suckers, taking them with their own roots; others take the best new branch from the upper parts, plant it upright, firmly setting it in earth mixed with dung, and heap up earth around it to the point where shoots grow from it. Some take billets one cubit long, as thick as a hand, put them in planting holes and earth them up, aslant, like the olive. Some rub the seed, newly gathered, along a rope plaited from sedge and place it in a ditch.[2]

Some think they fruit better if planted on their heads.

Myrtle likes to be well trimmed all round: this makes the plant grow straight and tall, suitable for use in basketry and for arrows.

---

1. Cato, *On Farming* 151 gives instructions on growing cypress.
2. Compare 5.44 and Pliny, *Natural History* 17.62, where Demokritos is cited for the method of growing a myrtle hedge by spreading the seeds on a rope.

Irrigate with human urine and especially sheep's urine, which it particularly likes.

It bears seedless fruit if irrigated with warm water.

It is grafted on its own kind, also white on black and the converse, and on wild pear, and apple, and medlar, and pomegranate.

If rose is grown alongside it, both plants flourish and bear fine fruit.

8. *Keeping myrtle berries.* Same author.

Put the myrtles in unpitched vessels, seal, and you will have them in best condition for a long time. Others put them up with their branches.

9. *Box.* Same author.

Box is grown from cuttings, layers and boughs[1] put aside in the nursery after 13th November. Being evergreen it likes damp sites.

10. *Story of the Aleppo pine.*

Pitys was a girl who was changed into a plant because she had two admirers. Pan was in love with her and so was Boreas, the north wind; both tried to persuade her, and she preferred Pan. Boreas was angry with her, threw her against the rocks, and consigned her to death. Earth, sorry at her suffering, produced a plant that bore her name. Though she has changed her nature her affection remains constant: the box tree crowns Pan with its wreaths, and mourns when the north wind blows on it.

11. *Planting Aleppo pine.*

The cones are planted, much like almonds, from October to January. They are harvested in June, before the *etesiai* begin to blow and before the kernels burst their shells and begin to fall.[2]

---

1. I don't know how this differs from the other two.
2. Compare Palladius, *On Agriculture* 12.7.9–12.

12. *The lentisk tree.*[1]

Lentisk likes wet places. It is planted after 1st January. They say it bears three crops [each year]; if the first crop is good, it means that the first sowing [of grain] will produce a good harvest, and similarly with the other two.[2]

13. *The willow.*

Willow likes swampy and watery places with damp and cold air. It is planted in February from layers and slips.

Demokritos says that the fruit of the willow, ground and mixed with beasts' fodder, makes them fat. Ground and taken in drink it makes humans sterile, which is why Homer says: *Alders, poplars and fruit-wasting willows.*[3]

14. *Oak galls.*

Holly oak should be planted before 1st March. They say that if the holly oak bears plentiful fruit it foretells a poor harvest.[4]

15. *Story of the rosemary.*[5]

Libanos [second element of Greek *dendrolibanos* 'rosemary'] is a Syrian name, whether applied to a mountain or to a plant.[6]

The rosemary was once a young boy, a devotee of the gods. Irreligious men were angry at this and killed him. Earth, honouring the gods, sent forth a plant bearing the dead boy's name. Although he changed his nature he did not abandon his devotion to the gods. Hence one pleases the gods much more by offering incense than by dedicating gold to them.

1. Greek *schinos*: *Pistacia lentiscus* L.
2. Similarly Aratus, *Phenomena* 1.1051 ff.; cf. Cicero, *On Divination* 1.15.
3. Eustathios, *Commentary on Odyssey* 10.510, is neutral on whether willows lose their fruit or whether a drink made from their flowers causes sterility.
4. Similarly Aratus, *Phenomena* 1.1047 ff.
5. Greek *dendrolibanon*: *Rosmarinus officinalis* L.
6. The mountain is the Lebanon range; the plant was frankincense. The name 'tree-incense' was apparently applied to rosemary because its aroma resembled frankincense (Pliny, *Natural History* 24.101).

16. *Growing rosemary.*

They say that rosemary grows from seedlings and cuttings: this is done by putting them straight into the ground and watering them.

It has a pleasant and heavy aroma, so *Demokritos* says, and helps the fainting.

It is planted on in March.

17. *Story of the rose.*

If surprised by the beauty of the rose, they say, consider the wound of Aphrodite. This goddess loved Adonis, but Ares loved her. So Ares, in anger, put an end to Adonis, thinking that his death would cure her love. Finding out about this, she hurried to Adonis's aid, and in her haste stepped on a rose while wearing no sandals. Its thorns pricked the sole of her foot. The rose, formerly white, was changed by the *ichor* that flowed from the wound to the colour that we now see. Ever since that time it has been red and scented.

Others say that when the gods were carousing in heaven and plenty of nectar was ready to serve, Eros was leaping in the dance, knocked with his wing the stand on which the mixing-bowl stood and upset it. The nectar fell down to earth and gave a red colour to the flower of the rose.

18. *Roses; how to make them more aromatic; how to ensure that they do not fade.* Didymos.

If you grow garlic alongside roses it will have a better aroma.

If you want to have roses continuously, plant one each month, manure them, and you will have them all the time.

Roses are grown in various ways. Some transplant whole rooted plants; some separate them out with their roots, trim both the roots and the shoots to the length of a palm, that is, four fingers, and plant each separate shoot, about a cubit apart.[1]

Some weave them together in wreaths for the aroma and so plant them.

1. A second version of this method is given later in the chapter.

It is worth knowing that roses planted in dry places are more aromatic; it is the same with lilies.

Roses planted in tubs and pots produce early if they get the same care as gourds and melons. If you want already-planted roses to fruit early,[1] trench around the plant at a distance of two palms and pour on warm water twice a day.[2]

The dew found on roses, if cleanly gathered on a feather and applied to the eyes with a lancet, cures ophthalmia.

You can keep fresh blooming roses if you put them in *amorge* so that the fluid covers them.

Some pull up green barley with the roots, put it in an unpitched pot, add unopened roses, cover and store; others spread the green barley on the floor and add roses.

Demokritos says that if the rose is watered twice a day during the heat of summer it will fruit in January.

Florentinus says that the rose can be cleft-grafted and bud-grafted to apple bark, and roses will come in apple season.

Zoroaster says that one who sees the first swelling rosebuds, and rubs his eyes with three of them without picking them off the plant, will have no eye trouble for a whole year.

Some keep roses fresh by slitting a green reed that is still growing, putting the buds into it, and fastening it carefully with papyrus so that no air enters.

If roses that are beginning to open are smoked with sulphur you will immediately have them white.

If you have only a few plants and want more, take the shoots, divide them, cut them to about four fingers or a little more, and plant them; when they are as year old, transplant them one foot apart, and dig them in, working the ground carefully and removing all weeds.[3]

I believe the nature of the rose tends towards divinity. It makes a perfume that is of no poor quality; it is an ally in cases of painful eyes, and it is highly useful in many other ways.

---

1. The reference is not to rose hips but to the flowers of the rose. For other instances of *karpos*, literally 'fruit', used in the sense of 'flower bud', see Theophrastos, *History of Plants* 3.3.5 with Hort's note; Aelian, *On Animals* 1.35 with Scholfield's note.
2. Similarly Pliny, *Natural History* 21.21; Palladius, *On Agriculture* 3.21.2.
3. Similarly Palladius, *On Agriculture* 12.11.

19. *Story of the lily.*

Zeus fathered Herakles on Alkmene. He was a mortal, but Zeus wanted to give him a share of immortality, and so put him to Hera's breast while she was asleep. Full of milk, the baby turned his mouth away from the teat, but the milk still flowed from it plentifully even when he was taken away. The milk that flowed into the sky created what is called the 'milky way'; what fell to earth and spread over the soil gave a colour like milk to the flower of the lily.

20. *Lilies.* Anatolius.

If you want to produce purple lilies, take the stems when they flower, tie ten or a dozen of them together and hang them in the smoke. The stems will produce rootlets like little bulbs. When it is time for planting, soak the stems in lees of red wine until you can see that they are purple and fully macerated; then take off [the bulbs] and plant them, pouring a quantity of the lees on each, and the new plants will produce purple flowers.[1]

Lilies keep fresh for a whole year in the following way. They pick them with their stems while they are not yet open but still in bud; they put them in new and untreated, i.e. unpitched, earthenware vessels, cover the vessels and put away. Stored in this way they keep fresh for a whole year. Whenever in the meanwhile you want to take out some for use, put them in the sun to revive and open.

If you want lilies to keep on flowering, plant some of the bulbs twelve fingers deep, others eight, others four, and you will have lilies over a long period. It is possible to do this with other flowers too.

Florentinus says that lilies will flower red if one inserts cinnabar between the layers of the bulb while taking care not to damage them. If one adds different dyes as desired it is possble to produce lilies of each colour.

21. *The iris.* Leontios.

The Illyrian iris, the small and very light kind, is planted out from newly-formed plants from January until April.

---

1. Similarly Pliny, *Natural History* 21.26.

22. *Story of the violet.*

The violet, *ion*,[1] comes from the person whose name it bears. Zeus fell in love with Io, coupled with her and tried to obscure the fact from Hera by changing the nature of the evidence: having been caught, in order to conceal his transgression he changed his human lover into a cow. Earth, honouring Zeus's beloved, allowed this cow to feed on certain flowers, which then took their name from hers. Their colour tells the girl's whole story: they blush like a virgin, they are purple like a cow,[2] they are white as Io when she became a star; whatever colour they may be, she was also.

23. *Growing violets.* Tarantinos.

Purple violets and all other colours, golden and brown, are planted after 15th March and after 1st May. Violet leaf is cooling and aids in cases of inflammation. The oil of violets, rubbed on the skin, cools the feverish.

The white violet[3] is likewise grown in vegetable beds. It is transplanted in January and until 7th February.

24. *Story of the narcissus.*

The cause of suffering was even stranger than the suffering: Narkissos was a boy who loved himself and by this love killed himself. He was remarkable for his beauty: this was the root of his love and his mishap. He went to a spring, wishing to drink; stood and regarded his own image and thus became both lover and beloved; as lover of himself he was destroyed. He came to the spring and was attracted to his reflection as to a beloved woman; succumbing to desire, reaching out for himself, he fell into the waters of the spring. Thus as he sought relief of his suffering he found extinction. He gained by his death, to the extent that he was transformed into a flower whose name preserves his memory.

1. Greek *ion*: *Viola* spp., especially *Viola odorata* L.
2. Greek *porphyra* extends from dark red to brown and purple.
3. Greek *leukoïon*: *Viola alba* Besser.

25. *Growing narcissus.* Didymos.

The narcissus is grown from self-rooted seedlings[1] that begin to sprout in March and are planted on. Its flower is extremely cold.

26. *Growing saffron crocus.* Florentinus.

Saffron[2] is grown from self-rooted seedlings produced when the flower falls.

The flower comes before the leaf. Saffron is harvested when it has a good colour, by taking the stamens from the interior of the flower and drying them for 3 or 4 days; then the extremity is cleaned and the white removed, and they are put into pots, pressed down as much as possible.

Diophanes says that the saffron should be dried in the shade.

27. *Marjoram, cost*[3] *and balm.*

Marjoram is grown from seed and is planted on in April and May. It has a pleasant and very hot aroma. Cost and balm are planted similarly from self-rooted seedlings in November. They are pleasantly scented.

28. *On* misodoulon *or basil.*[4] Sotion.

I know of no use for the basil, the so-called *misodoulon*. Those who eat it become manic, lethargic and hepatic; it is a sign of these ill effects that goats, which eat everything, avoid basil alone.

If it is chewed and left in the sun it produces scorpions.

It is especially inimical to women. It has such a physical antipathy to them that if a whole basil plant with the root is placed under a dish of food, a woman, albeit unaware of this, will not dare to take food from the dish until the basil is removed.[5]

1. *autorrizos* (ter). Is this what the word means here?
2. Greek *krokos*: *Crocus sativus* L.
3. Greek *kostos* here refers evidently to the garden plant *Tanacetum balsamita* L., costmary. The same word is used in the medical prescriptions for the spice costus or putchuk: see 6.7 and note.
4. Greek *okimon*: *Ocimum americanum* L. This identification of *okimon* with what was later called *basilikon*, 'basil', is made by *Suda* s.v. Some dispute it.
5. This is what Owen says, and it's logical, but the Greek seems to mean the opposite.

29. *Story of ivy.*

The plant ivy was once a young man, a dancer to Dionysos. Dancing to the god he tripped and fell to earth, and Earth, honouring Dionysos, sent forth a flower of the same name, a growth that preserved the young man's character: emerging from the ground it grows entwined with the vine, entwined as was the young man when he danced.

30. *Growing ivy.*

Ivy likes water.

It is planted before 1st November and after 1st March.

Ivy will produce fine bunches of berries if one one burns three shells, pounds them, and sprinkles them over it; or if one sprays the bunches with alum.

Black ivy turns white if white earth is soaked and poured on the roots for eight days.

Damegeron says that if one puts three bunches of black ivy berries in clean linen and ties them with linen thread, for three days, to one who is splenetic, the person so treated will be freed of the sickness.

Book 12

1. *What is sown and what is planted out month by month in the latitude of Constantinople.*[1]

In January seakale[2] is sown, along with orach[3] and fenugreek.

In February parsley is sown along with leek, onion, chard,[4] carrot, beetroot, savory, salad mixture (i.e. *dikardion, phrygiatikon, rigitanon*, white cabbage[5]), sprouting broccoli, coriander, dill and rue. *Maroullin* lettuce, chicory, *thridakin*,[6] *phrygiatikon, polyklonon* and *komodianon* are planted out.

In March local chard, orach, *dikardion, maroullin, rigitanon* are sown. *Maroullin*, chicory, *phrygiatikon*,[7] *polyklonon* are planted out.

In April, towards the end, are sown chard, orach and *dikardion* with *rigitanon*. From March and April white cabbage is planted out, as is *maroullin* with *rigitanon* and on its own.

In May are sown chard, orach likewise and individually, and *rigitanon*; chard and *maroullin* are planted out.

---

1. This chapter is fully discussed by Koder 1973.
2. Greek *thalassokrambe*: *Crambe maritima* L.
3. Medieval Greek *chrysolachanon*: *Atriplex hortensis* L.
4. Greek *seutlon, seutlomolochon*: *Beta vulgaris* ssp. *cicla* (L.) Koch.
5. Greek *leukokrambe* and variants: *Brassica oleracea* convar. *capitata* (L.) Alef. var. *alba* DC. Cf. *Prodromic Poems* 3.178 *krambin kardiai ... chionatai*, 'snow-white cabbage hearts'.
6. Simeon Seth p. 64 makes *maroullia* and *thridakinai* synonymous, 'lettuce'; here *maroullin* and *thridakin* are varieties, though *maroullin* is also the general term.
7. *Rigitanon* and *phrygiatikon* are both geographical names for unidentified salad vegetable varieties.

In June chard is sown, likewise *dikardion*, and little leeks are planted out, mud-covered, in damp soil; so are chard, mallow[1] and *maroullin*.

In July endive and chard are sown, leek is planted in dry soil and immediately watered so that the root will not spur as it wastes away. *Maroullin* must be planted out, and endive, and chard; beet and mallow must be planted out individually.

In August endive is sown, and chard, and root turnip,[2] and early turnip for shoots,[3] and white cabbage. Leek, endive and chard are planted out. Radish in general is sown, also rocket and cress.

In September chard, late endive and rough-country turnip are sown. Root turnip, turnip to be taken as shoots, *broumalitikon* endive,[4] chard with it, coriander and radish are planted out.

In October *maroullin*, chicory, *komodianon*, *polyklonon* and *thridakin* are sown for the new year. Turnip, beet, endive, cress, rocket, and white cabbage are planted out.

In November fenugreek is sown. Rough-country turnips are planted out, also late endive, beet individually, mallow individually. Coriander is sown.

In December *maroullin*, chicory, *polyklonon*, *thridakin* and *komodianon* are sown.

2. *Making a vegetable garden.* Florentinus.

Gardening is essential to life. For health and convalescence a garden should be developed not at a distance from the house but in proximity to it, where it will give enjoyment to the eyes and pleasure to the sense of smell; and not downwind[5] of the threshing-floor, so that the plants will not be killed by the chaff.

The vegetable growing enthusiast needs to give thought to four matters, good quality seeds, suitability of soil, water, manure. Good seeds will reproduce the kinds from which they came. Suitable soil

---

1. Greek *malache*: *Malva sylvestris* L.
2. Greek *gongylis*: *Brassica rapa* L.
3. Greek *gongylosparagon* (Italian *broccoli di rapa*).
4. Perhaps named after the *Brumalia*, celebrated on 24th November (see 1.1, 1.5).
5. *Kat' anemon* clearly must mean 'downwind' here, though at 5.33 and 5.48 it has to mean 'upwind'. Elsewhere, too, its meaning varies: compare Aristotle, *History of Animals* 541a26; Plutarch, *Moralia* 972a, 979c.

will produce fertile plants. Water will nourish vegetables and make them bigger. Manure will make the soil looser, and this makes easier the penetration of water, the development of roots, and the growth of plants.

3. *Soil suited to vegetables.* Didymos.

The best earth for gardening is neither clayey nor excessively rough, nor does it develop large cracks in summer. Clayey soil freezes in winter and dries out in summer, rendering plants weak and thin if it does not kill them; with some difficulty clayey soil can be made suitable if mixed with an equal quantity of manure. Soil that develops cracks is altogether useless. Rough soil cannot nourish and cannot hold water, but a few sites that are rough and sandy are good for vegetables because they have plenty of mud, which feeds the roots. Hence you will easily recognize soil suitable for vegetables: dissolve it in water, wash it, and if you find that it has plenty of muddy matter, you may determine that it is fertile and good for vegetables. If it has more watery matter, it is not good.

You may determine as unsuitable for vegetables any soil that, when worked in the hand like wax, you find to be extremely sticky.

4. *What manure is suitable for vegetables.* Same author.

The best manure for all vegetables is ash: it is very light, it is hot by nature, it kills fleas and borer beetles and all such vermin. The second best manure is pigeon dung, which is also effective at killing vermin: if a small proportion of this is used it will give the same result as a whole application of any other. Some prefer ass dung to that of pigeons because it makes the vegetables sweeter. Goat dung is also very good and can give the same results. If you have none of these, use other animals' dung, but not fresh: fresh dung generates vermin. It must be a year old and must have been often turned with forks.

5. *How all kinds of vegetables can be grown on waterless sites.* Vindanionius.

Select the area of land you require, dig down to about one foot or one cubit depth, remove the soil thus dug, take tiles and scatter them over the dug area, then dig in fresh, sieved, soil with very dry manure, then plant or sow the vegetables. Instead of the tiles some people dig the site and then level it off with mortar or lye as they would a trough, then dig in the soil and manure, then plant. Whether using mortar or tiles, give attention to the vertical surfaces that surround the dug area: secure them, too, with mortar or tiles, so that in either case the water used to irrigate the garden will not seep through. Having done this they then work the garden just as in a well-watered site, relying on rainwater in winter, irrigating in summer. They have no need for much water, having by this arrangement saved the whole of the winter rain at the site and prevented it from running off into neighbouring land.

Some people who have no plentiful supply of water make two vegetable gardens, one for the winter, watered by the rain, and the other for the summer, in a well-shaded, north-facing location.

6. *How to make the garden flourish and flower.* Demokritos.

The garden will flourish if you pound lotus,[1] add it to water, and sprinkle over.

Or grind fenugreek with water and sprinkle the vegetable beds.

Or drop an ass's skull in the middle of the garden.

7. *So that vegetables will not be eaten by flea beetles*[2] *or damaged by* phtheires[3] *or birds.* Anatolios.

Vegetables will not be eaten by flea beetles if you mix a little bitter vetch with the seed when sowing. This is particularly appropriate to radishes and turnips.

Others, working with analogy and antipathy, plant or grow rocket – especially alongside cabbage, which is particularly attacked by flea beetles.

If you want your crop to be free of other pests as well, soak the seeds in the juice of houseleek before sowing.

1. Greek *lotos* has several meanings: here possibly clover, *Trifolium* spp.
2. Greek *psylla*, literally 'flea': here *Phyllotreta* spp., commonly likened to fleas because they jump.
3. *Phtheir* (not mentioned in the text of this chapter) is literally 'louse'.

You will protect garden and field seeds from all vermin if you soak them before sowing in the juice of the pounded root of squirting cucumber.

Vegetables will not be eaten by pests if you sow the seed in a tortoise shell.[1]

8. *So that there will not be caterpillars[2] in vegetables or trees.* Apuleius.

Put some ash from burning vine stems in water for 3 days and sprinkle the vegetables with it.

Or smoke the trees or vegetables with asphalt and native sulphur.

Likewise there will be no caterpillars if you soak the seed beforehand in ash or lye from burning fig wood, and then sow. You will destroy existing caterpillars if you mix urine and *amorge* in equal parts, boil the mixture over a fire, then cool it, and sprinkle it over the vegetables.

If you take caterpillars from another garden and cook them in water with dill, cool this and sprinkle it over the vegetables, you will kill any caterpillars that are on them.

When there are a lot of caterpillars some people bring a woman, ritually pure, to the garden, barefoot, her hair loose, wearing only one dress and nothing else at all, no underclothing or other item. In this state she must walk around the garden three times, then cross it and leave it. This will immediately drive the caterpillars away.[3]

You can kill them with the smoke of burning the mushrooms that grow under walnut trees.[4]

Or burn bat droppings and the stems (not the bulbs) of garlic in such a way that the smoke wafts through the whole garden.

---

1. It is not clear what this means. Palladius, *On Agriculture* 1.35.5, suggests putting the seed to dry in a tortoise shell before sowing.
2. Greek *kampai*, here meaning caterpillars in general.
3. Compare Aelian, *Nature of Animals* 6.36 and Palladius, *On Agriculture* 1.35.3, adding that the woman must be menstruating. Pliny, *Natural History* 28.78, citing Metrodoros of Skepsis, adds further detail and remarks that the discovery was made in Cappadocia because of the quantity of insect pests there.
4. I cannot suggest an identification.

9. *How to destroy leek moth larva.*[1] Diophanes.

Take the fresh bowel of a sheep, full of the faeces and unwashed; bury it, not deep but near the surface. You will find that it fills with these leek moth larvae. If you do the same thing a second time you will collect them all together, and so take and destroy them. The creature is attracted to dung and is soon trapped by this method.

10. *Interplanting to help vegetables.* Fronto.

In general, all vegetables are helped when rocket is sown alongside them.

11. *To harm the gardener.* Africanus.

Dissolve goose droppings in brine and sprinkle over the vegetables.

12. *Mallow and its medicinal use in various illnesses.* Damegeron.

Mallow well boiled and eaten on its own cures sore throat; eaten with olive oil and *garon* it is effective in relieving constipation. Its leaves, chopped, with willow leaves, are always rather useful in plasters: they prevent inflammation, stop bleeding, quickly close a wound and treat dislocations and bruises. They cure stings of widow spiders and pests, if you pound onions and leeks to a paste, mix them with mallow leaves, and apply.

One who rubs on [to the skin] the juice of wild mallow with olive oil will not be stung by wasps;[2] the juice cures any who fail to do this and are stung.

The leaves of mallow, pounded and applied, cure the sting.

Mallow rubbed on [to the skin] likewise treats sycosis[3] and women's private ailments. The juice, dropped into the ears, stops earache; mixed with honey and drunk it cures hepatics and restores epileptics to consciousness.

---

1. Greek *prasokouris.* The identification with *Acrolepiopsis assectella* (Zeller, 1839), leek moth, was made by André 1950; see also Davies and Kathirithamby 1986 p. 167.
2. Similarly at 15.10.
3. Greek *leichen.*

This plant's juice also cures nephritics and those suffering from sciatica. The decoction, drunk, treats dysuria and is useful in difficult childbirth.

13. *Lettuce, its medicinal use, and how to grow it white and shapely.* Florentinus.

Lettuce is a wet and cold vegetable; for this reason it is helpful with feverish ailments. It is a food that suppresses thirst and induces sleep; it also encourages lactation. When boiled it becomes more nourishing; it also suppresses libido, which is why Pythagoreans call it *eunouchos* 'castrato' and women call it *astytis* 'impotent'.[1]

If you want to have shapely lettuce, tie around their hair (their upper parts, that is) two days before you pick them. This will make them white and shapely. Sand poured over them also whitens them.

Lettuce gives appetite for food; clears phlegm; inhibits sexual acts; when taken with sweet wine or vinegar, tempers bile; with hyssop and vinegar, is good for the hypochondria; cooked in rose oil and swallowed, stops cholera. Its juice reduces swollen bowels; rubbed on with woman's milk, it heals erysipelas. Its seed, ground and drunk, cures a scorpion sting; it helps with pain in the chest.

Lettuce induces sleep in healthy subjects when eaten; also in those who are sick, if without their knowledge it is placed under them,[2] and particularly if with the left hand, before sunrise, one picks from the earth a whole lettuce with the roots and places it under the patient's bedding. Its juice, rubbed on the face of one who cannot sleep, will put him to sleep.

If you want to grow saucer-shaped lettuces with many leaves and with no stalk, remaining close to the ground, transplant them and water them; then, when they are palm-sized, dig around them to expose the roots, smear fresh cow dung on them, then earth them up and immediately irrigate them. When they are full-grown divide each plant with a very sharp knife and place [in the cut] an unpitched potsherd, so that they will continue their growth outwards and not upwards.

---

1. Similarly Lykos fragment 57 Diels-Kranz as quoted in *Epitome of the Deipnosophistai* 69e.
2. Repeated in different words later in this chapter.

Eating lettuce frequently, especially if sweet, hinders the dimming of sight and produces sharp-sightedness.

Eating plenty of lettuce relaxes the bowels; eating a little constipates them.

They soothe a cold.

Travellers will not be upset by frequent changes of water[1] if they eat lettuce at breakfast before any other food. Drunkenness will also be prevented if one eats lettuce first.

Aromatic lettuce will be produced if a lettuce seed is inserted in a citron seed and sown.

The seed, drunk, inhibits ejaculation; it is thus prescribed to those who have frequent wet dreams. 5 or 3 leaves or a single leaf of lettuce will induce sleep in one who is confined to bed, if the lettuce is secretly placed under the mattress in such a way that the ends broken off the stalk point towards the foot and the outer ends towards the head.

14. *How to grow lettuce that produces celery, rocket, basil and the like from the same root.* Didymos.

Take a piece of goat or sheep dung, however small; pierce a hole in it; hollow it out neatly and pack inside it the seeds of the kinds of vegetable listed, or any you choose. Bury at a depth not less than two palms, after scattering manure and covering with fine soil; then water lightly. When the seed sprouts, water it, sprinkling manure frequently. When it forms a stalk, give it additional care, and you will have lettuce blended with the other kinds thus brought together. Others crush 2 or 3 goat or sheep droppings, crottels as they are called, mix the seeds with them, put them in linen, tie this up and bury it, then follow the same method already described; in this way they get lettuce variously blended.

15. *Beet and how to make it grow bigger.* Sotion.

If you want to produce bigger and whiter beet, smear the roots with fresh dung; then, as with leeks, divide the shoot and insert a flat stone or potsherd.

---

1. The assumption is that it was the change of water that caused digestive disorders in travellers.

Beet leaves, having a purgative property, relax the bowels when eaten in soup with olive oil, *garon* and a little natron.

The juice of raw beet leaves is a treatment for scurf and head lice.

The juice of beet leaves mixed with wax, melted, applied on a cloth, heals all roughnesses and swellings. It also cures leprous patches and alopecia.

16. *Various vegetables and their medicinal effects.* Varro.

Having recently puzzled out some therapies that I found in the hexameters and elegiacs of the learned *Nestor's Garden of Health*, I have finally written them down: since I am mentioning various vegetables, I decided it was essential, particularly for farmers' use, to set out the therapies derived from them.

17. *Cabbage and its medicinal effects.* Paxamos.[1]

It is necessary to know that cabbage is best sown in a salty place. Therefore, when it has three leaves, sprinkle it through a sieve with fine natron so that it looks frosted. Some use ash instead of soda, because it also kills caterpillars.

Cabbage lightly boiled opens the bowels; thoroughly boiled it constipates.

Here are the medicinal effects of cabbage. For women cabbage brings on menstruation, especially if its juice is drunk with sweet wine. Boiled and eaten before other food it treats consumptives. If cabbage is boiled and mashed, and then mixed with the water in which it was boiled, and cooled and used as ointment, it soothes fresh wounds, old wounds and swellings. The decoction cures gout and arthritis, mixed with barley meal, coriander, rue and a little salt, and applied as liquid. Cabbage juice mixed with Attic honey helps the eyes when applied to the corners.

Additionally it is nourishing, so that children grow more quickly when they eat cabbage; and anyone who has eaten bad mushrooms will survive if he drinks cabbage juice.

---

1. Compare Cato, *On Farming* 156–157.

Cabbage juice treats those who are jaundiced and splenetic if drunk for 40 days with white wine. Drunk with black wine it stops a cough. Cabbage leaves rubbed on remove sycosis; applied, they immediately cure bites of pests. Cabbage, mixed with 'round' alum[1] soaked in vinegar, treats itch and leprosy. The ash from burning cabbage roots helps burns. Cabbage juice taken with olive oil, and held [in the mouth] for a long time, stops ulceration of the mouth and tonsils and swelling of the uvula. The juice with wine, applied as liquid, helps the ears. Cabbage, bruised and applied, gives great relief to those who are feverish owing to disease. Boiled, and eaten by itself before other food, it treats the voice and bronchial conditions; hence voice-trainers use it. Cabbage seeds or leaves, bruised, blended with silphium[2] and vinegar, and applied, cures bites of rats and those bitten by dogs, including mad dogs; these patients are also given as a drink the water from boiling the leaves (previously rinsed and dried). Cabbage, emulsified and applied, 'melts' the spleen. Eaten raw beforehand cabbage stops sleeplessness and prevents the appearance of dream images.

Nestor in his *Garden of Health* says that the cabbage is the tear of Lykourgos. When Dionysos, to escape from him, sank under the sea, Lykourgos, bound by the vine, shed a tear, and a cabbage – says Nestor – grew from this tear; this is why the cabbage and the vine have a mutual antipathy. Indeed, if cabbage ever approaches closely to vine in the fields, either it is immediately caused to wither, or the vine withers. Because of the enmity between them, if owing to a head cold the uvula or 'grape'[3] sags into the throat, the juice of raw cabbage dripped on the head will make the 'grape' withdraw to the roof of the mouth. If cabbage and vine happen to grow side by side, then, as the stem of the vine grows, and it is about to approach the cabbage, it will not go on straight but will turn back, aware, somehow, of the antipathy. If one sprinkles the smallest quantity of wine on to boiling cabbage, it will stop boiling and its colour will be lost.

1. Compare Dioscorides, *Materia Medica* 5.106; Pliny, *Natural History* 35.187.
2. Greek *silphion*: the now-extinct spice from Cyrenaica.
3. The logic depends on the fact that (in Greek) one usual term for the uvula is 'grape'.

So those who want to drink a lot of wine and not get drunk should eat raw cabbage beforehand.[1]

It is necessary to know that cabbage seed when it is aged produces kale.[2]

18. *Asparagus.* Didymos.

Asparagus likes sifted soil. It is sown in spring. Make planting holes of three fingers and place 2 or 3 seeds in each. The planting holes should be about one span apart. The seeds so planted should not be disturbed in their first year, except to take the shoots.

If you want to produce a lot of asparagus, grind finely the skulls of wild rams, spread [the bonemeal] on the asparagus beds, and water. Some, more unexpectedly, say that if whole rams' skulls are perforated and buried, they will produce asparagus.[3]

If you want to have asparagus throughout the year, when you harvest it cover the top roots at once: thus treated the plant will produce more asparagus.

This vegetable does not like watering (it prefers dry soil); but if one waters it in autumn it will produce tenderer and healthier shoots.

19. *On gourds*[4] *and melons:*[5] *their therapeutic uses, how to make them seedless, and how to grow them early.* The Quintilii.

They will be without seeds [if you do] as follows. The first little stem or stalk of the gourd or melon plant should be covered with earth, like vine stems, so that only the tip of the stem emerges. When it lengthens, cover it again, to the third knot, and cut the side-shoots

1. Supported by Cato, *On Farming* 156.1 and other ancient sources: see Dalby and Grainger 1996 p. 50.
2. Greek *raphanos*, a less-desirable *Brassica* cultivar such as kale or kohlrabi.
3. Compare Dioscorides, *Materia Medica* 2.125; Pliny, *Natural History* 19.151 (both refuse to believe it).
4. Greek *kolokynte*: bottle gourd, *Lagenaria siceraria* Molina (Standl.), and perhaps watermelon, *Citrullus lanatus* (Thunb.) Mats. & Nakai.
5. Greek *sikyos*: *Cucumis melo* L., melon (including chate melon). My thanks to Harry Paris for assistance with the identifications in this chapter.

that emerge above ground along its length, leaving only the last – the third, that is. You will get gourds or melons without seeds.

You will also make melons and gourds seedless if for three days before sowing you soak them in sesame oil.

You will produce early melons and gourds in the following way. Put sieved earth mixed with manure into boxes (or pots which are no longer usable), making it fairly wet. Ahead of the usual season, at the beginning of spring for example, plant seeds. When there is sunshine and warmth, and in order to give them sufficient water, put the planting-boxes outdoors, but at sunset bring them indoors under cover; do this regularly, and water them by hand if necessary. When the frosts are completely over, take them to a spot that is dug over and bury the boxes or pots so that their lips are at ground level, and then care for them as normal.

If you remove their growing tips, they will fruit more quickly.

You will grow them long if you put water in a mortar or some other container and place it about five or six fingers away from them. One the next day the melons will have grown to that distance. If there is no water in the container, the melons will bend and grow away from it; that is how much they like moisture and hate dryness.

You will give them whatever shape you wish if you make pottery containers and, when the fruits are still small, enclose them and tie them, because they will fill moulds and shapes. So if you cut a reed to length, hollow it out, reassemble and tie it, and put the melon or gourd into it when it is still small, it will grow to the whole length and fill the reed.[1]

Gourd is emollient to the stomach. It cures pains in the ear if the juice is dropped into the ear. Melon seed alleviates painful urination and is diuretic.

These fruits will not be damaged by flea beetles if, while they are still small, you stick twigs of oregano [into the earth] around them. This kills any existing beetles and and prevents the creation of others.

If a baby, still suckling, has fever, putting it to sleep with melons of the same size will cure it immediately, because all the heat will be drawn into the melons.

---

1. Similarly Palladius, *On Agriculture* 4.9.8 citing Gargilius Martialis.

The root of the squirting cucumber, dried and pounded and drunk in sweet wine, or with mead, is a remarkable cure for vomiting.

If you want to have melons containing no water, when you dig the hole where you will plant the melons fill it up to half depth with chaff or dry sticks, then add earth and plant without watering.

Some make them good for the bowels as follows. They crush roots of the squirting cucumber, soak them in drinking water for two or three days, and water [the melons] with this liquid for five days; they repeat this five times. They become better for the bowels if after the seeds sprout you hoe the roots, put a bit of hellebore to the shoots, earth it in, and leave it.

Put melons in good-tasting (not vinegary) lees of white wine, fill a jar, seal it, and they will stay fresh. They also keep if placed in brine.

You will keep melons at their best if you hang them in a jar in which there is a little vinegar, but they do not touch the vinegar; then seal the jar so that air does not enter it, and you will have fresh melons in winter.

Keep melons as follows. Take fresh ones, chop them, boil water and pour it over them, let them cool in the open air for a whole night, then put them in strong brine. They will keep a long time.

You will make gourds purgative if you steep the seed for a night and a day in scammony.[1]

You will grow big melons and gourds by planting the seed upside down.

20. *Musk-melons.*[2] Florentinus.

They are distinctly cooling. They are very useful to one who wants to vomit at a particular time: after meals they remove phlegm, bringing up a large quantity, and clear the head.

You will make musk-melons smell of roses if you store the seed with dried roses, knead together, and sow.[3]

They can quench thirst caused by fever.

---

1. Byzantine Greek *askamonia*: *Convolvulus scammonia* L.
2. Greek *melopepon*: *Cucumis melo* L. var. *melo*.
3. Similarly Palladius, *On Agriculture* 4.9.6. The Latin term is *melo*.

[Produce of the melon-bed.] [1]

You will make any produce of the melon-bed sweet if you steep the seeds in milk and honey, dry them, and sow them.

If you steep the seeds of these plants in the juice of houseleek, you will keep them free of attack.

A menstruating woman must not enter the melon-bed; this will wither the [existing] fruit, and what comes afterwards will be bitter.

21. *Turnip and its seed.*

Turnip is not good at treating human disease, but it can treat injuries of animals if placed under the hooves and fastened there.

Turnip seed produces cabbage in the third year, and vice versa.

22. *On radishes.* [2] Same author.

Radishes will be sweet if their seeds were steeped in whey mixed with honey, or in grape juice.

They are useful to the phlegmatic; they also treat the nephritic, especially if one boils their outsides with wine and takes [the decoction] at breakfast before other food. Eaten with honey they cure coughs. Their seeds, roasted and taken with honey, stop coughs and breathing difficulties; given in childbirth they ensure fullness of milk; they arouse to the sexual act; they harm the voice; one who takes them at breakfast will be safe from poisoning by drugs. Their juice, taken in water, is an antidote to mushrooms, even the deadly ones. If one carefully anoints and rubs the hands with this juice, one can touch pestilent creatures fearlessly and safely. [3]

If put on scorpions they immediately kill them. Taken in water they cure dropsy. They thin the spleen. Their juice, drunk in sweet wine before bathing, treats jaundice. They purge the upper digestive tract if one takes them with honey, holds back for a little, and then vomits; they are good at causing vomiting and also arouse the appetite

1. Melons, watermelons, gourds and (whenever these were introduced) cucumbers and gherkins. They are grown in a separate melon-bed (Greek *sikyelaton*) because of their creeping habit.
2. Greek *raphanis*: *Raphanus sativus* L.
3. Similarly at 13.8.

of anorectics. They alleviate quartan fevers if one takes them in quantity and vomits. If at any location the water is bad, it becomes relatively health-giving when boiled up with radishes.

It harms nothing but the teeth.

When boiled they are a useful food to those who are spitting blood.

One who after eating radishes is stung by a scorpion not only will not die but will rapidly recover.[1]

Radish ground to a paste and placed on injuries caused by torture will rapidly heal the bruises.

It clears off warts and restores hair lost in alopecia.

Eaten last in the meal it purifies the breath.

23. *Celery.* Florentinus.

Celery will grow big if you collect the seed in three fingers, tie it up in an old cloth, rub it with manure, and immediately water.[2]

It will also grow very big if you dig right around the roots, add chaff, and water.

Celery will be crisp if you gently press and roll the seed before planting.

Eating celery makes women more inclined to sexual acts. For this reason women who are nursing should not be encouraged to eat celery, and particularly because it may stop the milk.

It improves the odour of the mouth, however. If those with bad-smelling mouths eat celery they will remove the bad odour. They say that those on the stage eat celery to sweeten their mouths.

Celery rubbed on with bread is a treatment for erysipelas. Its decoction, used in a bath and drawn up over the body, expels stones, treats dysuria, and cures the kidneys.

24. *Mint.*[3] Same author.

Mint is thought to have no use. Even a wound to which it is applied will not be easily cleaned; while if it is added to milk and the rennet

---

1. Similarly at 13.8.
2. For further explanation see 12.29.
3. Greek *hedyosmon*: *Mentha* spp.

is added afterwards, the milk will not curdle. It is also not conducive to sexual acts.

25. *Rue, cultivated and wild.*[1] Same author.

Rue does not like manure. It likes hot and sunny places; in winter it should be scattered with ash. Because of its hot nature it has an antipathy to frost. It is necessary to take care that a menstruating woman does not approach it or touch it at all: that kills it at once.

If one plugs the ears with tender hearts of rue it will cure headache.

The juice of wild rue, mixed with woman's milk and anointed, gives sharpness of sight. It clears clouding of the eyes and early cataracts in humans and other animals, if one mixes two parts of Attic honey with one part of rue juice and anoints. The wild rue itself, eaten and drunk, has the same effect. The fruit of wild rue, drunk, for 15 days, kills an unborn child: it is by nature antipathetic to pregnant women. Drunk with wine it stops pain, including that of the bites of vermin. Also, drunk, it aids epileptics and clears pains in the chest; with wine or rose oil it cleans out the ears.

26. *Rocket.*

Rocket seed, drunk in wine, treats rat bites; it expels roundworms, thins the spleen, and when mixed with ox bile and vinegar it cleans up black bruises.

It cures moles.

Rocket, mixed with honey, cleans up spots on the face. Drunk in advance with wine it lessens the pain of a whipping.

Three leaves of wild rocket, taken in the hand, cure jaundice.

Rocket sown alongside all other vegetables improves them.

Rocket helps with smelly armpits.

27. *Cress.* Same author.

Cress seed mixed with beanmeal, one part of lye added, cures scrofula and carbuncles; cabbage leaves should be used instead of a bandage.

---

1. Greek *peganon agrion*: *Peganum harmala* L.

Drunk with mint and wine it expels roundworms and tapeworms. Drunk together with goat's milk it cures [maladies of] the chest. Smoked it drives away snakes.

They say that those who eat cress develop a sharper intellect.

It is rather unconducive to sexual acts. With honey it cures cough. It is applied to spreading ulcers. Its juice stops hair loss.

Cress shoots treat small ulcers and scurf on the head, if applied with goose fat.

With yeast, it brings boils to a head.

They say that its juice, applied through the ears, cures toothache.

28. *Chicory or endive.*[1] Didymos.

Chicory, or rather endive, is good for the stomach when dipped in vinegar and eaten. The juice, drunk without admixture, is extremely useful to those spitting blood. When ground and applied to the left nipple it cures those with cardiac ailments. Its juice is given to those with pain in the liver: plants are previously dried briefly in the sun and then ground.

If after new moon one turns towards the moon and swears in its name not to eat chicory or horsemeat for 40 days, one will suffer no toothache.

29. *Leeks.* Sotion.

Sotion advises, after sowing the leeks, that the leek-bed should be trodden immediately, not irrigated, and left untouched for three days, then irrigated on the fourth: this is the way in which they do best.

Leeks will be sturdiest if you mix sand with the soil when planting them. They will also grow big if when transplanting them you put a potsherd or flat stone underneath them and do not water them. Again, they will grow big if when transplanting them you pierce the head of the leek, into the centre, not using iron but a wooden peg or a sharp reed or the like, and insert a leek seed. The inserted seed makes the leek heal and swell. Some insert not a seed of the same kind but a turnip seed: this too makes it heal and grow bigger.

1. The two Greek words are *seris* (classical) and *troxima* (medieval): *Cichorium endivia* L.

Leeks will be much bigger if you collect the seed in three fingers, tie it up in an old linen cloth, rub it with manure, and immediately water. All the seeds together will produce one big leek. The same happens with celery.[1]

If one eats cumin before leeks, one's breath will not smell.

If you place ground leek on bites of pests and widow spider stings they will be more quickly cured by other drugs.

Boiled leek, taken with honey, is capable of treating all affections of the throat. Its seed, drunk together with sweet [wine], cures dysuria. Eaten regularly it darkens the eyes and is bad for the stomach. The juice, drunk with diluted honey, is helpful to those bitten by vermin; leek, [ground and] applied, also helps. As drops with vinegar and frankincense, or milk, or rose oil, it cures earaches and tinnitus and also boils that are painful at night.

Well-cooked leeks should be eaten frequently; they are as nourishing as meat.

This vegetable is good for those with pain in the side.

30. *Garlic.*

Garlic grows best where there is white earth.

Garlic, when eaten, expels intestinal worms and is diuretic. It aids those bitten by vipers and by mad dogs, when applied to the bite, and also when chewed. Burnt, mixed with honey and applied as ointment it cures black eyes and alopecia. Kept in the mouth it stops toothache. With olive oil and salt it treats eruptions and helps the dropsical. It also removes moles and sycosis. Eaten cooked or raw it alleviates chronic coughs, soothes a painful throat and clears the voice. If one eats garlic in advance one will be immune to pests and other noxious creatures. Ground and applied it cures the wounded; it is also very helpful if drunk with wine. It is rather useful to those unable to digest their food. It provokes urination, cures nephritis, prevents disease arising from bad water.

If you want sweeter garlic, bruise it before planting.

There is cultivated, garden garlic; there is also wild garlic ('snake garlic' as it is called). Wild garlic is more effective than cultivated in the therapies already listed.

1. See 12.23.

You will grow sweeter garlic if you add olive-pressings when planting.

It will be without odour if you sow and gather when the moon is under the earth.

Some say that it will give no odour if, after eating garlic, one chews a raw broad bean.

31. *Onions.*

When planting on onions remove their tails and tops, and they will grow big.

Twenty days before transplanting, dig and dry out the ground to remove all dew; then plant, and they will be much bigger, and if you peel the bulbs before setting them they will be bigger still. They will be finest in red earth, just as garlic in white earth.

To keep onions without rotting, drop them into hot water, dry them in the sun, and after drying store them, not touching one another, in barley chaff.

Onion, ground, with honey, is suitable to apply to any wound.

One who selects a tender onion each day and eats it at breakfast with honey will stay healthy.

So onion will make an ulcer healthy, whereas garlic, applied to the healthy body, will ulcerate it.

Onions, smeared on with vinegar in the sun, remove leprous patches; rubbed on they cure alopecia rather quickly. Their juice is good for purulent ears; as an ointment it relieves sore throat; it acts against dimmed sight. Baked onion is given to cure a cough.

32. *Hartwort.* Paxamos.

Hartwort,[1] chewed, treats sufferers from *nephritis* through urination. Its water, drunk one hour before bathing alongside a sweet drink, treats those with jaundice through perspiration. Hartwort, chewed with honey vinegar and vomited, purges the upper digestive tract, and treats *melancholia, anorexia* and quartan fever.

---

1. Greek *kaukalides*: *Tordylium apulum* L.

33. *Pennyroyal.* Leontinos.

Pennyroyal – dried, pounded and taken after a meal – aids digestion. Dried, chewed and applied to the eyes it cures ophthalmia at its height; once having tried it, you will prefer to use this on your eyes than the best-recommended eye-drops.

34. *Dill.*

Eating dill blurs the eyesight.

35. *Spearmint.*[1] Damegeron.

Skimbron, called spearmint by some, arouses the appetite and provokes urination. It likes temperate, dry air and a sunny site not shaded by any trees. It grows underground and spreads. It is sown and planted. If sown it is harvested only in the third year, but if one plants the top of the root (the eye, as some call it) from which the shoots grow, it can be harvested in that same year.

36. *Grape hyacinth bulbs.*[2] Anatolios.

Grape hyacinth bulbs will grow big if, as with leeks, you put a potsherd under the roots of the bulbs when you plant them.

Bulbs are planted from the new moon of November to the new moon of February.

37. *Squill.* Berytios.

If the flower of squill grows up like a staff, and does not quickly wither, it is a sign of a good harvest.

38. *Sorrel.* Africanus.

The fruit of wild sorrel, drunk with wine, cures heart [ailments] and dysentery; wrapped around the left arm it cures childlessness in women. The root of wild sorrel cures jaundice and dropsy; boiled

---

1. Greek *sisymbrion* (here also *skimbron*): probably *Mentha spicata* L.
2. Greek *bolbos*: *Muscari comosum* (L.) Miller.

with vinegar and used as poultice, is said to cure leprosy, also sycosis and leprous patches.

39. *Artichokes.* Varro.

Plant artichokes in November; then they will be full grown and will fruit in spring. When planted in spring it is hard for them to bear fruit in the same year; they will be dry, and their fruit scanty. Take the artichoke plants that grow beside the bigger stems, using a sharp pruning-hook to remove them at ground level (having previously dug away the earth around) and take some root with them. Plant them in ground that is dug over, adding old manure, and during the summer water them rather frequently: this will give you tenderer and somewhat plumper fruit.

You will make the artichokes aromatic if you steep the seed in water of rose, lily, bay or another aromatic species for 3 days and then sow. You will grow them without spines if you smooth off the sharp points on the seeds by rubbing them on a stone.

Some assert that at whatever date you plant artichokes, they will fruit at the same date, and in this way you can have artichokes all through the year.

You will produce bay-flavoured artichokes if you take a bay berry, pierce it, insert the artichoke seed in the hole, and so plant it. Again, they grow without spines if you peel a lettuce root, cut it into small sections, insert an artichoke seed in each section and so plant it.

Mice find artichoke roots very good to eat and will go a long way for them. We will keep them off by wrapping the roots in wool, or putting to the roots either pig manure or the ash from burning figs – either because of antipathy, or because they turn away from the smell.

You will produce sweet artichokes if you steep the seeds in milk and honey, dry them, and plant them.

40. *Purslane.* Paxamos.

Purslane, applied as a poultice, cures *erysipelas*. The leaf, placed under the tongue, makes one less thirsty.

41. *Growing mushrooms.* Tarantinos.

Cut down a black poplar. Dissolve yeast in water and pour it over the stump as it stands in the ground, and poplar mushrooms will soon grow.

If you want the earth to bear mushrooms for you, choose mountain soil that is thin and has previously grown mushrooms. Collect reeds and brushwood and anything that burns well, and when you see the sky cloudy as if heavy with rain, start a fire. You will then have mushrooms growing of their own accord. If no rain comes when you are making your bonfire, sprinkle fresh, clean water over the burned area in imitation of rain, and mushrooms will grow there, though poorer ones. Those nourished by rain are better.

Book 13

1. *Locusts.*[1] Demokritos.

Much has been said by early authors on driving away locusts. I have selected the more convenient methods to record here. If a cloud of locusts approaches, everyone should remain indoors; they will then fly past the farm. If the locusts arrive before this precaution can be taken, they will not land on anything that has been sprinkled with bitter lupins or squirting cucumbers boiled down in brine: that would immediately kill them.[2]

They will also fly past the farm if you catch some bats and hang them in your highest trees.

If you catch some of the locusts and burn them, [the others] will be stupefied by the smell: some will die, while others will fold their wings and wait to be caught, or will be killed by the sun. This arises from antipathy. Moreover, if you catch and burn a scorpion you will also catch the rest of the locusts, or drive them off.

The same works with ants, as experience shows; probably it would be similar with other such creatures.

You will drive off the locusts if you prepare a *garon* made of locusts, dig holes, and fill them with the *garon*. If you then go out before dawn you will find them in the holes, heavy with sleep. How you then kill them is up to you.

Locusts will not land on anything sprinkled with water in which wormwood, or leek, or knapweed[3] has been boiled down.

---

1. Greek *akris*: perhaps chiefly the desert locust, *Schistocerca gregaria* Forsskål, 1775.
2. Similarly Palladius, *On Agriculture* 1.35.12.
3. Greek *kentaurion*: *Centaurea* spp., e.g. *C. salonitana* Vis.

2. Brouchos.[1] Didymos.

Dig three mustard seeds in at the root of the vine around the stock. Where mustard is planted the smell kills the *brouchos*.

3. *Weasels.* Africanus.

Steep sal ammoniac, add wheat to the mixture, and scatter this around the places where weasels often go. They will either die of eating it, or will keep away.

They say that if one catches one of the weasels, cuts off its tail or testicles, and lets it go alive, one will not find any more of them afterwards on the same farm.

4. *House mice.* Paxamos.

House mice[2] are killed if you put down black hellebore[3] with barley meal.[4]

Or the seed of squirting cucumber with black hellebore and colocynth and barley meal.

They will also run away from copper sulphate,[5] and the seeds of oregano, celery and love-in-a-mist[6] burned as incense.

If you put oak ash near the hole they will get the itch from the ash and will die.

If you mix iron filings with yeast and put this where there are numerous mice, they will try eating it and will die.

If you want to blind the mice, pound spurge,[7] mix it with barley meal and honeyed wine, and put it down for them; they will eat it and will be blinded.

---

1. Another locust, perhaps *Locusta migratoria* Linnaeus, 1758.
2. Greek *mys katoikidios*: *Mus musculus* Linnaeus, 1758.
3. Greek *elleboros melas*: *Helleborus* spp., e.g. *Helleborus cyclophyllus* Boiss.
4. So Pliny, *Natural History* 25.61. For book 25 Pliny lists none of the sources named in the *Geoponika* (but he does list 'Apollodorus Tarentinus').
5. Greek *kalakanthon*. The word has several other meanings; Needham identifies here with *glaukion*, 'juice of the horned poppy'. A similar prescription against mosquitoes at 13.11.1.
6. Greek *melanthion*: *Nigella damascena* L.
7. Greek *tithymalon*: *Euphorbia* spp.

Anatolios and *Tarantinos* in *On the Granary*, in discussing the damage done by house mice, use those same preparations.

If you catch one, skin its head, and let it go, the others will run away.

If they eat the root of bramble, mixed with butter, bread and cheese, they will die.

Some people pound and sieve white hellebore[1] and the bark of dog's-bane[2] and make this into cakes with barley meal, eggs and milk, and put it into their holes.[3]

Mice will run away if haematite is burned as incense, and if green tamarisk is smoked.[4]

Anatolios says that if you pour *amorge* into a copper basin and put it down at night inside the house you will collect all the mice together. As to other methods he does not differ from *Didymos*.[5]

5. *Field mice.* Apuleius.

Apuleius prescribes ox bile to be smeared on the seeds; field mice will then not touch them.[6]

It is better to pound together the seed of hemlock[7] with hellebore and barley meal; or squirting cucumber or henbane[8] or bitter almonds and black hellebore, and add an equal part of barley meal; then knead in olive oil and place around the mouseholes. They will eat this and die.

Some farmers in Bithynia have succeeded by blocking the holes with oleander leaves,[9] so that as the field mice hurry to get out they will take the leaves with their teeth. When they bite them they will die.

---

1. Greek *elleboros leukos*: *Veratrum album* L.
2. Greek *kynokrambe*: *Trachomitum venetum* (L.) Woodson (syn. *Apocynum venetum*) or, according to Liddell and Scott, *Cionura erecta* (L.) Griseb.
3. The same preparation, attributed to Paxamos, is recommended for killing mole rats at 13.7.
4. Tamarisk burns well even when green owing to the wax content of the wood, according to Plants for a Future (www.pfaf.org).
5. Whose views are not given. Evidently at least one attribution is missing.
6. Similarly Palladius, *On Agriculture* 1.35.9.
7. Greek *koneion*: *Conium maculatum* L.
8. Greek *hyoskyamos*: *Hyoscyamus niger* L.
9. Greek *rhododaphne*: *Nerium oleander* L.

Take a piece of paper and write on it: *I conjure any mice caught here to do me no harm and to prevent other mice doing so. I give you the following land* (and name it). *If I find you still here, I take the Mother of the Gods to witness, I will cut you into seven pieces.* After writing this, fix the paper before sunrise against a natural rock in the field where the mice are (the writing must be visible on the outside). I included this instruction rather than omit anything, but I reject such practices (may they not be true!) I advise others to do the same, and never to use such ridiculous methods.

6. *A cat.* Sotion.

A cat will not bite any bird under whose wing you have fastened wild rue.[1]

7. *Mole rats.* Paxamos.

If you want to destroy mole rats[2] take white hellebore and the bark of dog's-bane, pound and sieve with barley meal and egg, steep in wine and milk, make into cakes and put into their holes.[3]

Pierce a wooden pot, or any similar narrow device, fill it with chaff and a sufficient quantity of cedar oil and brimstone. Where the mole rat lives, stop up all the smaller holes so that smoke will not get out through them, and put the base of the pot into the larger hole so that the air will draw through, sealing the hole around it in some way, and blow through so that the smoke carries in all the smell of the cedar oil and brimstone. If you go around all the mole rats' nests and carry out the same procedure, you will destroy them all.[4]

8. *Snakes.* Florentinus.

No snakes will enter the farm if you plant wormwood or mugwort[5] or southernwood around the farmstead; you will drive away those

1. Repeated at 14.15. The reference may be to hens or chickens in particular (see note at 14.15); see also 14.4.
2. Greek *aspalax*: *Nannospalax leucodon* (Nordmann, 1840) and possibly *Spalax graecus* Nehring, 1898, which was once familiar in southeastern Europe.
3. The same preparation is recommended for killing house mice at 13.4.
4. Similarly Palladius, *Agriculture* 1.35.10.
5. Greek *artemisia*: *Artemisia vulgaris* L.

that are already there if you make smoke with white lily root or stag's horn or goat's hoof.

You will drive away all snakes if you chop and mix asafoetida, love-in-a-mist, galbanum, hyssop, brimstone, pellitory-of-Spain,[1] hog's fennel,[2] and goat's hoofs, grind them, add sharp vinegar, form into small balls and make smoke with them. The smoke of any one of these alone will drive off snakes.

Some say that fronds of pomegranate leaves ward off noxious creatures; this is why, for safety's sake, they are included among the leaves spread in *stibades*.[3]

Snakes will not trouble the pigeon-house if in its four corners you write *Adam*: if it has windows, write it at these too.[4]

Demokritos says that a snake does not move when an ibis feather is thrown at it; it dies when oak leaves are thrown on it,[5] and when someone who has taken no food spits into its mouth.

Apuleius says that a snake, when struck once with a reed, is stupefied, but when struck several times becomes stronger.[6]

When a snake is going into its hole, if one catches its tail with the left hand one will easily pull it out again; if with the right hand it will be impossible to get it out. Either it will escape, or the tail will break off.

Tarantinos says that a snake will not approach the smeared juice of dragon arum,[7] or the smeared juice or seed of radish;[8] those who merely carry these things will not be harmed; those bitten by a snake are cured if rose root is applied.

Florentinus says that a snake does not approach where there is deer fat, or knapweed root, or the stone called lignite, or dittany, and the excrement of eagle or kite.[9]

---

1. Greek *pyrethron*: *Anacyclus pyrethrum* (L.) Link.
2. Greek *peukedanon*: *Peucedanum officinale* L.
3. Mats or bedding used in outdoor dining.
4. Repeated at 14.5. Needham notes that *ADAM* stands for the four corners of the world (*Anatole, Dysis, Arktos, Mesembria*: east, west, north, south).
5. Repeated at 15.1.
6. Repeated at 15.1.
7. Greek *drakonteia*: *Dracunculus vulgaris* Schott.
8. Similarly at 12.22.
9. Partly repeated at 15.1.

[...] mixed with storax and smoked they drive pests away.[1]

In treating those bitten by a viper, first give them to drink the juice of manna ash leaves – in wine if they have no fever, in wine diluted with water if they are feverish. Apply the pressed-out leaves to the bite as a poultice.

Put physalis root[2] to a cobra[3] and you will send it to sleep.

Emulsify caltrops in water and place this mixture in the snakes' hole: it will drive them away.

If you sink jars of salt fish around the farmhouse, all the pests will fall into them; you can then stop up the jars, take them outside the farm boundary, and burn them.

9. *Scorpions.* Diophanes.

If you catch one scorpion and burn it, other scorpions will run away.

If you rub your hands carefully with radish juice, you can pick up scorpions and other such creatures without fear and without danger; and radishes, placed on scorpions, destroy them immediately.[4]

You will cure the sting of a scorpion by sealing the spot with a silver signet-ring.

Smoking with sandarac,[5] galbanum and butter or goat fat will drive away scorpions and all such creatures.

By frying a scorpion in olive oil and anointing the place where someone has been stung by a scorpion you will alleviate the pain.

Apuleius says that someone stung by a scorpion should sit on a donkey, facing backwards towards the tail; the donkey will suffer the pain and will fart.

Demokritos says that if someone stung by a scorpion immediately says to the donkey: 'A scorpion has stung me,' he will not suffer the pain: it will be transferred to the donkey.[6] The gecko has an antipathy

1. This sentence does not link grammatically to the preceding one: there appears to be something missing.
2. Greek *halikakabos*: possibly *Physalis alkekengi* L.
3. Greek *aspis*: asp or Egyptian cobra, *Naja haje* (Linnaeus, 1758).
4. Similarly at 12.22.
5. Greek *sandarache*: resin of citronwood, *Tetraclinis articulata* (Vahl) Masters, the same species whose wood was used to make dining tables in classical Rome.
6. This and the previous item are repeated at 15.1.

for the scorpion; so if you dissolve a gecko in olive oil and anoint the sufferer with the oil, you will cure him of the pain. The same author says that those stung by a scorpion are treated by placing a rose root[1] [on the sting].

Plutarch fastens a hazelnut on the legs of couches, so that scorpions will not climb them; he says that a scorpion will not go near a hazelnut.[2]

Zoroaster says that lettuce seed, drunk in wine, is the treatment for one stung by a scorpion.

Florentinus says that when someone has just been stung by a scorpion, if you drip fig sap on the sting the poison will not spread further. Also, if the sufferer eats squill, he will not suffer, so long as he says that the squill is sweet to the taste.

Tarantinos says that if you are holding the plant *sideritis*[3] you can pick up live scorpions and not be stung by them.

10. *Ants.* Paxamos.

If you catch and burn some ants you will drive away the rest of them, as experience has proved.

If you spread cedar oil around their holes, ants will not come on to the threshing-floor.

Ants will not attack a heap of grain if you draw round the heap with white earth, or put wild oregano[4] around it.

You will drive ants from their holes if you burn snail-shells with storax,[5] pound them and put them in the ant-hills.

Likewise you will drive ants away if you pound together oregano and brimstone and sprinkle this around the ant-hills.

Ants are completely destroyed if you put Cyrenaic silphium resin,[6] dissolved in olive oil, to the ant-hill.

1. Greek *rodon*: *Rosa* spp.
2. Not found in any of Plutarch's surviving works, this is Plutarch fragment 185 Sandbach.
3. Unluckily for those tempted to rely on the statement, this name was applied to many plants, most often *Stachys heraclea* All. and *Sideritis romana* L.
4. Greek *agrion origanon*: *Origanum* spp., e.g. *Origanum onites* L., *Origanum heracleoticum* L.
5. Greek *styrax*: Resin of *Styrax officinalis* L. or *Liquidambar orientalis* Mill.
6. Greek *opos Kyrenaikos*.

Ants will not attack trees if you smear the trunks with bitter lupin seeds kneaded with *amorge*, or with pitch mixed with oil or boiled.

Ants will not attack a honey pot, even if its lid is off, if you put white wool around it or draw round it with white earth or red earth.

Some dissolve silphium resin in vinegar and pour it into their holes.

If we tie dense ivy around the trunks of vines we will soon find not only ants but also beetles under the shade of the ivy, ready to be caught and destroyed.

Ants are completely destroyed by the smoke from burning the root of squirting cucumber, or if catfish, especially mudfish,[1] is burned on a slow fire.

When one ant is taken away the others will leave the nest.

If with the thumb of the left hand one takes an ear of corn that was being carried by an ant, and puts it into red leather, and ties it around a woman's head, it will serve to make her sterile.

When some ants are burned others will be driven away by the smell.

I have heard it said that a dead ant is carried away by another ant on its shoulders.

You will keep ants off by mixing bull's bile and pitch with *amorge* and smearing the base of the trunk [of a tree] with this. Red earth mixed with pitch and smeared on has the same effect. Some hang the fish called *korakinos*[2] in the tree, and destroy ants in that way.

11. *Mosquitoes.* Demokritos.

Horsehair stretched across the door and through the interior of the house destroys mosquitoes and prevents them from entering.

Copper sulphate and love-in-a-mist, smoked, drive them away.

If you soak a sponge in sharp vinegar and hang it at your head and at your feet [when in bed], the mosquitoes will not bite you.

---

1. Greek *silouros*, a catfish such as *Silurus glanis* Linnaeus, 1758; *silouros Alexandrinos*, the dried Nile catfish or mudfish *Clarias anguillaris* (Linnaeus, 1758). See Dalby 2003 pp. 233, 299–300.
2. See note on 20.9.

You will drive the mosquitoes off if you steep rue and sprinkle the house; and boil fleabane and sprinkle the house with the decoction; or boil galbanum, or incense, or cumin.

The mosquitoes will not bite you if you place a flowering sprig of hemp beside you when going to sleep.

They will not come near you if you rub yourself with manna in vinegar and olive oil.[1]

They will retreat from the smoke of vinegar, wood and oregano.

Dung, smoked and smeared on the walls, drives off mosquitoes.

They will retreat if you smoke the outer walls with 1 scruple fleabane, 2 scruples ammoniac incense, 2 scruples storax, 2 drams burned trumpet-shells,[2] crushed together.[3]

A sponge soaked in vinegar, hung from the ceiling, will bring them all together.

Mosquitoes will not harm someone in bed who is lying on hemp leaves.

Steep rue in water, or boil fleabane and sprinkle the house: this will drive off the mosquitoes.

Smoked bdellium[4] also expels them.

12. *Flies.* Berytios.

Bay pounded with black hellebore and soaked in milk or sweet wine or hydromel,[5] or in water, and sprinkled, will kill flies.

If you pound cassia with olive oil and rub it on they will not land on you.

To drive them off, burn copper sulphate. A decoction of elderberry leaves, sprinkled, also drives them off.

Anatolios says that if you want to gather them all into one spot, dig a hole, pound oleander leaves and put them in it: you will collect them all there.

1. Manna, the excretion of insects found on the leaves of certain tree species, had various uses in ancient medicine; see Donkin 1980.
2. Greek *keryx*: probably *Charonia tritonis* (Linnaeus, 1758).
3. Something resembling silphium: Dioscorides, *Materia Medica* 3.84; used in imitations of more expensive aromatics, ib. 2.24, 3.48.
4. Greek *bdellion*: resin of *Commiphora mukul* (Hook. ex Stocks) Engl.
5. See 8.28.

Flies will not harm cattle if you boil bay berries, [mix them] with olive oil and rub them with it.

Flies will never settle on your beasts if you rub them with lion fat.

Hellebore soaked in milk or grape syrup, with arsenic, kills flies.

If you anoint with a paste of alum and oregano, they will not settle.

13. *Bats.* Africanus.

If you hang plane leaves in their path, they will not approach.

Smoked ivy kills bats.[1]

14. *Bugs.*[2] Didymos.

Liquid pitch and the juice of squirting cucumber put on a bed kills the bugs. Otherwise squill chopped up, made into a paste with vinegar and spread on the bed with a sponge.

Otherwise, smear the joints of the beds with citron leaves, boiled, with olive oil.

And, mix bull's or goat's bile with sharp vinegar and smear the bed and the walls. The same effect is produced if you make a paste of old olive oil and natural sulphur and coat the bed with it.

There will be no bugs if you boil fish glue and coat the beds. You will kill existing bugs if you mix boiled *amorge* into ox bile with olive oil and sprinkle it on them.

Or make a paste of ivy or caper leaves in olive oil and smear it on the beds. If sprinkled, this also kills bugs that are on the walls.

An effective poison is made as follows. A saucer of stavesacre,[3] the same quantity of finely chopped squill and a spoonful of sharp vinegar are pounded finely together, warmed, and smeared on the site. One part of cedar oil and four parts of sweet wine gives the same effect; also if you smear goat or calf bile, the same quantity of sweet wine, and vinegar.

1. Repeated at 15.1.
2. Greek *koris*: *Cimex lectularius* Linnaeus, 1758.
3. Greek *staphis agria*: *Delphinium staphisagria* L.

Florentinus says that just as smoking bugs kills leeches,[1] smoking leeches kills bugs, as long as the couch is curtained off with drapes so that they get no relief from the smell.

Millipede, dried and smoked, gives the same effect.

And pounded ivy leaves.

And 10 leeches.

Demokritos says that feet of hares or deer, tied on to the bedposts behind the headboard, stop bugs.

When travelling, if you fill a vessel with cold water and put it under your bed, they will not bite you while you are asleep. Pouring hot water on them, as people always do, kills the existing bugs but it does not prevent their rapid reappearance.

15. *Fleas*[2] *in the house.* Pamphilos.

Dig a hole; grind oleander leaves and place in it: they will all gather there.

Wormwood or squirting cucumber root,[3] steeped in brine and sprinkled, destroys them.

Or sprinkle a decoction of fleabane.

Or, mustard seed destroys them, and oleander, boiled in both cases, and sprinkled in the room.

After sweeping the floor, scatter sieved slaked lime: this kills them.

Otherwise, soak the floor repeatedly with *amorge*; then grind wild cumin and mix with water, and grind 10 drams of squirting cucumber seed and add to the water; sprinkle this in the room and you will make the fleas split.

Or soak wormwood and squirting cucumber root in seawater, or spurge-olive root –

And some black poplar leaves pounded and soaked in water.

– or caltrops boiled in water.

Sprinkling sharp salt, also seawater, destroys them.

1. Compare 13.17.
2. Greek *psylla*: principally *Pulex irritans* Linnaeus, 1758.
3. Similarly Palladius 1.35.8.

If one places a bowl in the middle of the house, and draws a circle around it with a pure iron blade (especially one that has killed a man) and sprinkles the rest of the house, outside the circle, with the liquor from pounded stavesacre or bay leaves that have been soaked and boiled in brine or seawater, this will collect all the fleas in the bowl.

Or write on the entrance door, when no one is looking, before 15th May, [...][1]

Also bury an earthenware vessel so that its lip is at ground level, smear it with bull's fat, and it will collect all the fleas, even those that are in garments.

If you ever go into a place where there are fleas, say *Och! Och!* and they will not bite you.

One who digs a small hole under the bed and pours goat's blood into it will collect all the fleas to that spot and will attract those from other garments;[2] even the fleas in the thickest and double-pile carpets, where they nestle when they are full, can be got out if these are placed inside a wooden chest or earthenware vat.[3]

16. *Beetles.* Zoroaster.

Kantharides will not damage the vines if you soak some of these *kantharides* and with them smear the whetstone with which you are to sharpen your pruning-hooks.[4]

If you burn galbanum with old dung you will drive them off.

Otherwise, by smoking the roots of squirting cucumber you will chase them off.

Aristotle says that the smell of roses kills dung-beetles[5] and the smell of perfume kills vultures;[6] the explanation is that a good smell is a bad smell to these creatures.

Many people put a wreath of ivy on the ground around the stock of each vine; they then find the beetles in the shade of the ivy and kill them.

1. The words are missing from all manuscripts.
2. I.e. in addition to those in clothes that are being worn.
3. Along with a bowl of goat's blood? The instruction is not clear.
4. Similarly 5.49 (see note there).
5. Greek *kantharos*: beetles mainly of sub-family *Scarabaeinae*. Repeated at 14.26.
6. Repeated at 14.26 and 15.1.

17. *Leeches.* Anatolios.

If an ox or other quadruped swallows a leech while drinking, squash some bugs, let the animal smell them and it will immediately eject [the leech].

18. *Frogs.* Africanus.

Frogs will stop their croaking if you light a candle and put it on the river-bank.

Book 14

1. *Pigeons.* Florentinus.

Keeping pigeons is extremely advantageous to those engaged in farming, notably because they produce useful manure, also because their chicks are necessary in the removal of illnesses.[1] Their keeping also brings no little profit. They are only fed by their keepers for two months each year: during the rest of the year they get their own food by foraging. The pigeon is also a very prolific creature. Every forty days it conceives, lays, hatches and feeds its chicks, and this throughout the year. With the sole exception of the period from the winter solstice to the spring equinox the pigeon lays all year round, and you may see pigeons, while still feeding up their chicks, carrying and laying eggs once again. The young, as soon as they are full grown, begin to lay at the same time as their parents. This creature likes to eat grass pea, bitter vetch, fenugreek, pea, lentil, wheat, and also the so-called darnel that grows in the wheat.

You should prevent them flying off, because they might lay elsewhere: they should not be distracted into flying out but occupy themselves in producing young. If there is a shortage of food allow only those with young to fly out, because these, when they have fed, will quickly return bringing food for their chicks.

2. *To make pigeons stay and mate.* Didymos.

Smear the doors, windows and corners of the pigeon-house with oil of balsam of Mecca,[2] and they will stay.

---

1. A curious claim unsupported elsewhere in the text.
2. Greek *opobalsamon*: *Commiphora opobalsamum* Engl.

Pigeons will not fly away if you soak cumin and lentil in honey water and scatter this around.

If you give them honey water to drink, or boil lentils in must and give them to eat, you will encourage them to mate.

The following prescription is also given to prevent pigeons flying away. Mix together sifted potsherd and cost and aromatic old wine and give it as food to those going out foraging.

Some knead together boiled barley meal with dried figs, add one part of honey, and give as food.

Others give cumin to those going out foraging.

Pigeons will stay if you put a bat's head on the tower.[1]

Or, at flowering time, place in the pigeon-house fronds of wild vine with the flowers.

3. *To make pigeons stay and attract others to join them.* Africanus.

If you smear the pigeons with perfume they will bring in others from outside.

If you throw cumin seeds to those going out foraging you will retain them and make many others join them, attracted by the smell of cumin.

If you take chaste-tree seed, soak it in old wine for three days, then take bitter vetch and soak in the wine, and throw this to pigeons, you will entice them: noticing the smell on the air, other pigeons will all enter the dovecote.

You will make pigeons come in more quickly if you smoke the pigeon-house with sage[2] and frankincense.

4. *To stop the cat disturbing the pigeons.* Sotion.

On the windows and entrances to the pigeon-house, and on additional spots inside it, place and hang sprigs of rue. Rue has something antipathetic to predators.

---

1. In this instruction *pyrgos* 'tower' is used in place of *peristereon* 'pigeon-house'. A third term, *kalia*, is used below (translated 'dovecote').
2. Greek *elelisphakos*: *Salvia* spp.

5. *To stop snakes entering the pigeon-house.* Demokritos.

Snakes will not trouble the pigeon-house if in its four corners you write *Adam*: if it has windows, write it at these too.[1]

You will drive off the snakes if you smoke with hog's fennel.

6. *The pigeon-house.* The Quintilii.

During calm weather, make a building, secured against the entrance of wild animals, and plaster it carefully. In the walls, from floor to roof, make nesting-places – some call them *sekoi*, but we say niches[2] – where the pairs of pigeons will live and lay their eggs. Each niche must have doors by which it is entered. Inside the building dig a relatively large pool so that they can drink from it and wash in it, and so that people do not have to disturb the birds frequently (because that is very bad for them) in order to provide them with water. It is, however, not ruled out for people to enter. The building has to be swept out sometimes; the dung has to be taken away; and the inside has to be checked for possible threats, in case it is attacked by snakes or other such creatures.

Aiming to prevent attack by pests, I chose a particular site with no buildings near, but quite isolated, and fetched pillars to it, eight in number but it could have been more,[3] depending on the size of the intended structure. I set them up not in a straight line, but in a circuit, and then placed capitals on each, and then, on top of the capitals, architraves of stone (but if I had no stone I could have used very sturdy timber architraves)[4] and on these I erected two buildings to a height of seven cubits, with a window in their western walls for light, and a window on the east with a hatch in it for the birds to go out for food, and a door on the south side so that the person who

1. Repeated from 13.8.
2. The preferred Greek word is *kythrinos*. *Sekos* really meant 'sheepfold'; *seka* was a word used by shepherds to call their sheep home.
3. The words 'eight in number but it could have been more' are omitted in two manuscripts and in the Latin translation. It is indeed hard to see how two buildings of useful plan can be erected on eight pillars arranged in a circle.
4. I.e. horizontal beams spanning the pillars. The words 'of stone, but if I had no stone I could have used very sturdy' are omitted in the same two manuscripts and in the Latin translation.

looks after the birds could enter. That was how I made the pigeons safe. pests could not enter using the pillars because they were very carefully plastered with mud and smoothed off, while cats and other animals could not jump in because there were no other buildings nearby from which they could make their attack.

One who wishes to set up a pigeon-house should not begin with young pigeons but with broody ones. If there are ten pairs to start with they will multiply quickly.

7. *Poultry.* Florentinus.

Domestic fowl should be housed in relatively warm and waterproof buildings in which smoke is produced. On the walls we will place nesting-boxes in which they can lay, making them from board and spreading chaff on the bases so that new-laid eggs will not drop on a hard surface and break. Rods on which the birds can perch should project from the walls. For their food they should be given boiled barley or millet or wheat bran or darnel, the so-called *zizanion*, which is excellent food for them, or tree-medick leaves in water: this also makes them very prolific. When they are laying it is important to ensure that they do not eat grape pips, because this makes them sterile.

Hens that feed on their own eggs can be prevented from doing so as follows: extract the white from an egg; then, around the yolk, the yellow that is, inject liquid gypsum so that it will solidify. Next time they are greedy they will be able to get nothing out, and will stop spoiling their eggs.

They fatten well and get very plump if they are housed in a dark, warm building, with their pinions plucked, and are fed on barley meal kneaded in water.

Others use meal of barley and darnel mixed, or barley and linseed with raw bruised wheatmeal. Others add pearl barley; others again pour in some wine.

Some soak wheat bread in good wine and give them this.

Most people feed them on millet.

One who wishes to keep poultry must choose hens that are particularly fertile. This is learned from practice and experience, but there are certain useful pointers.[1] Those that are golden-coloured, with extra claws, with a high comb, with black wings, and big-bodied, bear the male easily and are better layers and lay bigger eggs that produce finer chicks. No more than fifty birds should be kept in the henhouse – overcrowding kills them – and one-sixth of the total should be cocks. Eggs, as soon as laid, should be taken and placed in bran in a vessel.

When we want the hens to hatch their eggs we put clean chaff under them with an iron nail somewhere in it: this seems to protect against all mischances.[2] Not more than 23 eggs should be put under a good bird; fewer under those that are not so good, depending on their capacity; but it should always be an odd number, and this should be done under a waxing moon, that is, from new moon to the 14th of the lunar month. Eggs covered between then and the next new moon die. Eggs to be hatched should be those laid from when *zephyros* begins to blow until the autumn equinox, that is, between 7 February and 22 September: these should be set aside so that chicks can be raised. Those laid before or after this period, and all 'firstborn' eggs, should not be covered: they are sterile and unproductive.

The best period for covering eggs is from the spring equinox, that is, from 24th March. Eggs should be put under the older birds, not those that are in their prime for laying. They are in their prime for laying when one year old, and particularly when two years old; when older than this, less so.

Those that have spurs, like cocks, should not be allowed to hatch eggs: they will make holes in them. After the eggs have been placed, the birds should be put in the henhouse and shut in, so that they will cover them all day and all night. The henhouse should be opened at dawn and dusk, to give their usual food and drink, and then shut again; the birds that do not willingly go back inside should be made to do so. The hand whose job this is should turn the eggs every day so that they are evenly covered. Four days after they are laid, the eggs can be checked for fertility, by eye, by holding them up to the sun. If something fibrous and bloody can be seen inside, it will be [fertile];

1. An almost identical sentence occurs at 14.16, in the first paragraph of a chapter attributed to Florentinus.
2. Compare Columella, *On Agriculture* 8.5.12.

if it is clear, it should be discarded as sterile. Other eggs can be set for covering in place of those rejected. There is no need to worry that eggs will die if they are frequently and gently turned: such treatment never does them any harm. Do not set a single hen to covering eggs, but always three or four on the same day. Chicks just hatched can be taken immediately from each hen and placed under the one that has fewest (while eggs not yet hatched can be shared among all the hens still sitting to be covered and so hatched) but the one that has fewest should never be given more than thirty chicks.

Cold is the worst enemy of the domestic hen.[1]

You can test whether eggs are good by putting them in water: any egg that floats is empty and useless, while those that are full will sink to the bottom. Do not test them by shaking them, because this may destroy the life in them.

Some put eggs of other kinds under the domestic hen. It is worth knowing that they hatch pheasant eggs, just like their own, in 21 days. Peacock and goose eggs are hatched in 29,[2] so if you calculate the days as stated they will be hatched about seven or eight days after the hen's own chickens.

In Alexandria in Egypt there are fowl called *monosiroi* from which fighting-cocks are bred. They lay two or three times in succession. Each successive brood is taken from them to be raised separately, and each bird sits for 42 or 63 days.

8. *How to hatch chickens without a hen.* Demokritos.

You can have plenty of chicks without any bird to cover them by adopting the following method. On the same day on which you put the [new-laid] eggs under the laying hen, take chicken dung, pound it fine, sieve it into incubating jars; on it place hens' feathers; on this place the eggs, upright with the narrow end upwards, and put more of the dung all around them until they are completely covered. Leave them for two or three days; after that, turn them daily, taking care that they do not touch one another, so that they are evenly 'covered'. After the twentieth day, when eggs covered by

1. Expanded at 14.9.
2. 20 and 27 according to Varro, *On Agriculture* 3.9.10.

hens begin to hatch, those in the incubators will begin to break open as well. For this reason people label them with the date of laying so as not to lose track of the days. On the twentieth day, then, take off the shells, give the chicks some bits of food by hand, put them in a basket with some hens' feathers in it, take them to the hen, and she will look after all of them.

To provide their food, take barley-yeast and bran and soak in water; also take donkey or horse dung, put [all this] into the jars, and after three days maggots will develop suitable for feeding the chicks.

9. *Caring for chickens.* Didymos.

Chicks are put straight into a basket and suspended over a little smoke. For two days they take no food.

Seal the vessel from which they are fed with cow-dung.

When they first begin to feed, for fifteen days they get pearl barley with cress seed and wine, soaked in water. The place they are in is smoked with one of the products that drive pests away.

For the first forty days they must be always under cover; it is essential to keep them in a well-warmed hutch. The cold is their worst enemy.

An antipathy has been discovered that prevents chickens being attacked by cats [...] soaked in advance. If this is given them to drink they will not be attacked.

If rue is fastened under the wings of birds no cat or fox or other such creature will bite them;[1] all the more so if fox or cat bile is kneaded into their food, *Demokritos* assures us.

10. *Producing eggs with writing.* Africanus.

Grind oak gall and alum with vinegar until they are as thick as black ink. Write on the egg whatever you wish and let the ink dry in the sun. Then dip the egg in strong brine, dry it, boil it, take off the shell and you will find the writing [on the white].

If you cover the egg with wax, then inscribe writing on it – scraping the wax entirely off the shell to form the letters – and then

---

1. See note at 14.15.

leave the egg soaking in vinegar overnight, on the next day you can take off the wax: you will find that the vinegar has made [the shell] translucent in the shape of the letters.

11. *Making hens produce large eggs; keeping eggs.* Leontinos.

You will make hens produce large eggs if you crush Laconian pots, mix the powder with bran, moisten it with wine and give it to them; or mix a saucer of crushed pot with two *choinikes* of bran and give as food.

Some who want large eggs to be produced crumble up red earth and mix it with their food.

Hens do not 'miscarry' if you cook white of egg, pound an equal quantity of dried raisins, and give them the mixture before their other food.

Some fumigate the henhouses, the nesting-places, and the hens themselves with brimstone, asphalt and pine-wood; or they put some scrap of iron, or nail-heads, and sprays of bay in nesting-places; these serve as antidote against divine portents.[1]

In winter, store eggs in chaff; in summer, store them in bran.

Others rinse eggs in water, roll them in fine salt, and keep them thus.[2]

Some dip them in warm brine for 3 or 4 hours, then take them out and put them away in bran or chaff.

Of those that are kept in brine or salt, some will go bad.

Whether eggs are full or empty can be determined by putting them in water; an empty egg will float but a full one will sink.

12. *To stop cocks crowing.* Same author.

Soak oregano and give it this to drink.

Or wash with urine.

Or rub its 'nose' with garlic; or put garlic in water and give it this to drink.

---

1. Literally 'signs from Zeus', and sometimes meaning simply 'thunder and lightning', but here rather 'abortions and monstrous births'.
2. More fully Columella, *On Agriculture* 8.6.1.

13. *To blind hens.* Berytios.

Mix asafoetida with honey, soak wheat in this, and feed them with it.

14. *To prevent abortion in hens.* Pamphilos.

A hen will not abort its eggs if you bake yolk of egg, pound an equal part of dried grapes, and give it this before other food.

15. *To stop a cat harming a bird.* Africanus.[1]

A cat will not bite a bird if wild rue is tied under its wing.

16. *Cocks.* Florentinus.

One must select the most warlike of the cocks. This is learned from practice and experience, and from certain useful pointers.[2] The best cocks are those with compact bodies, with purple combs, with short beaks, alert, with black eyes, with rosy wattles, with stocky necks, with varied colours, with scaly legs that are rather sturdy than long and have strong spurs with sharp tips, and with big, bushy tails. In addition, those that are proud, vocal and tenacious in fighting, but not starting the fight, rather defending themselves vigorously when attacked; and those that do not retreat from predators but defend the females from the attack of such creatures.

Cocks should be given as food tree-medick seeds and [dried] leaves soaked in water – these are just as nutritious for them as fresh leaves.

17. *Particular treatments for poultry.* Paxamos.

You may treat the eyes of fowl by bathing the outer eye with human milk or with purslane juice; or pound together equal quantities of sal ammoniac, cumin and honey, and again apply as ointment; and also keep them in the dark.

---

1. Repeated from 13.6 (attributed there to Sotion) and 14.9. Greek *ornis* means either 'bird' in general or 'hen' in particular: the context here implies that 'hen' or 'chicken' is intended, or so the compiler understood.
2. See note at 14.7.

You will cure diarrhoea with a handful of barley grains and an equal quantity of wax, mixed with wine and formed into cakes, given to them before other food.

Or a decoction of apples or quinces as drink; good for the eyes too.

You will relieve them of lice thus: pound an equal quantity of roasted cumin and stavesacre, mix with wine and anoint the fowl; then wash with the water from boiling wild lupin seeds.[1]

Dirty drinking water gives them *koryza*, so they must be given clean water. You may treat *koryza* thus: chop cloves of garlic[2] finely, put it into hot olive oil and bring to the boil again: bathe their mouths with this. If they eat it, it will be an even better treatment. Stavesacre on its own or mixed with vetch also helps; also squill, cleaned and steeped in water, then given to them with barley grains. If the *koryza* is more serious, prick them under the cheek with iron, squeeze out what is around the eyes, and rub the wounds with fine salt. Some burn oregano, hyssop and thyme[3] and hold the bird's head over the smoke, also rubbing the beak with garlic. Some boil garlic in human urine and rub the beak with this delicately, avoiding touching the eyes.

18. *Peacocks.* Didymos.

Peacocks are best kept on man-made islands; they must at any rate have an area with plenty of herbage and parkland. Strong ones must be separated from weak ones: the better are troublesome to the poorer. Females start laying in their third year (younger ones either fail to lay, or do not feed their chicks). As food, in winter, give them before anything else beans roasted on the embers, six *kyathoi* to each bird; also give them clean water, because this makes them more fertile. When they are laying spread greenstuff or chaff all over the floor of the hutch so that the eggs do not break when

1. Greek *agrios thermos*: *Lupinus* spp., e.g. *Lupinus angustifolius* L., and perhaps the wild forms of the cultivated species, in the Balkans *Lupinus albus* subsp. *graecus* (Boiss. & Spun.) Franko & Silva; in the Near East *Lupinus albus* subsp. *termis* (Forsk.) Ponert.
2. Greek *skorda*: *Allium sativum* L.
3. Greek *thymon*: *Thymus* spp., e.g. *Thymus vulgaris* L.

they drop: they lay standing. They lay twice a year, and not more than 12 eggs in total. Eggs can be put under them, on the ninth day of the lunar month, to a total of nine, five of their own and four hens' eggs. Ten days later take away the hens' eggs and put others there instead, so that on the thirtieth day the peahens' eggs and the hens' eggs will hatch together. The young need be given no food for the first two days. From the third day we should give them barley meal kneaded with wine, bran bruised and boiled, and the tenderest leaves of leek pounded with green cheese.[1] After six months they can also be fed barley.

19. *Pheasants, guinea-fowl, partridges and francolins.* Varro.

These birds must be fed just as we have described for peafowl. They fatten when shut in. On the first day they take no food. On the next, give them honey-water or wine, and as food, raw bruised wheat or barley meal made into a paste with water. Give it to each of them separately, and bit by bit; then boil ground beanmeal, and pearl barley, and good millet, and linseed, and mix these with the wheatmeal, and add olive oil to make cakes from all this, and feed them till they cannot eat any more. Some add fenugreek for 5 or 6 days, so that the birds will be purged of their bile and cleansed. For the most part they are fattened for sixty days.

Health treatment for these species of birds is the same as that already described for domestic fowl.

20. *Partridges.* Berytios.

Partridges have a very hot temperament as regards mating; hence the males fight one another, jealous over the females. Whenever there is a group of female birds and two males, the males will immediately begin to fight, and the contest will only end when one of them is defeated and withdraws. All the females will then follow the male that came off better; he will then exultantly tread the defeated male, who will afterwards follow him among the crowd of females.

---

1. I.e. fresh cheese. Similarly Columella, *On Agriculture* 8.11.14; Palladius, *On Agriculture* 1.28.

21. *Hunting partridges and other game birds.* Anatolios.

You will quickly catch partridges if you throw them wheatmeal soaked in wine.

You will readily trap any game bird if you put out for it in vessels wine lightly diluted with water: after drinking it will immediately become drowsy and will not run away from its captors.

22. *Geese.* The Quintilii.

Choose the biggest and whitest geese. Make their enclosure in a place with plenty of grass and water. As food give them any pulses except bitter vetch;[1] feed them lettuce leaves, too, but do not let them eat dog's-tooth grass, which gives them indigestion.

They produce eggs three times a year, up to twelve eggs – some even more – and they must sit on some of these.

The chicks have to stay indoors for their first few days. If the weather is good we can lead them out to find their food. When they have fed well they can be led to water, too, but make sure they are not hurt by nettles or thorns.[2] Make sure, too, that in drinking they do not swallow goat's or pig's hair, which would kill them.

As soon as the chicks hatch from their eggs give them cooked barley meal and soaked wheat as food, with green cress.[3]

Geese are fattened in warm sheds: two parts of barley meal and four parts of bran, moistened with warm water and fed to them as much as they will eat. They eat three times a day and in the middle of the night and are given plenty to drink. After thirty days, if you want to make their livers large,[4] chop up dried figs very finely, mix them with water and give this to them as a drink for 20 days.[5]

---

1. Palladius, *On Agriculture* 1.30.3 evidently intends to forbid this same species, though the text varies (*excepto erobo/eruo/herbo*).
2. Similarly Palladius, *On Agriculture* 1.30.3.
3. Greek *kardamon*: *Lepidium sativum* L.
4. In the manuscripts this clause reads merely 'After they are large'. The extended version in the text is based on the Syriac text, on the repeated text later in this chapter, and on comparison with Palladius's *On Agriculture* (see next note).
5. This section is almost identical with Palladius, *On Agriculture* 1.30.4, where the method is attributed to 'the Greeks'. Part of it is repeated, with minor variation, below.

The eggs of each goose must be separately marked, and must be placed under the mother, because these birds will not sit the eggs of another. The eggs should be placed under for 9 to 11 days at the most, never less than 7.

They are broody for 27 days for the most part, or 30 if it is cold. For as long as they are broody, feed them with barley soaked in water.

After 30 days, if it is desired to make their livers large, chop up dried figs very finely, mix with water and put straight into their mouths for 20 days, or at the least 17.

Some, to make their livers large and the geese fat, feed them as follows. They shut them in and feed them with soaked wheat, or barley just as well: wheat fattens them quickly but barley makes their meat white. They must eat one or both of these foods for 20 days, twice a day giving up to 9 cakes, for 5 days, and increasing little by little for the remaining 15. At the end of the 50 days, boil mallow, soak dough in the mallow-water while it is still hot, and feed them this, repeating for 4 days. During the same days give them honey-water, changing it three times each day rather than always using the same; then for the remaining 6 days, with the dough as described, chop dried figs very finely and give them this. Thus after 60 days you will use both the goose and its liver, tender and white, which is to be removed and placed in a flat dish in cold water, the water to be changed once and then again.

The carcases and the livers of females are better.

Geese are not one-year animals: they live two and up to four years.

23. *Ducks.* Didymos.

Ducks are called *nessai* by some.[1] They should be kept in secure enclosures so that they cannot fly off. Sow dog's tooth grass in their enclosure, and throw into their pond, as food for them, wheat or millet or barley or raisins. At intervals they will also take locusts, or shrimps and similar lake and river creatures.

---

1. Greek *nessa* (the classical word) and *nekton*: chiefly mallard, *Anas platyrhynchos* (Linnaeus, 1758).

Those who want to have them tame should look for [duck] eggs at lakesides, put these eggs under their hens; the hens will raise them, and the result will be tame ducks.

They are fattened by increasing their food, like most other birds.

If one observes where they get their water and replaces the water with black wine, after drinking they will fall down and let themselves be caught. Lees of wine have the same effect.

24. *Turtle-doves, quails, thrushes and other small birds.* Same author.

Turtle-doves are fattened with broomcorn millet and foxtail millet and simply by drinking (they like [...]).[1] Quails take millet, wheat, darnel and pure water.

Because quails may graze on hellebore, putting those who afterwards eat them at risk of convulsions and vertigo,[2] millet should always be boiled along with them. Anyone who eats them and becomes ill should drink the water in which the millet was boiled. Myrtle berries have the same effect. This is also very helpful in the case of deadly mushrooms. Millet offers another natural benefit to humans: one who has previously eaten millet bread will not be hurt by any poisonous creature.

Thrushes are kept in a warm hutch. Perches should be set in the walls, and fronds of bay or some other bush at its corners. Their food is placed on the floor, which must be clean: dried figs well soaked in water, crushed, pounded and mixed with wheatmeal or raw bruised wheat; also myrtle berries, lentisk fruits, ivy berries, bay berries, olives and the like. They are made fatter with broomcorn millet, foxtail millet and very clean water. Small birds are fed on broomcorn millet, foxtail millet and cracked emmer steeped in clean water.

---

1. The sentence has become garbled. It probably once explained (compare Columella, *On Agriculture* 8.9.4) that they like fresh and very clean water, as given to pigeons and hens.
2. This is a real risk, now usually attributed to hemlock rather than hellebore. See Lewis and others 1987; Rizzi and others 1991.

25. *Jackdaws.* Leontinos.

You will drive away jackdaws if you catch one and burn it. The others, seeing this, will fly off, thinking that there are snares in your property.

You will prevent jackdaws and all wild birds from approaching if you soak black hellebore in wine and put it out [as bird food] with barley grains.

It will be good if before they settle on a field you drive them away with some kind of noise. The noise of castanets or of a bull-roarer is enough to frighten them off.

26. *Vultures.* Aristotle.

Aristotle says that the smell of perfume kills vultures and the smell of roses kills dung-beetles,[1] because a bad smell is these creatures' salvation. Also that vultures do not mate, but fly into the south wind, and having conceived in that way, lay their eggs after three years.

---

1. Repeated from 13.16.

Book 15

1. *Natural sympathy and antipathy.* Zoroaster.

Nature knows many things that are antipathetic and sympathetic to one another, as *Plutarch* says in book II of his *Symposium Questions*. It is necessary, I have decided, to list some of the stranger of these reactions in the present work: I have been anxious not only to collect what is useful to lovers of farming but also to ensure that my writing is agreeable to lovers of literature. Learn, then, that an elephant in musth becomes tame when he sees a ram, and shudders at the squealing of a piglet. A wild bull becomes calm and tame when tied to a fig tree. A horse, once bitten by a wolf, will be good and swift. Wolf-bitten sheep have sweeter flesh but their fleece produces lice. These reactions are mentioned by Plutarch. *Pamphilos* in *On Natural Effects* says that horses that tread in the footsteps of wolves become torpid in their limbs. A wolf touching squill becomes paralytic; hence foxes place squill in their dens against the wolves. If a wolf first catches sight of a man it makes him weak and tongue-tied, says *Plato* in the *Republic*, but if the man sees the wolf first it becomes weaker. A lion stepping on holly oak leaves becomes torpid; he is frightened of a cock and its crowing, and runs away if he sees one. If a hyena should step on the moon-shadow of a dog, for some natural reason it will crawl away with the motion of one climbing down a rope.[1] *Nestor* says in *Panacea* that when the

---

1. A variant, or perhaps rather a misunderstanding, of the information in Aelian, *Nature of Animals* 6.14: 'When the moon's disc is full, the Hyena gets the rays behind it and casts its own shadow upon the dogs and at once reduces them to silence, and having bewitched them, as sorceresses do, it then carries them off tongue-tied …' (A. F. Scholfield's translation, vol. 2 p. 27).

hyena sees a man or a dog asleep it stretches itself out alongside the sleeper. If it finds its body to be longer, then by its own length it turns the sleeper mad through a natural effect, and bites his arms, and he cannot defend himself. If it finds itself to be shorter it runs away as fast as it can.

If approached by a hyena, make sure that it is not on your right side, because if so you will be stupefied and will not be able to protect yourself. If it approaches on your left side, attack it boldly and you will certainly kill it.[1]

Holding a hyena's tongue in one's hand will be the greatest protection from attack by dogs.

A crab, attacked by an octopus, sheds its claws.

Bats are killed by the smoke of burning ivy.[2] Vultures are destroyed by the smell of perfume.[3] A snake dies if oak leaves are put on it. A snake will not move if an ibis feather is thrown on it. An adder if struck once with a reed is stupefied, but if struck several times it becomes stronger.[4]

If you ward off a viper with a frond of Valonia oak it will cower in fear.

If a tortoise eats snake it will be sick, but if it then eats oregano it will be cured.

Storks nest their chicks in plane-tree leaves to keep off bats. Swallows nest them in celery against cockroaches;[5] ring-doves[6] in bay leaves; falcons[7] in wild lettuce; shearwaters[8] in ivy; ravens in

1. The last two stories are related to one cited from Aristotle by Pliny, *Natural History* 8.106 and by Aelian, *Nature of Animals* 6.14: 'The Hyena ... has in its left paw the power of sending to sleep ... When it finds any creature asleep it creeps softly up and puts what you might call its sleep-inducing paw upon the creature's nose, and it is suffocated and overpowered.' Not found in surviving works of Aristotle, this is Aristotle fragment 369 Rose.
2. Repeated from 13.13.
3. Repeated from 13.16 and 14.26.
4. These three items are repeated from 13.8, where they are attributed to Demokritos and Apuleius.
5. Greek *silphe*: chiefly *Blattella germanica* Linnaeus, 1767.
6. Greek *phatta*: *Columba palumbus* Linnaeus, 1758.
7. A possible identification of Greek *kirkos*: *Falco* spp., chiefly *Falco peregrinus* Tunstall, 1771.
8. A possible identification of Greek *harpe*: *Calonectris* spp.

chaste-tree leaves; hoopoes[1] in maidenhair fern; crows in procumbent vervain;[2] larks[3] in dog's-tooth grass (hence the proverb: *Twisted dogstooth lies in the lark's bed*), thrushes in myrtle, partridge in a reed bed, heron[4] in a crab[-shell], eagle in adiantum.

Theophrastos and *Aristotle* say that not only is it the case that animals reproduce their kind; some arise spontaneously and are born from rotting earth; some animals and plants change from one kind to another. The *kampe*, for example, changes into a different, winged creature called the *psyche*;[5] the fig tree *kampe* changes into a *kantharis*,[6] while the water-snake changes into a viper when ponds dry out. Some believe that such changes happen in accord with the seasons, like the change between hawk[7] and hoopoe and that between the robin[8] and the summer bird called the redstart;[9] it is the same with the beccafico[10] and the blackcap,[11] because, these, too, change into one another: the beccafico appears about fruiting time and the blackcap immediately after the vintage.[12]

If seabirds have sores around their beaks, they are cured with oregano.

A scorpion is killed if kale is put on it.

If one stung by a scorpion sits upright on an ass, facing its tail, the ass will suffer in his place and will show this by farting. If one stung by a scorpion says in an ass's ear: 'A scorpion has stung me,' he will no longer feel the pain: this will be transferred to the ass.[13]

Ants destroy the interior of the grain they store, so that it will not grow.

1. Greek *epops*: *Upupa epops* Linnaeus, 1758.
2. Greek *peristereon ho hyptios*: *Verbena supina* L.
3. Greek *korydos*: *Alauda arvensis* Linnaeus, 1758.
4. Greek *erodios*: chiefly *Ardea cinerea* Linnaeus, 1758.
5. *Kampe* here has its usual meaning 'caterpillar', and *psyche* 'moth or butterfly'.
6. A 'small beetle', here no doubt the fig bark-beetle, *Hypoborus ficus* Erichson, 1836.
7. Greek *hierax*: *Accipiter* spp.
8. Greek *erithakos*: *Erithacus rubecula* (Linnaeus, 1758).
9. Greek *phoinikouros*: chiefly *Phoenicurus phoenicurus* (Linnaeus, 1758).
10. Greek *sykallis*: *Sylvia hortensis* (Gmelin, 1789).
11. Greek *melankoryphos*: *Sylvia atricapilla* (Linnaeus, 1758).
12. So Aristotle, *History of Animals* 632b31.
13. These two items are repeated from 13.9, where they are attributed to Demokritos and Apuleius.

If seeds during sowing touch the ox's horns, they [yield grain that] does not respond to fire; they are called horn-struck.[1]

The magnet stone or *sideritis* attracts iron. It loses this power if garlic is rubbed on it, but recovers it if bull's blood is poured over it. The *elektrion* stone or amber attracts everything light and chaff-like, but not basil. There are two kinds of *aetites* stone,[2] one dense and solid, the other rarefied and empty. The dense kind, if fastened to men, assists their potency; the light kind, tied to women, promotes childbearing. The coral stone, lying in a house, keeps away all murder and deceit –

Chips of ebony have the same effect; so do the roots of camel's thorn, and the aromatic pimpernel,[3] and dried squill lying in the doorway of the house.

– The lignite stone, smoked, drives pests away. The same stone, steeped in cold water, and brought to the fire, catches fire and burns brightly, says *Nestor* in *Panacea*, but if oil is poured on to it the fire goes out. The asbestos stone is more powerful than fire, and does not burn however long it is in the fire.

Likewise the salamander,[4] the least of creatures, has its origin in fire, lives in fire, and is not burned by it.

Bulls become dizzy if their nostrils are smeared with rose oil.[5]

A male goat will not run away if you cut his beard.[6]

2. *Bees, and how they are 'ox-born', from an ox carcass.* Florentinus.

The place where the bees are to be should face the winter and spring sunrise so that they will have warmth in winter and the breezes will cool them in summer. The best water for the swarms is what flows through coarse gravel, clear and not turbid and therefore productive of health and of pure honey; you should place pebbles and pieces of wood just about water level for them to settle on

---

1. See 2.19.
2. Literally 'eagle-stone'; see Pliny, *Natural History* 36.39.
3. Greek *anagallis*: *Anagallis arvensis* L.
4. Greek *salamandra*: *Salamandra* spp.
5. Repeated at 17.11.
6. Repeated at 18.9.

and drink without effort. If there is no naturally flowing water, well water should be drawn into clean troughs or basins, which should be placed close to the bees so that they are not exhausted by fetching water. They particularly like to browse on thyme: when they can do so freely they will make the largest quantity of honey and will produce new swarms. Sage, savory and tree-medick are the foods that bees like best; new swarms especially choose tree-medick and find it their easiest source. The best hives,[1] that is, containers for the swarms, are made from beechwood boards, or from fig, or equally from pine or Valonia oak; these should be one cubit wide and two cubits long, and rubbed on the outside with a kneaded mixture of ash and cow-dung so that they are less likely to rot.. They should be ventilated obliquely so that the wind, blowing gently, will dry and cool whatever is cobwebby and mouldy. This creature likes solitude and is troubled by the approach of humans. The beekeeper should therefore build a wall of gappy stones around them so that they can fly into the holes and escape the dew and any predatory birds. Bees like their usual pastures and do not willingly go into strange localities; they should, therefore, normally be kept in the same place. If there is a need to move them, at the demand of a purchaser or for some other reason, it must be done gently and during the night; the hives should be wrapped in skins; they should be set in place before dawn. When it is done in this way the combs will not be damaged and the creatures will not be injured.

When they browse on spurge and taste its juice they develop diarrhoea: it is necessary to remove and pull up any that is growing nearby, and to treat them by grinding the skin of pomegranate, the rind that is, sifting it through a fine sieve, kneading with honey and austere wine, and feeding it to them.[2] If they are infested by *phtheires*[3] you will treat them by burning and smoking branches of apple and of wild fig. You will cure them of weak eyesight using the smoke of oregano leaves.

---

1. The word here is *angeion* 'vessel', a reminder that, in spite of these instructions, early hives were most often earthenware vessels.
2. There is a problem with the text, but the meaning is hardly in doubt.
3. Literally 'lice'.

Just as bees take twenty-one days to develop from an ox carcass, the new swarms, too, emerge in the same number of days. The kings are found at the top of the combs: leave one in each hive and destroy the rest, otherwise the bees will gather around each king, start a civil war, and stop working. The best kings are those coloured yellow and half as big again as a bee; next best are those of varied colour, rather dark, twice the size of a bee. You should remove from their pasture spurge, hellebore, thapsia,[1] wormwood, wild fig[2] –

And everything that kills bees.

– because if they take from these plants they make poor honey. You must destroy their predators: these include wasps, tits,[3] bee-eaters,[4] swallows, crocodiles and lizards. Drive off and destroy everything that kills bees. When any humans approach the bees are hard to control and will attack, particularly any who smell of wine and perfume; they also attack women, especially those who have been making love. Their hives should be carefully smeared with flowers of thyme or of white poplar, so that they will like these containers and stay in them.

Or pound a mixture of equal parts of the herb nard[5] and of myrrh, mixed with four parts of honey, and smear the hives.

Juba, *king of the Libyans*, says that bees must be developed in a wooden box; *Demokritos*, and *Varro* in Latin, say that they must be developed in a building, which is better. The method is as follows. You require a large building, ten cubits high, ten cubits wide, all sides equal. You should make one entrance to it and four windows, one in each wall. Drive an ox into it, thirty months old, well-fleshed, rather fat, and have plenty of young men standing around it who are to beat it vigorously with cudgels until they kill it, smashing the bones as well as the flesh; but they should take care not to make it bleed (because bees do not develop from blood) and therefore not to strike the early blows too hard. Immediately all its orifices,

---

1. Greek *thapsia*, sometimes called 'deadly carrot': *Thapsia garganica* L.
2. There is some mistake. Wild fig has nothing to do with honey-bees, and it would be a bad idea to extirpate it even if it were possible. From the parallel passages in Palladius (*On Agriculture* 1.37.5) and the Syriac *Geoponika* it appears that an earlier text specified squirting cucumber, not wild fig.
3. Greek *aigithallos*: *Parus* spp.
4. Greek *merops*: *Merops apiaster* Linnaeus, 1758.
5. Greek *nardos botane*: probably hazelwort, *Asarum europaeum* L.

eyes, nostrils, mouth and the natural excretory passages, should be stopped with clean, fine cloths smeared with pitch. Then they should spread plenty of thyme on the ground, place the ox supine on this and immediately leave the building, sealing the door and windows with clay so that no air or wind or anything else can get in or ventilate it. In the third week it may be opened up on all sides to admit light[1] and fresh air except where any strong wind might enter; on that side the opening should remain closed. Then, when the substance seems to have been sufficiently aerated, the building should again be sealed with clay as before. Eleven days after this, open up and you will find it full of bees swarming on each other like bunches of grapes, and nothing left of the ox except the horns, the bones and the hair. They say that the kings develop from the brain and the other bees from the flesh. Kings also develop from the spinal marrow, but those from the brain are better than the others in size, beauty and strength. You will already have observed the first metamorphosis of the flesh and its development into living creatures, their birth and origin as it were, because when the building was opened you will have seen small white things, all alike, not fully formed and not yet quite living creatures, multiplying on the carcass, motionless but slowly growing. You might see their wings develop and divide, and the creatures taking on their proper colour and gathering around their king and beginning to fly – but only a short distance and with trembling wings because of their lack of practice in flying and the weakness of their limbs – and settling on the windows, their wings whirring as they urge and press one another, longing for the light; it is better if the opening and re-sealing of the windows, as described, is done every other day, because when the bees have not yet fully taken their form it is important that they should not be killed by suffocation through excessive enclosure and the failure to admit air when needed. The beehive should be placed near the building. When the door and windows are opened and they fly out, smoke thyme and mezereon:[2] with the smell you will attract them towards the beehive, drugged

1. Those intending to follow this procedure should know that the windows have shutters, not glass panes; when they are sealed, light is entirely excluded.
2. Greek *kneoron*: *Daphne gnidium* L.

by the scent of the flowers, and with the smoke you will gather them in easily. Naturally, as makers of honey, bees like fragrance and flowers.

3. *Bees.* Didymos.

The bee is the wisest and cleverest of all animals and the closest to man in intelligence; its work is truly divine and of the greatest use to mankind. Its social life resembles that of the best-regulated cities. In their excursions bees follow a leader and obey instructions. They bring back sticky secretions from flowers and trees and spread them like ointment on their floors and doorways. Some are employed in making honey and some in other tasks. The bee is extremely clean, settling on nothing that is bad-smelling or impure; it is not greedy; it will not approach flesh or blood or fat but only things of sweet flavour. It does not spoil the work of others, but fiercely defends its own work against those who try to spoil it. Aware of its own weakness, it makes the entrance to its home narrow and winding, so that those entering in large number to do harm are easily destroyed by the guardian bees. This animal is pleased by a good tune: when they are scattered, therefore, beekeepers clash cymbals or clap their hands rhythmically to bring them home. This is the only animal that looks for a leader to take care of a whole community: it always honours its king, follows him enthusiastically wherever he goes, supports him when he is exhausted, carries him and keeps him safe when he cannot fly. It particularly hates laziness; bees unite to kill the ones who do no work and use up others' production. Its mechanical skill and near-logical understanding is shown by the fact that it makes hexagonal cells to store honey.

4. *To stop bees flying away.* Same author.

The bees would not fly away if you smeared the mouths of their hives with the dung of a cow that has calved once.

When the swarm has settled and taken up residence, take the king gently and cut off the extremities of his wings; if he stays inside the others will not move elsewhere.

Bees will not fly away if you grind together leaves of wild and cultivated olive and rub this on the hives in the evening.

Or smear the walls and interior structures with honey-water.

[Seasonal care of bees.]

As food for young bees put out wine mixed with honey, in basins, and in these place leaves of many-flowered savory[1] so that they do not drown. To feed your swarms in the best possible way whenever they stay at home because of wintry weather or burning heat and run out of food, pound together raisins and savory finely and give them this with barley cakes. When the first ten days of spring are past, drive them out to their pastures with the smoke of dried cow-dung, then clean and sweep out their hives: the bad smell of dung disturbs them, but cobwebs are an obstacle to them. If there are many combs in the hives, take away the worst, so that they are not made unhealthy by overcrowding. Do not take more than two swarms from any hive: they will be underfed and weak.

5.   *When to harvest honey.* Same author.

The best time to harvest honey and combs is at the rising of the Pleiades – according to the Roman calendar, at the beginning of May; the second harvest is at the beginning of autumn;[2] and the third, when the Pleiades set, around October. It is not done on fixed days, however, but according to the completeness of the combs; if you harvest before they have finished making them the bees are angry and stop working. They do the same if you take all the produce away, leaving the hives empty. You should leave one tenth for them in the spring and summer; in the winter you should take one-third, and leave two-thirds for them, so that they will not be discouraged and will have food. Before harvesting drive them off with the smoke of cow-dung.

1. Greek *thymbra polyanthos*: probably *Satureja thymbra* L.
2. Autumn begins early in this calendar; the second harvesting is identified as 'summer' below.

Or the harvester should be smeared with the juice of the male wild mallow known as tree-mallow,[1] against the stings.

Lemon-balm smeared on, and lentisk flower, are also helpful.

6. *To avoid being stung when gathering honey.* Paxamos.

Take flour of roasted fenugreek, add the decoction of wild mallow with olive oil so that it has the consistency of honey; anoint the face and bare skin with this thickly, take it into the mouth and blow into the beehive three or four times.[2]

Set fire to cow-dung in a pot, place it at the entrance to the beehive and leave the smoke to penetrate for half an hour; then lift and hold the pot outside so that there is plenty of smoke outside, and harvest [the honey].

If you want to get rid of young wasps use the same preparation [as above] but mix flour of lentil with the rest.

7. *Honey and its improvement.*[3] Diophanes.

The best honey is Attic; the best Attic honey is from mount Hymettos. Island honey is also good: the best Sicilian is from Hybla,[4] the best Cretan is *Akramanmorion*,[5] the best Cyprian is *Chytrion*, the best Koan is Kalymnian.[6] It should be translucent and pale yellow in colour, smooth to the touch, remaining in a long string when pulled, readily raised to a point and slow to sink back, thick when it reluctantly separates; and it should have a good aroma. All honey solidifies over a long period; Attic, however, remains liquid, but darkens in colour.

---

1. Greek *malache agria arren* and *dendromalache*: *Lavatera* spp., e.g. *Lavatera arborea* L.
2. Compare 15.10.
3. Compare Dioscorides, *Materia Medica* 2.101–103.
4. Many sources confirm the excellence of Hymettian and Hyblaean honey.
5. There are several different manuscript readings and editiorial conjectures. Whatever the original spelling, its meaning is not known.
6. Kos and Kalymnos are different islands, but the statement still makes sense because Kos dominated Kalymnos and probably marketed its honey. Compare Strabo, *Geography* 10.5.19.

Cook poorer honey, because that will improve it; eat the best honey raw. It is not only pleasant to those who eat it, but prolongs their lives, so that those who in old age eat nothing but bread with honey live the longest. It also keeps the senses active.

Demokritos, asked how men could be made healthy and long-lived, said: apply olive oil outside and honey inside.

Is honey unadulterated? dip and touch it. If it is unadulterated, it will touch more cleanly.[1]

8. *To prevent enchantment of beehives, fields, houses, animal sheds and workshops.* Leontinos.

Bury the hoof of the right foreleg of a black donkey under the threshold of the entrance, and pour on liquid unburnt pine resin (this is found in Zakynthos, thrown up from a lagoon, just as asphalt is thrown up from a pool at Apollonia near Dyrrhachion),[2] salt, Heracleotic oregano,[3] cardamom[4] and cumin. Each month bring bits of bread, squill, a twist of white or red wool, chaste-tree, vervain,[5] brimstone, pine torches, and amaranth,[6] pile them up, throw on a *panspermia*,[7] and leave it all there.

9. *To kill the drones.* Demokritos.

If you want to kill the drones, at the beginning of evening sprinkle the insides of the lids of the hives with water. Around dawn, open the hives and you will find the drones settled on the drops of water on the lids, because, being always full of honey, they get thirsty; greedy for water, they cannot keep away from the moisture on the lids. Thus it is possible to kill them all, none escaping.

They are big, without stings, and lazy.

1. Or possibly 'set fire to it: if unadulterated it will burn more cleanly'. Beckh comments (1895 p. 449) that the text here is 'hopeless ... I have never managed to set fire to honey, and have never touched it without getting sticky.'
2. See Pliny, *Natural History* 6.99, 31.82, 35.178
3. Greek *origanon Herakleotikon*: *Origanum heracleoticum* L.
4. Greek *kardamomon*: *Elettaria cardamomum* (L.) Maton.
5. Greek *hiera botane*: *Verbena officinalis* L. or *Verbena supina* L.
6. Greek *amaranton to hyperythron*: perhaps *Amaranthus graecizans* L. or a similar species.
7. A ritual mixture of 'all seeds', or, at least, all that were useful to humans.

[Box-tree honey.]

Aristotle says that honey from the box-tree has a heavy smell. If healthy people eat it they go out of their minds, but if epileptics eat it they are cured at once.[1]

10. *To avoid being stung by wasps.* Paxamos.

One smears oneself with the juice of wild mallow.[2]

---

1. Aristotle, *On Marvellous Things Heard* 831b22.
2. Similarly at 12.12; compare 15.5, 15.6.

Book 16

1. *Horses.* Apsyrtos.

Mares from whom we are to breed foals should be sound, of sufficient size, fine-looking, with broad bellies and flanks. In age they should be not younger than three nor older than ten. The stallion for breeding should be large-bodied and sound in every part.

The mating season is from the spring equinox, that is, 22nd March, until 22nd June, so that the foal will be born in the most suitable season of the year and will have fresh fodder. The mare carries her foal for 11 months and 10 days. Foals conceived after the summer solstice are degenerate and useless.[1] The stallion should be freed from work at mating time. He should cover a female twice a day, not more than that, at dawn and dusk. If after once mating she will not take the male again, bring him back to her after 10 days, and if she still will not take him, keep her apart: she is already pregnant. When they are carrying, ensure that they are not over-tired and that they do not spend time in cold places, because cold is bad for pregnant mares. We shall make the males eager to mate by rubbing their nostrils with the secretion from the females' sexual parts.

You can tell whether a colt will be a good one from its physical and mental qualities as follows. As regards the body it should have a small head, black eye, flared nostrils, short ears, a delicate neck, a long mane, slightly curled and falling on the right side of the neck, a broad and muscular chest, big shoulders, straight arms, a firm belly, small testicles, a spine preferably double or at least not humped, a long tail with curled hair, straight legs, muscular haunches, a well-shaped

---

1. Compare Columella, *On Agriculture* 6.27.3.

and evenly structured foot, a small 'frog', a solid hoof: from all these signs it will evidently be a good and big horse. Mental points are judged as follows: if it is not timid, or frightened by things that appear unexpectedly, and likes to be first in the herd of colts, not yielding to a rival but pushing it aside, and when faced by rivers or lakes not waiting for another to go first but going ahead bravely itself.

Begin to tame the colts when they reach 18 months, putting a halter on them at that stage. Hang the bridle at the manger, so that they will be accustomed to its touch and will not be worried by the noise of the bits. Break them when they are three years old and before they feed on grass.

We will know the age and maturity of horses, and all animals without cloven hoofs, and more or less all horned animals too, by the shedding of their teeth. When the colt is thirty months old it sheds its first front teeth – we call them incisors – and middle teeth, two above and two below. At the beginning of its fourth year it sheds another two below, one from each side, and likewise two above; it then produces its canine teeth. At the completion of its fourth year and starting on the fifth it sheds the remaining teeth, one on each side both below and above, and produces cupped teeth in their place. Starting on its sixth year the cups in the first are filled. Starting on the seventh year it has all its teeth full, with no cups. After this stage it is no longer easy to verify a horse's age.[1]

A horse will never be ill if you tie a stag's horn to it.[2]

2. *Signs in horses.* Pelagonios.

Some count among the finest horses those with differently-coloured eyes (they say Alexander of Macedon's horse Boukephalos was of this kind),[3] with a thin and long tongue, with a flat or a rather hooked face. It needs to be high-necked, skittish, grey, ticklish, upright, with a full and thick neck – not short-necked, that is – with a compact stomach, tight-flanked, not too small, the veins well-marked and neat over the whole body, the colour solidly black; but *Plato* likes

---

1. Similarly Palladius, *On Agriculture* 4.13.8.
2. Repeated at 16.3.
3. Compare *Hippiatrica Berolinensia* 13.1, ascribed to Apsyrtos.

them white: thus both extremes of colour are approved. Bay[1] is also counted among good [colours for] horses – and they may often be of other colours too.

Another sign of a good horse is that when it stands it is not content to be still but paws the ground as if longing to run.

3. *Cures for various diseases.* Apsyrtos.

If the horse loses weight, feed it a double quantity of parched wheat or pounded barley, and let it drink three times a day; if it remains thin, add bran to the wheat, and ensure gentle exercise. If it lacks appetite, add to its food nightshade[2] and leaves of germander soaked in drinking water, and steep in water the barley and vetch that you feed to it; or grind two *kyathoi* of love-in-a-mist, mix with three *kyathoi* of olive oil and give[3] with one *kotyle* of wine. If it is nauseous, treat it by giving garlic mixed into one *kotyle* of wine. If it also suffers from dysuria, we mix the whites of ten eggs with the preceding and give by mouth.

Neither oxen nor horses will be ill if you tie a stag's horn to them.[4]

4. *Fever.* Same author.

Fever is to be treated by bathing with warm water. In winter keep in a warm place: the horse must not get cold. Feed on vetch or wheat meal, as little as possible, and give lukewarm water to drink. Rub the whole body with wine and warmed olive oil; purge via the bowels; bleed from the neck, or the veins of the throat or chest, or from the foot. The knees should be rubbed with hot vinegar. When it seems to be recovering, wash in hot water.

If it is feverish and thin from overwork, give – for three days or more, until healthy – a mixture of one *kotyle* goat's milk, one *metron* frumenty, half a *kotyle* olive oil, 4 eggs, juice of pounded purslane. If it is feverish from disease in the throat or head, keep it warm and rub the palate with a mixture of salt and oregano, pounded and

---

1. Greek *phoinikizon*, a colour approaching dark red (*phoinix*).
2. Greek *strychnos*: black nightshade (an edible species), *Solanum nigrum* L.
3. 16.14 indicates that liquid medicines might be given by mouth using a horn.
4. Repeated from 16.1.

blended in olive oil; warm the feet and knees with hot water, rub around the mouth with pounded nightshade and wine lees, and feed with moss or green plants, without barley. If it bleeds from the nostrils, pour into the nostrils the juice of coriander or a decoction of asafoetida.[1]

5. *Ophthalmia*. Same author.

If the eye is phlegmy, smear under it a mixture of male frankincense[2] (another source gives: lamb's marrow; one dram of either), saffron, cuttlebone, one dram, rose oil 10 drams, white of 4 eggs.

Another for phlegmy eye: equal parts frankincense, frumenty, Attic honey.

6. *Cataract*. Same author.

Sal ammoniac should be mixed with Attic or other fine honey as ointment.

Or apply same quantity of butter.

Or powdered cuttlebone, puffed on through a reed.

Or asafoetida root, pounded with olive oil, smeared under, twice a day.

Or rocket seed, pure, as it comes, puffed on to the eyes and left until its bitterness has caused the eyes to wash and clean away their weakness.[3]

7. *Nerves*. Same author.

A horse troubled by nerves is to have the [affected][4] parts and the head washed in warm water; then put in a small jar a mixture of equal quantities of ox fat and myrrh with sulphur, cover the horse's head, warm and smoke with this mixture.

---

1. Identical with *Hippiatrica Berolinensia* 1.23, ascribed to Anatolios.
2. 'Frankincense that hangs suspended in a globule', according to Pliny, *Natural History* 12.61; 'the best kind', according to the chauvinistic lexicon of Liddell and Scott 1925–1940.
3. This sentence isn't clear to me.
4. This is what 'parts' means elsewhere in book 16, but what 'parts' are affected by nerves?

8. *Bowels.* Same author.

If there is diarrhoea, bleed from the veins of the head, and let the horse drink barley meal stirred into lukewarm water. If it does not improve, pour olive oil into the nostrils.

Pomegranate rind stops diarrhoea; so does Syrian sumach, either of them pounded and given by mouth.

9. *Colic.* Hierokles.

Wash in hot water and cover the horse. Then give by mouth 5 drams myrrh, 6 *kotylai* old wine, 3 *kotylai* olive oil, mixed to a smooth fluid and divided into three parts; warm the belly with seawater or with a decoction of myrtle berries in water.

Also give a mixture of germander leaves, or southernwood, or bitter almonds, with austere black wine.

Or pomegranate rind with water.

Also helpful are equal quantities of celery and melon seed, each mixed with equal quantities of wine and honey and given to drink.

Or cardamom seed ground, with water, or lucerne seed – sprinkled on in the way that barley is scattered.[1]

Horses with dizziness are given a clyster of a decoction of beet in water with 40 drams natron and 30 drams olive oil.

Dissolve and warm natron in wine and administer.

Alternatively urinate on the ground and smear the horse's belly with the mud; this will stop the colic.

10. *Pneumonia.* Same author.

Sharp vinegar, warmed and injected, cures diseases established in the lungs.

Or human urine with 20 drams melted pig's fat; but it must not be the urine of a menstruating woman.

11. *Cough.* Same author.

When it has just begun to cough, give it to drink barley meal mixed with vetch or broad bean. If the cough is established you should give

---

1. As barley is scattered over the head of a sacrificial animal.

two *kyathoi* honey, same quantity of liquid pitch, same of olive oil, and 24 drams butter, heated, with a moderate amount of old pig's fat. If this does not stop it, pound leek with olive oil and salt, mix into wine and give by mouth.

Some give leek juice, olive oil and root of wild rue; some people add frankincense, and administer with olive oil.

12. *Unknown illness.*[1] Theomnestos.

Take blood from both shoulders and prepare the following medicine: pound a little rue with sorrel root and mix with 2 drams opopanax into three *kotylai* of water. Feed night and day with wheatmeal made into a paste with water and given as a drink.

If the disease attacks a herd of horses, the smaller ones should be given three *kyathoi* of *garos* and olive oil, the larger ones twice that quantity.

13. *Dysuria.* Apsyrtos.

Some place an onion, the skin removed, around the penis.

Others: ground celery seed with two *kotyloi* of wine; or an onion with the same quantity of wine; or they give, with wine, either pigeon dung, or germander leaf, or dried myrrh bark,[2] or 5 drams natron with one head of garlic, pounded. Some simply use black wine.

14. *Blood in the urine.* Same author.

Give by mouth, daily for three days, cracked wheat, boiled, mixed with deer fat with a little wine.

Or one *kotyle* goat's milk, half a *mna* frumenty, 10 eggs, 3 *kyathoi* olive oil, all mixed and given using a horn.

15. *Ulceration.* Same author.

If the spine is ulcered, iris root is burned, pounded and sprinkled over.

---

1. See 17.14 for discussion of this term.
2. There is an error here. Frankincense bark was available in trade (it is called for at 20.2) but myrrh bark was not, so far as I can discover; even if it were, it would not need to be dried.

Or the ash of burned cannabis seed, mixed in honey, is spread on, after previously rubbing the [affected] parts with old urine.

16. *Inflammation.* Same author.

Any inflammation is treated by being spread with salt and olive oil, or germander leaf burned and mixed into wine, or mullein boiled in wine.

17. *Plaster for joints.* Pelagonios.

8 drams frankincense, same quantity galbanum, 12 drams wine lees, 4 drams each of heated pine resin, natron and sulphur, one *kyathos* Egyptian mustard, same quantity cardamom, 100 bay berries, one *mna* dried figs, a few oleander leaves, a sufficient quantity of gypsum: the dry ingredients are to be ground, added to the liquids, and applied as poultice to the spine.

18. *Mange.* Same author.

Equal parts of liquid pitch from cedar,[1] pine resin and alum, mixed with vinegar and applied under sunlight.

After rubbing the affected parts with hot ash, wash off until they begin to bleed, then throughly grind litharge and alum, mix into lentisk oil and smear on.

Or equal parts of *aphronitron*,[2] flower of salt and wheat flour, mixed into vinegar and spread on.

Or rub with lye; then take the ash of burned caper root, mix with pork fat, and smear over.

19. *Leeches.* Apsyrtos.

If it swallows a leech, lay it supine, mix hot olive oil with wine and give by mouth using a horn.

Or you can cure by burning bugs near its face, or killing them in its nostrils: the leeches will immediately fall out or die. This can be done with cattle and other domestic animals.

1. Greek *kedros*: *Juniperus* spp.
2. Native sodium carbonate: compare Pliny, *Natural History* 31.112–113.

20. *Curing the bites of scorpions and other poisonous creatures.* Hippokrates.

The wounded part should be smeared with ox dung.

Or pounded nightshade, or spurge, or henbane seed, or linseed oil, or alum, or native sodium carbonate, or roasted salt: any one of these will help if smeared on.

You can also treat it with water filtered through a cloth and poured into the nostrils.

For local affections of horses, asses and mules, taking blood is an appropriate treatment.

21. *Asses suitable for mating.* Apsyrtos.

We will select and keep asses suitable for mating as we do with horses. Certain breeders, sensibly, tame wild asses, because free-ranging stock are better breeders than animals kept enclosed. Asses can be readily tamed, will then serve any purpose just as well as those originally tame; once tamed, unlike other animals, they never revert to the wild, and their offspring resemble them. Asses should mate a few days before the summer solstice. Females carry their young for twelve months. It is better for mares to be covered by male asses than for female asses to be covered by stallions; some, wisely, put newborn asses under mares to suckle: the milk that they get is better, they are more friendly to horses because brought up among them, and more willing to work. They suckle for two years, just as foals do. Asses are useful for breeding between the ages of three and ten. Ensure that those for breeding are well-shaped, because their offspring will resemble them. Some, sensibly, clothe the ass (or stallion or other animal) that is about to mount in a cape of the colour that they wish the offspring to be. Whatever the colour of the cloth worn by the male when mating will be the colour of the offspring.[1]

[Lameness in asses.]

You can treat lame asses by washing the whole foot with hot water and cleaning around it with a scalpel. When this is done pour over

---

1. Identical with *Hippiatrica Berolinensia* 14.9, ascribed to Anatolios.

it old urine, hot, with salt, wipe carefully, and apply fat, that of goats preferably or, if none, of oxen, by pressing in with a hot iron implement. Repeat the treatment till cured.

22. *Camels.*[1] Didymos.

Didymos says in his *Georgika* that camels can withstand thirst for up to three days.

Mange in camels is treated with cedar oil.

A camel will not mate with its mother or its sister.

Didymos, again, says that the Bactrian camel in the mountains bordering on India mates with wild boars native to those mountains; from boar and [female] camel are born the camels with two humps, just as mules are born from horses and asses. These inherit many characteristics from the male parent: their bristly hair, their remarkable strength, the fact that they seldom slip in mud because their strength keeps them stable, their ability to carry twice as much as other camels. They are naturally called Bactrian because Bactria is their region of origin. I have seen – he says – racing camels competing alongside horses and winning.

Florentinus in his *Georgika* says that he saw a *kamelopardalis*, a giraffe, at Rome; I saw one at Antioch, brought there from India.[2]

1. Greek *kamelos*: *Camelus* spp.
2. Compare Pliny, *Natural History* 8.68.

Book 17

1. *Cattle.* Florentinus.

Before the 30th day of mating the cows should not be allowed to fill themselves with food, because the leaner they are the more easily they will be impregnated.

2. *Cows or heifers.* Same author.

Choose cows that are sturdy, oval in body shape, well-sized, with good horns, flat-faced, black-eyed, small-jawed, snub-nosed, with flared nostrils, with a long and thick neck and a good chest, with blackish lips, deep-flanked, flat-backed, big-eyed, with a long tail reaching the heels, with plenty of hair, with short shoulders; the legs straight, firm, rather thick than long and not rubbing together, with feet not excessively splayed in walking and not divided, with smooth and regular hoofs; the hide soft and not woody. The best are distinguished as fine-bred by their yellowish colour and black legs. It is ideal if a cow has all these physical features; if not, most of them.

[Understanding in cattle.]

Cattle recognize the cowherd's voice. They know the names they are given. They respond to a commander's commands.

3. *Bulls.* Didymos.

For two months preceding mating the bulls should not be pastured with the cows. They should get plenty of green food, and if the pasture does not give them enough, [add] chickpeas or bitter vetch or barley steeped in water. Before their third year and after their twelfth they are not suitable for breeding, and the same is true of the females.[1]

Separate them from the females for a two-month period; then take them to the herd and do not restrain their impulse.

4. *Preventing weakness in oxen.* Demokritos.

Steep ground vetch and give this to drink once a month.

[Injuries.]

You can treat injuries in cattle by coating with a paste of wild mallow.

5. *Mating.* The Quintilii.

The proper time for mating is the middle of spring.[2] If the cows are unwilling to take the bulls, take the inner layers – the softest part, and what might be called the fat – of a squill bulb, pound it in water, and rub it on the sexual parts of the cows after washing. If bulls are reluctant to mount, burn the tail of a goat, pound it, knead it with wine, anoint the penis and testicles of the bull with it, and he will be aroused immediately. This works not only for bulls but for other animals, and for humans too. To end the state of arousal, anoint with oil.

The *polyspermos* and the plant called *polygonos*[3] also make animals more potent.

6. *Predicting the offspring.* Africanus.

Those who want to predict whether a cow will produce a male or a female should observe the mating carefully. If the male mounts her

1. Compare 17.10.
2. Compare 17.10.
3. Possibly the plants elsewhere called 'male *polygonon*' and 'female *polygonon*', identified respectively as knot-grass, *Polygonum aviculare* L., and mare's tail, *Hippuris vulgaris* L.

from the right side, this shows that the offspring will be male, and if from the left side, female. If you wish a male to be produced, tie off the left testicle at the time of mating; if a female, tie off the right.

Some people, relying on natural sympathy, arrange the mating when the wind is in the north if they want a male to be produced, and in the south if they want a female.

7. *Horsefly or gadfly.*[1] Sotion.

We know that the sting of gadflies drives cattle mad. Gadflies will not come near them if you pound bay berries, boil them up in water and sprinkle this in the field where they are pastured: the gadflies will fly off, owing to natural antipathy.

If cattle are stung nonetheless, one smears around the sting with ground white lead mixed with water.

8. *Care of calves.* Didymos.

We feed cows that are suckling their calves on tree-medick or lucerne: with this food they produce more milk.

Calves should be castrated in their second year; after this castration is not appropriate. The cuts should be coated with ash and litharge, then, after three days, liquid pitch and ash with the addition of a little olive oil.

9. *Preventing exhaustion in working oxen.* Demokritos.

Boil olive oil and terebinth oil and coat their horns with it.

10. *From what age cattle must be prevented from mating.* Varro.

They should not mate before their second year, so that they calve in their third year – but in the fourth year is better. For the most part cows go on calving till their tenth year. Bulls are mature in their third year.[2] The season for cattle to mate is from the rising of Alpha

---

1. The Greek words are *myops* and *oistros*: chiefly *Tabanus bovinus* Linnaeus, 1758.
2. Compare 17.3.

Delphini, that is, around the beginning of June, for forty days.[1] Cows carry their calves for 10 months.

Barren and weak cows, and those of advanced age, should be removed from the herd; caring for unproductive animals brings no profit.

11. *Preventing cattle being troubled by flies.* Africanus.

Grind bay berries to a paste, boil, mix with olive oil and rub the cattle with this.

Or smear them with ox fat.

Bulls whose nostrils are smeared with rose oil become dizzy.[2]

12. *Fattening cattle.* Sotion.

You will fatten cattle if when they come from their pasture you give them as feed, on the first day, chopped cabbages steeped in sharp vinegar; then, for 5 days, sifted chaff mixed with wheat bran; on the 7th day, 4 *kotylai* of milled barley, and gradually increase this feed over the next 7 days. In winter give them their first feed about cockcrow, their second about dawn, then let them drink, then the remainder of their food about evening; in summer the first feed at dawn, the second about the third hour, then let them drink, then the third feed about the ninth hour, and let them drink again. Give them their feed rather warm in winter, cold in summer. Wash around their mouths with urine to remove phlegm, clean their tongues by removing the worms with tweezers (they get worms in their tongues) and rubbing their tongues with salt. Give attention to their bedding.

13. *Care; to prevent them swallowing bones.* Paxamos.

Neither hens nor pigs should approach the cows' manger, because the dung of either, if eaten, will harm them.

The cattle will not swallow bones if you burn a wolf's tail at the manger.

1. Compare 17.5.
2. Repeated from 15.1.

14. *Unknown illness.*[1]

Almost all illnesses of animals are unknown: how would one discover them? whom would one ask about an internal disorder of an animal? But by pouring into the nostrils ground asafoetida with unmixed black wine, you can treat any unknown illness.

Demokritos advises that for fourteen days at the beginning of spring you add squill and buckthorn root[2] to the drinking water of your cattle.

You can treat an ox that is suffering from evident illness as follows. Steep in advance each day, in the water they are to drink on that day, mountain sage and leek. Give them this as treatment; it is good for other domesticated animals as well as cattle.

Salt mixed with their food also helps them greatly.

Best and most healthy is *amorge* mixed with water, given little by little.

Lucerne helps too.

15. *Headache.*

It is necessary first to diagnose headache in cattle. When they put down their ears and do not eat, this is headache.

The tongue is smeared with thyme pounded in wine, and with garlic and fine salt.

Raw barley water diluted in wine also helps.

It will also help if you take a handful of bay leaves and put them in the mouth.

Or else pomegranate rind.

You can also treat with myrrh, an amount the size of a bean, dissolved in two *kotylai* of wine, poured into the nostrils.

16. *Diarrhoea.*

Pound buckthorn leaves, mix into a paste with asphalt, and give as food.

Some give as food pounded leaves of pomegranate made into a paste with pearl barley.

1. Compare 16.12.
2. Greek *ramnos*: *Rhamnus* spp., e.g. *Rhamnus alaternus* L.

Others give 2 *kotylai* of pearl barley and ground parched wheat, half and half, mixed with water.

17. *Indigestion.*

Indigestion in an ox is diagnosed by its not eating, belching frequently, moving its legs restlessly and emitting wind. We will treat it by giving hot water to drink and a *desme* of cabbage steeped in vinegar to eat.

Some boil the tender parts of cabbage, pound to a liquid with olive oil, and give by mouth through a horn; they then drive the ox outdoors to walk, keeping it warm with covers. This helps not only cattle but other grazing animals.

Some pound the leaves of wild olive or fresh fronds of other trees, add water to make a mixture, and give 6 *kotylai* of this for two days.

18. Bouprestis.

Some people pour olive oil into the nostrils of the cattle. Others pound fruits of the wild fig in water and, likewise, pour into the nostrils.

19. *Colic.*

An ox with colic does not stand still in one place or take food, and it groans. It can be given a little food, and the flesh near the hoofs should be pricked to bleed it.

People also prick around the tail to make blood flow, and wrap in a cloth.

Others make a blend of onion and salt, form into a suppository and insert well into the rectum, then make the animal walk.

Others pound natron, dilute it, and give by mouth.

20. *Feverishness.* Didymos.

A feverish ox will not go to its food, lowers its head, produces tears, is irritable, and is hollow around the eyes. They treat it as follows. Take dog's-tooth grass from shady sites, wash it and give as food –

Or vine leaves.

– It should be given very cold water to drink, better not under the sky but in the shade. Its ears and nostrils should be wiped off with a sponge soaked in water.

21. *Coughing.*

Milled barley, soaked, with the finest chaff, cleaned, and 3 *kotylai* milled bitter vetch: divide into three parts and give successively as food.

Some grind mugwort, soak in water, squeeze out, and administer before food for 7 days.

22. *Suppuration.*

If a wound becomes suppurated it must be cleaned by rinsing with old heated ox urine and wiped with wool; then apply a poultice with fine salt and liquid pitch.

23. *Lameness.* Florentinus.

If owing to a chill the ox is lame in one limb, the leg should be washed, the affected part opened with a scalpel and steamed with old urine; then sprinkle with salt and wipe with a sponge or cloth; then rub goat or ox suet and drop on to the affected part using a hot iron. If it is lame as the result of treading on a stake or the like, the same procedure can be followed, but melt wax together with old olive oil, honey and vetch flour, cool, and apply to the wound; then take finely powdered and sifted pot, mix with pounded figs or pomegranates, and apply this, wrapping it in a cloth and tying carefully so that nothing can slip in as long as it remains, because in this way it will heal; dress the wound on the third day. If it is lame because of a flux of matter, the part should be heated with boiled oil and sweet wine; then apply hot bruised wheatmeal. When it is soft, open it, rinse, and apply to the opened wound lily leaves, or squill with salt, or *polygonos*, or pounded leek.

24. *Mange.*

Mange and eruptions are cured by smearing on old ox urine and butter.

Some smear with a paste of pine resin or liquid pitch and sulphur, and cure in this way.

25. *Bile.*

The legs of oxen are to be cauterized down to the hoof, and frequently washed with hot water. Cover the animal with cloths; give no food.

26. *Chill.*

Administer asafoetida mixed into black wine.

27. *Grubs.*

People kill the maggots by sprinkling the wounds with cold water.

28. *Poor appetite.*

The food should be sprinkled with a sufficient quantity of *amorge*; then mix equal parts of olive oil and pine or terebinth resin and coat the horns with this down to the roots.

29. *Ticks.*[1] *[Blisters.]*

The ox should be turned on its back; as the head is thrown back the tongue can be examined for blisters. These can be burned off with sharp hot irons: then anoint the wounds with pounded wild olive leaves and salt, or fine salt and olive oil, or butter and salt.

Or give as food the root of dried squirting cucumber, ground with figs.

Or give two *kotylai* of barley meal and an equal quantity of flour of parched wheat, steeped in wine.

---

1. For ticks on sheep see 18.16. There is no text about ticks on cattle; the title is now attached to material on blisters.

Book 18

1. *Selecting sheep; judging males and females.*
   Florentinus.

The best ewes for breeding are those that have plentiful soft wool, with hanks growing thickly over the whole body but particularly around the throat and neck, and with the whole belly thick with plenty of soft wool, and all the same colour; they should have good eyes, long legs and long tails: these are the best for lambing. The rams should be sturdy, good looking, with blue-grey eyes, a woolly face, good horns but short, ears covered with thick wool, a flat back, large testicles, and the same colour over the whole body. Rams and ewes are judged ready in their third year. One ram is enough to impregnate 50 ewes. One man can take charge of 20 sheep[1] with a boy to assist him. Sheep carry their lambs for 5 months.

The best sheep are those with straight wool; it has been determined that those with curly wool are unsound by nature.

2. *Their care and survival.* Same author.

There need to be several sheepcotes constructed on relatively flat ground, warm and dry, the floors of flagstones on an even slope so that the urine runs off. The mangers should be at the highest point of the floor, with racks fixed above them so that as they are taking their food they do not tread on it.[2] In summer they are also fed in the open air and spend the whole day outdoors, but when the sun is hottest they should be brought into the shade.

---

1. The number is much too small. Owen gives '120' without comment.
2. Accepting Owen's emendation: the text reads 'they do not leap over it'.

They should always be moved from places with hard winters to warmer places, and never the reverse, because cold is very injurious to them.[1]

To prevent noxious pests getting into the sheepcotes, you should make smoke in them by burning women's hair, or galbanum, or hartshorn, or hoofs or hair of goats, also asphalt, also cassia, or fleabane, or any other strong aroma, either singly or after pounding several together. As bedding for the flocks use horse-mint, and asphodel or pennyroyal or germander or fleabane or southernwood: plants of this kind repel pests. The feed to give them is tree-medick and lucerne or fenugreek or oats, and legume pods and barley chaff: these are best sprinkled with brine while on the threshing-floor. Fallen unripe figs and dried fig leaves are also suitable fodder for sheep. They should be driven out to pasture in summer before sunrise, while there is still dew, but in winter when the frost and dew are all cleared away.

There should always be an odd number of sheep in the flocks, because this has some natural influence on their survival and safety.

3. *Mating and lambing.* Didymos.

The rams should be separated two months before mating and given more plentiful food. When they have gathered flesh and strength, let them go to the females. The age at which rams are ready for mating is from 2 to 8; similarly with the females –

Be aware that rams go first for the older ewes, because they mate more quickly, and then for the young ones.

– but do not mate them beyond that age: it is injurious. Some who want to have lambs and milk almost all through the year extend the mating season, arranging mating at various times of year.

Rams gain vigour for mating when onions are mixed into their food, or the *polygonos* and *polyphoros* plant, which also encourages mating in other grazing animals. They should have water from their usual source, however, not from any other.

If one wants to produce more males, let the rams go to the ewes on a fine day when the flock is grazing on land that catches the north wind; if one wants females, they should have the south wind behind

1. Compare what is said of people and plants at 2.48.

them. It seems the rule holds good for sheep and for other animals too. Also if the right testicle is tied off the offspring will be female, as was said about cattle, and if the left testicle is tied off, male.

When the lambs are full of milk they should be penned apart: if they are left together the ewes tread on them.

For two months no milk should be taken; it is better if milk is never taken, because the lambs will then have the best possible nourishment.

Offspring of ewes that are lambing for the first time should be sold:[1] they are unfitted to survive.

4. *To make sheep follow you.* Africanus.

Block their ears with wool.

5. *To prevent a ram attacking.* Same author.

Drill through its horns close to its ears.

6. *To diagnose the colour of the lamb that a ewe is carrying.* Demokritos.

Open the ewe's mouth. If its tongue is black it will produce a black lamb, and if multi-coloured a multi-coloured lamb.

7. *To keep lambs free of illness.*

Give them ivy as food for 7 days and they will not be ill.

8. *When and how to shear sheep.* Didymos.

The time to shear sheep is when the ice is gone, before the summer comes, in the middle of spring. Wounds made in shearing should be coated with liquid pitch and the rest of the body with olive oil mixed with water or with the water from boiling bitter lupins.

It is better to coat with equal parts of wine and *amorge*, or olive oil and white wine, mixed together with wax and fat. This does not hurt the wool, stops scab, and also prevents suppuration.

1. Sold as 'spring lambs' for meat.

Note that sheep should be sheared after the first hour of the day, when the dew that fell on their wool during the night is dried off, after being well rubbed down, and preferably in the sun. When the sheep being sheared sweats well the sweat is taken off in the wool, making it softer and of a better colour.

9. *Male and female goats.* Florentinus.

Goats like mountainous districts, but in many ways they are like sheep. They mate at the same season and bear their young in 5 months as sheep do. They generally bear twins, and feed them and also offer no little profit in the milk, cheese and meat they give, not to mention their hair. The hair is needed for ropes, sacks and the like, and for nautical equipment, because it is not easily cut, nor does it naturally rot unless badly neglected.

Females for breeding should be selected that are sturdy, big and muscular, with smooth skin, thick hair and big, swelling udders. Such females are the best survivors too. The goat is sensitive to cold, indeed by nature it is continuously feverish: if the fever leaves it, it dies. Males are chosen that are big, with good flanks and large haunches, with thick, long, white hair, a short, thick throat and neck and a rather deep chest. The best time for mating them is before the winter solstice.

A male goat will not run away if you cut his beard.[1]

10. *How to make goats give more milk.* Same author.

Give cinquefoil to eat, before drinking, for five days.

Goats give a lot of milk if you fasten dittany around their bellies.[2]

11. *Preventing the* loimike nosos[3] *in sheep and goats.* The Quintilii.

If you emulsify a stork's intestine in water, and make each one swallow a spoonful, they will not get the disease.

1. Repeated from 15.1.
2. See also 18.12.
3. Literally 'the plague disease': unidentified.

12. *Milk, and how to make farm animals yield plenty of milk.* Africanus.

All farm animals produce plenty of milk if, after giving birth, they eat tree-medick or if you apply dittany to their bellies.

Milk warmed over a fire and stirred with a fig branch curdles.

Oxygala[1] placed in oil, or wrapped in terebinth leaves, remains fresh.

13. *Treatment of diseases of sheep.* Leontinos.

Take precautions so that sheep do not suffer from the *loimike nosos* in the first place. At the beginning of spring, pound together mountain sage[2] and garden horehound[3] and mix them in their drinking water for 14 days. Do the same in autumn for the same number of days. If the disease has taken hold of any, this treatment will help them.

Also useful is tree-medick given as fodder; also very tender roots of very strong reed soaked in their drinking water.

Those that are sick should be moved to a different enclosure, so that the healthy ones will not be infected by them and so that they themselves will regain health from the change of water and air.

14. *Hunting wolves.* Diophanes.

This is how to catch wolves. Blennies are small sea fish; some people call them *lykoi* 'wolves'.[4] They are used as follows in the hunting of terrestrial wolves. Take a large number alive by fishing. Crush them finely on a grinding-stone or in a mortar. Make a big charcoal fire on the mountain where the wolves live, and (while the wind is blowing) take some of the fish and throw it on the embers, and quickly mixing the fish blood with mutton flesh finely chopped, add this to the fish on the fire and then move away. As a strong smell develops from the fire, all the wolves in the neighbourhood will be

1. Literally 'acid milk': perhaps fromage blanc or cottage cheese.
2. Greek *elelisphakos oreios*: *Salvia* spp., e.g. *Salvia ringens* Sibth. & Sm.
3. Greek *prasion*: *Marrubium vulgare* L.
4. Greek *blennos*, usually identified as *Blennius* spp., not highly regarded as food except, it seems, by wolves ('normally used for fish soups': Davidson 1981 p. 134).

drawn to it. As they take the meat and inhale the smoke they will be stupefied and fall asleep; approach them while they are still in this narcotic state and slaughter them.

15. *Scab.* Didymos.

Scab will not take hold if one treats them as described above after shearing. If you omit to do this, you can cure it as follows. Strained unsalted *amorge*, the water from soaking bitter lupins, lees of white wine: an equal quantity of each is mixed in a vessel and heated, and the sheep is dipped in this and remains so for two days. On the third day it is to be washed in seawater or hot brine, and then in drinking water.

Others add cypress cones with the water.

Some smear with sulphur and *kypeiros* pounded with white lead and butter.

Some people smear with the mud formed when an ass urinates in the road.

Some people manage it better: they do not apply any of the preceding compounds to the scabby animal before shearing it and rubbing with old urine.

In Arabia they think the application of cedar oil sufficient, as they do with camels and elephants.

You can treat scab in sheep by washing with urine and rubbing on sulphur with olive oil.

16. *Ticks.* Same author.

If it has ticks or *krotones*, pound the roots of maple, add water to this and boil it; then part the wool of the animal from the head along the spine and pour the water over it, lukewarm, until it has run over the whole body.

Some people there use cedar oil alone.[1]

Some follow a similar procedure with mandrake root.[2] Ensure that the animal does not taste it: it is dangerous.

Some boil up *kypeiros* root and wash with this decoction.

1. Presumably 'in Arabia' (compare 18.15).
2. Greek *mandragoras*: *Mandragora officinarum* L.

17. *Various diseases.* Anatolios.

If the burning sun injures a sheep, so that it falls down suddenly and stops eating, squeeze out and administer the juice of wild beet, and make it eat this beet. If it has a breathing difficulty, cut the ears with iron and move it to a different location. If it has a cough, clean and pound almonds, mix with three *kyathoi* of wine, and administer through the nose. If the belly is swollen because of unhealthy grazing, treat by bleeding: open the veins above the lips and those under the tail beside the anus; also give 1½ *kotylai* human urine. If it swallows worms with its grass, do the same. If it has a leech, give hot sharp vinegar or olive oil. If it has an evident abscess, open it and insert into the wound fine roasted salt with liquid pitch. If it is bitten or stung by some pest, give love-in-a-mist with wine, and prepare and apply the same treatments already specified for oxen and others.

Wolves will not attack the farm animals if you fasten squill around their so-called 'guide'.

18. *Herds of goats.* Berytius.

We give the same care to goats as we do to sheep, both in their feeding and their illnesses; but their special features must not be overlooked. Unlike sheep they do not graze side by side; in flat pasture they graze restlessly, jumping and skipping away from each other, and they prefer mountain ridges. The best evidence that the goat has more understanding than other dumb animals is that when its eyes become dim it goes to a bed of spiny rush[1] and pricks them.[2]

19. *Cheesemaking.* Same author.

Most people curdle cheese using what some call juice and others rennet; the best is from kids. Roast salt also curdles milk, and the sap of the fig tree and its green shoots and leaves, and the hairy inedible parts of globe artichokes, and pepper, and the rough lining of the stomach of the domestic hen which is found in its droppings and looks like skin.

1. Greek *oxoschoinos*: *Juncus acutus* L.
2. To clear the cataract. Similarly Pliny, *Natural History* 8.201.

When animals are browsing tree-medick produces thicker and better milk, and much more of it.

Milk keeps for 3 days if, the day before you transport it, you pour it into a jar, boil it, and transfer it into another, stirring it with a fennel stalk or reed while it cools and sprinkle a little salt into it.

Fresh cheese keeps longer if safflower seed[1] made up in a little warm water, or also with warm honey, is added to it.

Cheese keeps if washed in drinking water, dried in the sun and put up in earthenware jars with savory or thyme, the cheeses kept apart from one another so far as possible, then sweet vinegar or *oxymeli* poured over until the liquid fills the gaps and covers them.

Some keep cheeses by putting them in seawater.

Cheese keeps white if stored in brine.

Firmer and sharper-tasting if smoked.

All cheese seems to last longer if kept in [dried] pulse, especially grass pea or garden pea.

If it is harsh or bitter because it is old, it should be soaked in raw bruised corn (that is, milled from unparched barley), then covered in water, and the floating [scum] removed.

20. *Testing milk.* Same author.

You can test whether milk has been watered by putting spiny rush in it, taking it out again and letting the milk drip on your nail. If it flows off quickly there is water mixed in it; if it stays it is pure.

21. *Quick way to make* melke. Paxamos.

The so-called *melke* is easy to make and especially good if into new earthenware pots you pour sharp vinegar and put them on hot ashes or a slow fire, that is, charcoal. When the vinegar simmers a little take them off the fire, so that it does not bubble over the pots. Then pour milk into the same pots, and put them away in a cupboard or chest or somewhere where they will not be disturbed. Next day you will have *melkai* much better than those made in the more troublesome way. After the first or second use, change the pots.

---

1. Greek *knikos*: *Carthamus tinctorius* L.

Book 19

1. *Dogs.* Varro.

We shall choose 'noble' dogs as guardians of our flocks. The type is not unknown: big in the body, strong and tenacious, high-spirited, with a loud, deep-pitched and terrifying bark. If anyone approaches, they do not attack madly and to no purpose, but in a disciplined way, knowing when to make their move, and thus more effective and harder to deal with.

Take care that shepherds' guard dogs have a raw skin wrapped around their necks, protecting the whole length of the throat and windpipe (so that even metal-tipped weapons will not penetrate), because if a wild animal gets its teeth in here, the dog will be killed; if some other part is bitten, it will merely be wounded.

Males and females should be matched for age and breed. Make sure that offspring of the same mother do not mate together.

Bitches carrying a litter should be fed with barley bread, not wheat bread: barley is best for growth. To go with this, boil mutton bones, without the flesh, and make a soup (the marrow from the bones will mix in and make it fatty): break the bread into small pieces and pour the soup over it, then break it up further and feed it to them. When they are nursing, feed them barley meal mixed with cows' or goats' milk and [with the soup] from boiled mutton bones as described. Let them have water to drink. We need to supplement the puppies' diet, too; what they get from the teat is not enough, and we should give them bread soaked in cows' milk and in the mutton-bone soup. Give them the bones, too, to strengthen and sharpen their teeth.

2. *More on dogs.* Fronto.

As to dogs, people choose males that are big-eared and big-bodied, black-eyed, with noses of regular colour, lips that are almost black or rather red, sharp teeth, large heads, flat chests, long limbs, solid and thick front legs, back legs that are straight or, if not, rather bandy-legged than knock-kneed, big feet that splay as they walk, distinctly-jointed toes, curved claws; the back straight all the way to the tail, the tail thick and gradually tapering from its root; a resounding bark; white colour; and, particularly in shepherd dogs, grey-blue eyes and a lion-like look, whether they happen to be shaggy or smooth-haired; they also choose dogs that are big-jawed, with a long neck (*auchen*) and a flat throat (*trachelos*) –

Note that this word *trachelos* denotes the whole circuit of the neck. In men *auchen* is the back part of the neck, because a man stands upright; in animals it is the upper part, because animals bow their heads. The word *deira* in men refers to the front part of the neck, in animals to the under part.[1]

– they choose females endowed with the same good points and also with big breasts and regular-sized teats: some dogs have them misshapen and woody. They may be shaggy or smooth-haired, but shagginess seems to induce fear in attackers.

They should mate at the beginning of spring in order to produce a litter around the summer solstice: bitches carry their young for three months. As soon as the puppies are born, remove the runts and any that are blemished: from seven you should keep three or four; from three keep two. Spread chaff under them to give them a soft bed, and keep them warm: this animal, too,[2] winters poorly. Puppies apparently begin to see after 20 days. They should be left with their mothers for two months and then gradually weaned.

People rub around the puppies' ears and between their toes with bitter almond pounded in water so that flies will not settle and bite them and so that ticks or *krotones* will not trouble them. They spur

---

1. This note does not suit its context here, or indeed any other part of the *Geoponika*, in which the word *deira* is never used. In the *Geoponika auchen* means the upper profile of the neck (I translate it 'neck') and *trachelos* means the lower profile (I translate it 'throat').
2. As is said of chickens (at 14.9) and others.

them to fight one another and do not let them back down. They teach them not to be cowardly and cringing but brave in their work, never giving in. They accustom them to the leash, a leather strap at first, later in some cases a chain. They do not allow them to get at dead farm animals, so that they do not get accustomed to attacking the living ones: it is hard to cure them of this habit once they have tasted the raw meat.

Dogs should be raised in packs, because by nature they defend one another.

So that wild creatures such as hyenas and wolves do not attack them, put around their throats and necks protective collars strengthened with iron and fitted with spikes two fingers apart.

If you want a dog not to run away, spread butter on bread and give it to him to lick. Or measure him from head to tail with a reed [...][1]

A dog will follow you if you tie another dog's skin in a cloth and let him sniff it.[2]

3. *Care of dogs.* Theomnestos.

Rabid dogs should be shut up and given no food for one day, then given some hellebore mixed with their food, and, after they are purged, fed on barley bread. You can give the same treatment to people bitten by rabid dogs.

You can kill fleas with seawater and brine; then rub on henna oil with hellebore and water and cumin and unripe grapes, or else [wild] cucumber root with water.

It is better to rub the body with *amorge*: this cures itchy animals.

Ticks and other diseases that give serious discomfort can be treated as explained for sheep.

---

1. According to Aelian, *On Animals* 9.54, 'measure its tail with a reed, smear the reed with butter and give it to the dog to lick'. It won't work without the butter.
2. This links with the Greek proverb *Chalepon choriou kyna geusai* 'It's hard when a dog has tasted the skin' (hard to break a habit, that is). See Gow's commentary on Theokritos, *Idylls* 10.11, and for the Latin equivalent Horace, *Satires* 2.5.83.

4. *Hares.* Demokritos.

It is said that the same animal is sometimes male and sometimes female: it changes its nature, sometimes impregnating as male, sometimes giving birth as female.

5. *Deer.* Xenophon.

Deer avoid a stretched rope with feathers attached to it because they are frightened by the movement of the feathers, but they forget this fear when they see men standing near them.

When they hear the music of pipes and reeds they do not run away but stay and listen to it and so are caught.

A deer by breathing or drawing breath perplexes a snake and attracts it to itself.

If one burns a deer's tail, makes a paste of this with wine, and smears it on the testicles and penis of an animal about to mate, one increases its sexual arousal; this is ended by smearing olive oil. The same effect occurs with humans.

6. *Pigs.* Florentinus.

People choose female pigs that are rather oblong and rounded in shape, with big bodies, exclusive of the head and feet: those with small heads and short legs are better, and those of uniform colour are a better choice than the piebald. They choose boars in the same way, and in addition those that are big around the neck and shoulders, with a thick 'mane' (we give this name to the bristles that grow behind the neck) and plenty of thick skin on the neck and back (called 'crackling' by butchers).

This animal likes to drink often, especially in summer. It winters poorly and is easily injured by the cold. Hence they make sties for them, and do not drive them out of these until the frost is ended.

Those who buy pigs judge them by pulling bristles out of their 'manes'. If they see these blood-stained, they say that the animal is diseased; if clean, it is healthy.[1] The best time for them to mate is

---

1. Repeated in different words at 18.7.

from when *zephyros* begins to blow[1] until the spring equinox, so that the litter will be produced in summer: the pig carries its young for four months. When they are pregnant people separate the boars from them; otherwise by going after them and assaulting them they will make them miscarry. A boar is capable of impregnating ten sows.

Piglets born in winter are underfed; they do not get enough milk because the climate is unsuitable for lactation; there is less milk in the udders, they press and hurt the teats with their teeth, and so their mothers drive them away.

After impregnation, when the litters are born, people leave them with their mothers for two months and then take them away.

[Other] people mate the mothers in such a way that eight months of each year is given to the production of piglets and four months to the rearing of the offspring.

Each sow that has produced a litter should be put in her own sty, so that they do not mix with piglets from other litters, and so that the mothers know their offspring and the piglets their mothers. If they mix, they are unable to recognize their mothers, and it is better if each feeds her own. The pig feeds largely on acorns. It is also fattened with wheat bran, and refuse from the threshing floor, and wheat. Barley is good for fattening pigs and also makes them productive in breeding.

Pigs do not suffer from the *loimike nosos*, or if they suffer from it they will be cured, if you put asphodel roots in the water they drink or frequently wallow in.

7. *Treatment of pigs.* Didymos.

Pigs will not be ill if you give them 9 river crabs to eat.

People recognize sick pigs by pulling bristles from their necks. If the bristles are clean they are healthy; if they are bloody, or with some thick secretion around the bristle, they are ill.[2] *Demokritos*, the writer on sympathy and antipathy, instructs that 5 *mnai* of asphodel root, chopped finely, be mixed with each pig's food: within 7 days health will be restored.

1. 7th February, according to 1.1 and other chapters.
2. Repeated from 18.6.

337

If they have fever, take blood from the tail. If they have a sickness of the tonsils, take blood from the shoulders. If they are affected by unknown disease they should be shut up for a whole day and night and not given any food or drink, then for a whole day and night be given pounded roots of squirting cucumber in water. [Continue to] give this as drink on the following day. After drinking this very heavily they will rapidly vomit up the cause of the disease.

Since pigs eat heavily they often suffer from disease of the spleen: water in which burning tamarisk wood has been doused should be given them to drink. Humans can be treated by giving them to drink wine, rather than water, in which tamarisk embers have been doused: *Demokritos* particularly advises this. *Demokritos*, again, asserts that better treatment for the spleen in humans will be effected by heating iron in the embers, dousing it in water, mixing this water with vinegar and giving this to the splenetic patient to drink.

When pigs are bitten by poisonous pests they can be treated with the same remedies prescribed above for grazing animals.

8. *Wild boar.* Demokritos.

If you want not to be attacked, carry crab's claws fastened around you.

9. *Salting of all kinds of meat.* Didymus.

Fresh meat keeps longest if washed and dried and put in dark, moist places, north rather than south-facing. Snow packed around it and chaff spread over it will make it taste better.

Animals whose meat is to be salted should be given no water on the day before [they are killed]. The salters should bone the meat. Roast salt is most suitable for salting. Earthenware to be used for salting is better if previously used for olive oil or vinegar. Salt kid, mutton and venison are best if after the first salting the brine and juices are removed, wiped clean, and fresh salt sprinkled on, and then the meat is placed among grape pips not separated from the grape skins, in such a way that the pieces of meat do not touch one another but the spaces between them are filled with pips. If you pour sweet grape juice on to them they will be better still.

Book 20

1. *Keeping fish.* Florentinus.

At an inland site fish ponds are to be made, as large as one wishes or as large as is practical. They can be stocked with fish that live in fresh water; in addition fish that are able to live in either can be brought from the sea. People living near a sea or lagoon will put in their artificial ponds whatever fish are commonest in the sea. Attention is needed to the kind of soil: if it is marshy, keep marsh-dwellers; if stony, keep rockfish. As food for sea fish and rockfish the tenderest greenstuff is thrown in and the tiniest fish (some also throw in fish gills and entrails) and chopped juicy figs and fresh cheese; also shrimps and gobies or whatever one has of that kind, or lumps of bran bread, or crushed dried figs.

There will be plenty of fish everywhere if you pound the plant *polysporos* (resembling *polygonos*) and throw it into the water where fish are kept.

2. *Bringing fish together.* Oppianos.

Pennyroyal, savory, oregano, marjoram,[1] 3 drams each; frankincense bark, myrrh, *sinopis*,[2] 8 drams each; pearl barley soaked in wine, ½ *mna*; roasted pig's liver, 24 drams; same quantity of goat fat; same of garlic; pound to an even mass, mix in some fine sand, and throw this in at the site one or two hours before you set the nets.

Others pound, sift and throw in the male larkspur plant, thus calling the fish to be caught by hand.

1. Greek *sampsychon*: *Origanum majorana* L.
2. Red lead from Sinope on the Black Sea.

Some take ½ *mna* of garlic, or the same quantity of roasted sesame; pennyroyal, oregano, thyme, marjoram, savory, stavesacre, 32 drams each; knead in 1 *mna* pearl barley, same quantity of cracked wheat; 18 drams frankincense bark; mix with earth and bran, and throw in.

3. *Catching river fish.* Didymos.

Mutton fat, roasted sesame, garlic, aromatic wine, oregano, thyme, dried marjoram, same quantity of each: pound, dip up with bread and throw in.

4. *Collecting all kinds of fish in one place.* Demokritos.

Blood of oxen, goats, sheep, pigs; excrement from the small intestine; thyme, oregano, pennyroyal, savory, marjoram, garlic, lees of aromatic wine, same quantity of each; fat or marrow of the same animals: all pounded together to an even consistency and made into lumps, to be thrown in at the site one hour before setting the nets.

5. *For all fish.*

Mix blood of a black goat and lees of aromatic wine with pearl barley; pound a goat's lung to the finest possible paste, knead with the other ingredients and use.

6. *Fishing.* Tarantinos.

I wished to inform you reliably, honoured friend, of their nature (in a word): their life, mating, nurture, the length of their lives; what kinds there are of sea fish, river fish and inshore fish; then, each kind individually, those that are scaly, spiny, smooth, soft-shelled; viviparous and oviparous; solitary and gregarious; those that are cannibalistic and those that never attack one another. I am quite determined to deal so fully with the subject that you will know everything of the life of the sea. More of that in due course. But I see that some are curious about the names of fish and devoted to that subject, and since answers are demanded I must deal fully with the question as to common and local terms, repeating for general readers what *Asklepios, Manetho, Paxamos* and *Demokritos* have explained on this subject.

7. *Bait for fish.*[1]

[...] grey mullet, sting-ray, rascasse, sturgeon, tigerfish, sardinelle, parrot wrasse, bluefish, red mullet, bonito, garfish, barbier, tunny, horse-mackerel, *sakoutos*, oblade, picarel, cephalus, octopus, thresher shark, bogue, *mys*, morme, *smylos*, cuttlefish, *phokis*, crayfish, electric catfish, rainbow wrasse, Nile carp, sarg, shrimp, *charakias*, sole, golden bream, *aleantris*, shad, *illos, anios, prospantamias*, young bonito. For marine small fry, goby, *genaris, dax*, schall, *galea*, bynni, grouper, *leukopis*, moray, tilapia, langouste, eel, horn-shell, *latilos*, purple-shell, bass, and for all on any occasion; also for small fry.

First of all is the bait for big fish, *illos*, bluefish, braize and all large kinds. As soon as this bait is placed on the hook and touches the water the small fish, fearing the arrival of the big ones, disappear. The big fish are attracted from their own lairs by the sympathetic pleasantness of the bait, even if two *stadia* distant; by sympathetic effect they play and fight with one another, and, enthralled by pleasure, do not try to wriggle away or to break the fishing-line.

8. *The compound for bait is:*

Mudfish, oats, 8 drams; red flying *paphoi*,[2] anise, goat's milk cheese, 4 drams each; opopanax, 2 drams; pig's blood, 4 drams; galbanum, 4 drams; render each separately to an even consistency, mix, pour in unadulterated austere wine, form pills as for incense, dry in the dark.

---

1. The text of 20.7–45 on fishing bait is particularly faulty. Chapter 20.7, evidently an introduction to the rest, seems to be quite incomplete. The context in part of this list and in some following chapters seems to be Egypt. Names of fish that cannot be identified have been left in Greek. Since nothing substantive is said about them, fish that occur only in this chapter have not been footnoted. For more on them and their identification see Thompson 1947; Davidson 1981; Dalby 2003.
2. Perhaps a blister beetle? The term is otherwise unknown.

9. *Another, excellent bait for very large tilapia.*[1]

8 scruples roasted lentils; 1 dram roasted cumin seeds; 4 drams raw betony;[2] 4 drams buckshorn plantain;[3] 1 dram bitter i.e. fresh *anthyllion*;[4] 4 drams *patetos* dates;[5] 1 dram castor.[6] Make all these into a paste, add dill juice, form into pills and use.

10. *For river fish, as used by ...anos.*[7]

Put calf's blood and finely-chopped calf's flesh in a Spartan cup and leave for ten days to use as bait.

11. *A bait to attract fish readily.*

Roast pearl barley, make into small lumps and throw in.

12. *Small river fish for fish traps.*

2 *mnai* barley bran, 1 *choinix* whole lentils: mix and moisten with sufficient real *garon*, add 1 *choinix* sesame. Scatter a little of this; throw it around. As soon as you scatter it all the small fry will approach; even if they are five *stadia* away they will come, but the big fish will retreat because of the smell. Use this and you will succeed.

13. *Schall.*[8]

4 dr. sesame, 2 dr. garlic heads, 2 dr. salted quail meat, 1 dr. opopanax: take, pound with gum, form pills and use.

---

1. Greek *korakinos*, the Nile fish *Oreochromis niloticus* (Linnaeus, 1758), syn. *Tilapia nilotica*, which was salted and available as far away as Rome (see also 13.10 and Dalby 2003 p. 233).
2. A possible identification for Greek *kestron: Stachys officinalis* (L.) Trevisan.
3. Greek *koronopodion: Plantago coronopus* L.
4. A name for several plants including *Ajuga iva* (L.) Schreber.
5. A very juicy kind that splits on the tree, according to Pliny, *Natural History* 13.45.
6. Greek *kastorion*, secretion of the beaver, *Castor fiber* (Linnaeus, 1758).
7. Perhaps *Oppianos*, to whom 20.2 is ascribed.
8. Greek *choiros*, in Egypt, was *Synodontis schall* (Bloch & Schneider, 1801).

14. *Eels.*[1]

8 dr. nereids,[2] 8 dr. river shrimps, 1 dr. sesame; take and use.

15. *Bait for marine grey mullet.*[3]

1 ball tejpat leaf; 10 peppercorns; 3 love-in-a-mist berries; a little flower of reed (some say, reed pith): pound and mix; then soak white bread in a cup of Mareatic wine,[4] take up the mixture with this, combine and use as bait.

16. *Marine grey mullet bait.*

Put a ram's penis into a new soup-bowl, cover with another soup-bowl and seal it so that it is air-tight; then give it to a glass-making workshop to bake from morning till evening and you will find it as tender as cheese. Make baits from it.

17. *Another for success in catching mature grey mullet and no other fish.*

4 dr. tunny liver, 8 dr. sea shrimps, 4 dr. sesame, 8 dr. cracked wheat, 2 dr. raw *auitoi*:[5] grind these ingredients, take up in drops of grape syrup, make pills and use as bait.

18. *The 'Ptollatos', a concoction to bring sea fish to one place.*

Take 3 limpets, those that grow on the rocks; remove the flesh and write the following text on the shells; to your surprise you will immediately see the fish arrive. The names are *Iao Sabaoth*. This is the name that the Ichthyophagoi use.[6]

---

1. This is the European eel (also familiar in the Nile), Greek *enchelys*: *Anguilla anguilla* (Linnaeus, 1758).
2. Greek *skolopendra thalassia*, literally 'sea centipede': probably *Nereis* spp.
3. Greek *kestreus thalassios*: several species including *Liza aurata* (Risso, 1810). The name 'marine grey mullet' distinguishes it from the Nile grey mullet, chiefly *Liza ramado* (Risso, 1810).
4. From the district of Mareia in Lower Egypt; well known from the 1st century BC onwards.
5. An unknown word.
6. The Ichthyophagoi ('fish-eaters') were a people of the western shore of the Red Sea.

19. *For red mullet[1] and large parrot-wrasse:[2] to be used in the water, and owing to its speed unsuited to small fish; a compound that works by sympathy.*

8 dr. flesh of river *typhlen*,[3] 8 dr. roasted whole lentils, 4 dr. river shrimps, 1 dr. tejpat: reduce these to paste, take up in egg white, make pills and use.

20. *For all large sea fish, such as bluefish,[4] dogfish,[5] grouper[6] and others like them.*

Cock's testicles and pine cone, roasted and ground. 8 drams testicles, 16 drams pine cones. Grind till it is like dough, mould into pills to serve as bait.

21. *For moray.[7]*

16 dr. river catfish, 8 dr. wild rue seed, 8 dr. veal fat, 16 dr. sesame: pound, make pills and use.

22. *For octopus and cuttlefish.*

16 dr. sal ammoniac, 8 dr. goat's milk butter: make smooth pills; rub on to ropes or on to sails without hems, and they will feed there and not go away. Be at hand quickly and gather into your boat crayfish,[8] horn-shells,[9] purple-shells[10] and whatever there is.

---

1. Greek *trigle*: *Mullus barbatus* Linnaeus, 1758.
2. Greek *skaros*: *Sparisoma cretense* (Linnaeus, 1758).
3. An unidentified Nile fish.
4. A possible identification for Greek *glaukos*: *Pomatomus saltator* (Linnaeus, 1766).
5. Greek *galeos*: chiefly the smoothhound *Mustelus mustelus* (Linnaeus, 1758).
6. Greek *orphos*: *Epinephelus guaza* (Linnaeus, 1758).
7. Greek *myraina*: *Muraena helena* Linnaeus, 1758.
8. Greek *karabos*: *Palinurus elephas* (Fabricius, 1787).
9. Greek *keryx*: *Charonia tritonis* Linnaeus, 1758.
10. Greek *porphyra*: *Murex brandaris* Linnaeus, 1758.

23. *Catch eels and bony fish as follows.*

8 dr. sal ammoniac, 1 dr. onion, 6 dr. veal fat. Make the hooks blue-green, smear them with the compound, cast them; the fish will come, attracted by the smell, and will give themselves up.

24. *Bait for all fish at any season.*

4 leaves Celtic nard, 1 tiger-nut,[1] Egyptian myrrh the size of a bean, cumin to fill three fingers, a handful of dill seed: pound, sieve and put in a small pot. At need take parasitic worm or earthworm, rinse, put in a container; press out wet *araulin* from the locality into your hand, mix with a sufficient quantity of the compound, put the worms into the mixture, rub them in, then take out and use as bait.

25. *For small fry caught with rods.*

1 *choinix* river shrimps are to be steeped in real *garon* from pickled little *korakinoi*, left to marinate for 2 days, and used as bait on the third. Fish with two rods, with four hooks each, yourself and an assistant, and you will take away so much fish that you will not be beaten by the round nets or the casting-nets of other workers.

26. *General bait.*

Make a paste of lentil soup with dry starch; mix in [...] and use.

27. *For all fish.*

Take out the flesh of snails, separating the tails; put your bait in these, not using as much as a full shell.

28. *For traps.*

The juice pressed from Egyptian balsam,[2] human dung, white bread, each pounded separately and then the three mixed: put this in the trap and you will succeed.

---

1. Greek *kyperis*: probably *Cyperus esculentus* L. or *C. auricomus* L.
2. Greek *myrobalanos*: *Balanites aegyptiaca* (L.) Delile, the source of zachum oil.

29. *Another for traps.*

I found it written that the Ichthyophagoi fish in this way: take the snail called *pomatia*[1] from the rocks, with their flesh, and fish with them.

30. *Marine grey mullet.*

One unit [each] of bones of parrot-wrasse, red mullet, cuttlefish, with fresh *sisymbrion*, that is, laver,[2] and with water, flour of spring wheat and cow's milk cheese: mix and use.

31. *Rascasse*[3] *only.*

Sawdust of mulberry wood, artichoke and sandarac, 8 dr., with 5 cabbage caterpillars[4] and wheat: pound the wheat till it is fine; add ajowan,[5] then add water, form into lumps and use as bait.

32. *Sea bream.*[6]

Grind locusts and worms in a decoction of love-in-a-mist, with flour of spring wheat; add water to the consistency of honey and use as bait.

33. *Garfish.*[7]

Knead calf's bile with pearl barley and olive oil and water, make little lumps and use as bait. Chew the same compound, spit it into the water, and they will come to it.

---

1. The escargot, *Helix pomatia* Linnaeus, 1758.
2. Greek *bryon*: *Porphyra* or *Ulva* spp. Some dispute is reflected in the text: '*sisymbrion*, that is, *bryon*' makes no sense as such, since the two words are never synonymous, but *bryon* and *–brion* were homophones.
3. Greek *skorpios*: *Scorpaena* spp.
4. Greek *kampe*, here no doubt the larval cabbage white, *Pieris rapae* (Linnaeus, 1758).
5. Greek *ammi*: Trachyspermum Ammi (L.) Sprague.
6. Greek *phagros thalassios*: *Pagrus pagrus* (Linnaeus, 1758). The Greek name distinguishes it from the Nile fish known as *phagros* in Greek and tigerfish in English, listed in 20.7 above: *Hydrocynus forskahlii* (Cuvier, 1819).
7. Greek *raphis*: *Belone belone* (Linnaeus, 1758).

34. *Tunny only.*

Burn 5 walnuts to ash: mix this into a paste with marjoram and combine with white bread soaked in water and with goat's milk cheese; make into lumps and use.

35. *Picarel.*[1]

Garlic pounded with bread, and cow's and goat's milk cheese, and white flour of spring wheat: make into a smooth and uniform paste, form lumps and place as bait.

36. *Sting-rays.*[2]

Soak pigeon dung and bread-wheat flour: knead.

37. *Another for the same species.*

Boil lettuce seed, add butter and bread-wheat flour: grind the result.

38. *Saupe.*[3]

Fresh laver from the rocks, in olive oil: set bait in this.

39. *Bluefish, bonito,*[4] *barbier.*[5]

Bake shad[6] and bone them; add laver and barley meal, combine, make lumps, use as bait.

40. *Horse-mackerel,*[7] *oblade.*[8]

Moisten ass's dung in the cooking liquor from green coriander; add bread-wheat flour, make lumps, use as bait.

1. Greek *smaris*: *Spicara smaris* (Linnaeus, 1758).
2. Greek *trygon thalassios*: *Dasyatis* spp.
3. Greek *salpe*: *Sarpa salpa* (Linnaeus, 1758).
4. Greek *amia*: *Sarda sarda* (Bloch, 1793).
5. A possible identification for Greek *kallichthys*: *Anthias anthias* (Linnaeus, 1758).
6. Greek *thrissa*: *Alosa* spp.
7. Greek *trachouros*: *Trachurus trachurus* (Linnaeus, 1758).
8. Greek *melanouros*: *Oblada melanura* (Linnaeus, 1758).

41. *Grey mullet, cephalus.*[1]

Bread from spring wheat, goat's milk cheese, unslaked lime: mix, pound, add seawater, make lumps from this, use as bait.

42. *Octopus.*

Fasten bogues, mormes and *aradoi*[2] to some stiff object and use as bait.

43. *Cuttlefish only.*

Wine lees, dry, pounded in olive oil. Go to the place and throw this into the sea. They will notice this, emit their ink, come to the place where they saw the oil, and you can catch them.

44. *Crayfish, morme.*

[...] tied to some strong object. Pound 10 purple-shells with olive oil and a little laver. Spit this on to the rock and you will catch them.

45. *Oblade.*

Take goat liver and put it on your hook.

We may have found another way to get a great number of fish: bait with a goat's or a donkey's hoof.

46. *Making* gara.

The so-called *liquamen* is made thus. Fish entrails are put in a container and salted; and little fish, especially sand-smelt[3] or small red mullet or mendole[4] or anchovy,[5] or any small enough, are all similarly salted; and left to pickle in the sun, stirring frequently. When the heat has pickled them, the *garos* is got from them thus:

---

1. Greek *kephalos*: the grey mullet species *Mugil cephalus* Linnaeus, 1758.
2. The first two are bream species (*Boops boops* (Linnaeus, 1758) and *Lithognathus mormyrus* (Linnaeus, 1758)); the third is unidentified.
3. Greek *atherine*: *Atherina hepsetus* Linnaeus, 1758.
4. Greek *mainidion* (and *mainis* below): *Spicara maena* (Linnaeus, 1758).
5. Greek *lykostomos*: probably *Engraulis encrasicolus* (Linnaeus, 1758).

a deep close-woven basket is inserted into the centre of the vessel containing these fish, and the *garos* flows into the basket. This, then, is how the *liquamen* is obtained by filtering through the basket; the residue makes *alix*.

The Bithynians make it thus. Take preferably small or large mendole, or, if none, anchovy or scad[1] or mackerel,[2] or also *alix*, and a mixture of all these, and put them into a baker's bowl of the kind in which dough is kneaded; to one *modios* of fish knead in 6 Italian pints of salt so that it is well mixed with the fish, and leaving it overnight put it in an earthenware vessel and leave it uncovered in the sun for 2 or 3 months, occasionally stirring with a stick, then take [the fluid], cover and store. Some add 2 pints of old wine to each pint of fish.[3]

If you want to use the *garon* at once, that is, not by ageing in the sun but by cooking, make it thus. Into pure brine, which you have tested by floating an egg[4] in it (if it sinks, the brine is not salty enough) in a new bowl, put the fish; add oregano; place over a sufficient fire, until it boils, that is, until it begins to reduce a little. Some also add grape syrup. Then cool and filter it; filter a second and a third time until it runs clear; cover and store.

A rather high quality *garos*, called *haimation*, is made thus. Take tunny entrails with the gills, fluid and blood, sprinkle with sufficient salt, leave in a vessel for two months at the most; then pierce the jar, and the *garos* called *haimation* flows out.

1. Greek *sauros*: *Trachurus trachurus* (Linnaeus, 1758).
2. Greek *skombros*: *Scomber scombrus* Linnaeus, 1758.
3. The quantities here are wrong in some way.
4. The egg is Casaubon's conjecture: the manuscript text is faulty.

Bibliography

A. C. Andrews, 'Index of plants' in *Pliny, Natural History books XXIV-XXVII* ed. and trans. W. H. S. Jones (2nd ed. Cambridge, Mass.: Harvard University Press, 1980) pp. 485-550.

W. G. Arnott, *Birds in the ancient world from A to Z*. London: Routledge, 2007.

Heinrich Beckh, ed., *Geoponica sive Cassiani Bassi scholastici de re rustica eclogae*. Leipzig: Teubner, 1895.

Ianus Cornarius, trans., *Constantini Caesaris selectarum praeceptionum de agricultura libri viginti*. Venice: apud Iacob de Burgofrancho, 1538.

Dorothy Crawford, 'Food: tradition and change in Hellenistic Egypt' in *World archaeology* vol. 11 no. 2 (1979) pp. 136-146.

Andrew Dalby, *Siren Feasts*. London: Routledge, 1996.

Andrew Dalby, ed. and trans., *Cato, On farming*. Totnes: Prospect Books, 1998.

Andrew Dalby, *Food in the ancient world from A to Z*. London: Routledge, 2003.

Andrew Dalby, Sally Grainger, *The classical cookbook*. London: British Museum Press, 1996.

Alan Davidson, *Mediterranean seafood*. Harmondsworth: Penguin, 1981.

R. A. Donkin, *Manna: an historical geography*. The Hague: Junk, 1980.

Stella Georgoudi, *Des chevaux et des boeufs dans le monde grec: réalités et représentations animalières à partir des livres XVI et XVII des Géoponiques*. Paris, 1990.

J. Koder, *Gemüse in Byzanz: Die Versorgung Konstantinopels mit Frischgemüse im Lichte der Geoponika*. Vienna, 1993.

David C. Lewis, Elizabeth S. Metallinos-Katsaras, Louis E. Grivetti, 'Coturnism: human poisoning by European migratory quail' in *Journal of cultural geography* vol. 7 (1987) pp. 51-65.

Anne McCabe, *A Byzantine Encyclopaedia of Horse Medicine: the sources, compilation, and transmission of the "Hippiatrica"*. Oxford: Oxford University Press, 2007.

Peter Needham, ed., Γεωπονικὰ: *Geoponicorum sive De re rustica libri XX Cassiano Basso scholastico collectore*. Cambridge, 1704.

T. Owen, transl., Γεωπονικὰ: *Agricultural Pursuits*. London, 1804-1805.

D. Rizzi and others, 'Clinical spectrum of accidental hemlock poisoning: neurotoxic manifestations, rhabdomyolysis and acute tubular necrosis' in *Nephrology, dialysis, transplantation* vol. 6 (1991) pp. 939-943.

R. H. Rodgers, ed., *Palladii Rutilii Tauri Aemiliani Opus agriculturae, De veterinaria medicina, De insitione*. Leipzig: Teubner, 1975.

R. H. Rodgers, 'Varro and Virgil in the Geoponica' in *Greek, Roman and Byzantine studies* vol. 19 (1978) pp. 277-285.

R. H. Rodgers, 'Κêpopoïïa: garden-making and garden culture in the Greek Geoponica' in *Byzantine Garden Culture* ed. A. Littlewood and others (Washington, 2002) pp. 159-175.

Margherita Rossi, Isabella Germondari, Paolo Casini, 'Comparison of chickpea cultivars: chemical composition, nutritional evaluation, and oligosaccharide content' in *Journal of agricultural and food chemistry* vol. 32 (1984) pp. 811-814.

A. F. Scholfield, ed. and trans., *Aelian, On the characteristics of animals*. Cambridge, Mass.: Harvard University Press, 1958-1959.

J. L. Teall, 'The Byzantine agricultural tradition' in *Dumbarton Oaks papers* vol. 25 (1971) pp. 35-59.

D'Arcy W. Thompson, *A glossary of Greek fishes*. London: Oxford University Press, 1947.

K. D. White, *Roman farming*. London: Thames and Hudson, 1970.

Index

This is an index of names and subjects, and of transliterated Greek words remaining in the translation. It is not a narrative index. For this, the reader should look at the list of books and chapters at the beginning of the text.